THAT
SUNNY DOME

A Portrait of Regency Britain

The shadow of the dome of pleasure
Floated midway on the waves;
Where was heard the mingled measure
From the fountain and the caves.
It was a miracle of rare device,
A sunny pleasure-dome with caves of ice!

A damsel with a dulcimer
In a vision once I saw:
It was an Abyssinian maid,
And on her dulcimer she played,
Singing of Mount Abora.
Could I revive within me,
Her symphony and song,
To such a deep delight 'twould win me,
That with music loud and long,
I would build that dome in air,
That sunny dome! those caves of ice!

From 'Kubla Khan' by Samuel Taylor Coleridge

THAT
SUNNY DOME

A Portrait of Regency Britain

Donald A Low

Dent   London, Melbourne and Toronto
Rowman and Littlefield, Totowa, N.J.

© Donald A. Low, 1977
All rights reserved
Made in Great Britain
at
Biddles Ltd, Guildford,
Surrey and bound
at the Aldine Press,
Letchworth, Herts
for J.M. Dent & Sons Ltd
Aldine House, Albemarle Street, London
First published 1977

First published in the United States
by Rowman and Littlefield, Totowa, New Jersey, 1977

This book is set in 11 on 13pt IBM Baskerville

Dent ISBN: 0 460 12008 5
Rowman and Littlefield ISBN: 0-87471-978-x

British Library Cataloguing in Publication Data

Low, Donald Alexander
    That sunny dome: a portrait of Regency Britain.
    Bibl. — Index.
    ISBN 0-460-12008-5
    1. Title
    941.07'3   DA521
    Great Britain — History — 1789-1820

Contents

Illustrations

Acknowledgments

It is a pleasure to thank the following individuals, who have helped me in a variety of ways during the writing of this book: Dr W. A. Cramond, Principal of the University of Stirling, and Professors T. A. Dunn and A. N. Jeffares, for their interest and support; Dr Roy Park, Fellow in English and Librarian of University College, Oxford, for many kindnesses and for the stimulus of his conversation; Dr Patrick Conner, Keeper of Fine Art, Royal Pavilion Art Gallery and Museums, Brighton, for generously sharing his time and specialist knowledge; Ron Stewart, Chief Technician, Audio-Visual Aids, University of Stirling, for photography, and Ann Hamilton and Shona McGee, Department of English Studies, University of Stirling, for help with typing. All errors of fact and interpretation in the book are entirely my responsibility. I wish further to record my thanks to the Trustees of the Carnegie Trust for the Universities of Scotland for the award of a research grant in the Spring of 1976 which made it possible for me to visit a number of the places about which I have written. Above all, I wish to thank my wife Sheona and Christopher and Kirsty for so cheerfully putting up with and encouraging an author in the house.

Acknowledgments for permission to reproduce photographs of works of art in their keeping are gratefully offered to the Directors and Trustees of: the British Museum, the National Gallery, the National Portrait Gallery, the Tate Gallery, the Victoria and Albert Museum, and the Royal Pavilion Art Gallery and Museums, Brighton.

For S.

Foreword

The Regency, or second ten years of the nineteenth century, when the future King George IV acted as ruler of Great Britain for his elderly deranged father, has long been recognized as an exceptional decade, both in terms of the historic events which it witnessed, and the incomparably fine literature which it produced. The Duke of Wellington's triumph at Waterloo falls within its span, as does the contrasting episode nicknamed 'Peterloo', when government troops rode down and killed peaceful political demonstrators. Meanwhile, Byron, Keats, Scott, Jane Austen and other writers were adding to the nation's cultural heritage. In name only an in-between time, the Regency exists unmistakably as a period in its own right — one of such restless energy and daring that it stands out from the long surrounding ages of George III and Queen Victoria as different, exotic, and somehow modern. It can be viewed as the true forerunner of our own time, the spirit of experiment and violent suffering of which have led one recent historian to speak of 'the Promethean twentieth century'. But while the Regency is in one sense startlingly familiar, it is also rich in period flavour; and to find a parallel to its many-sided national achievements, it is necessary to go back to the reign of the first Queen Elizabeth, when victory over the Spanish Armada was followed, during a time of marked social tension, by the literary masterpieces of Shakespeare, Marlowe and Spenser.

The central idea running through the Regency which is traced in this book is that of a varied quest for freedom. Britons had grown impatient of old ways, and after a long war which had been used as an excuse by the Government for delaying political and other reforms that were badly needed there was now a general desire not only for change, but also for freedom. Everywhere men and women were in search of some kind of emancipation, whether this involved them in political or social innovation like Robert Owen at New Lanark, or simply in 'doing their own thing' like Beau Brummell or the crowds who walked twenty miles to watch a boxing match. The Prince Regent set the example by commissioning his architects to spend very large sums of money on his palace of pleasure, the Royal Pavilion at Brighton. Journalists, engaged in what has been called 'the struggle for the freedom of the Press' from domination by party political interests, were committed in a quite different way to extending their areas of privilege. Working men in the Midlands who saw in the mechanization of industry a direct threat to their own livelihood took the law into their own hands by smashing knitting-frames and other machines. A little later, people in large cities like Manchester, which, despite a population of 100,000 still had no Member of Parliament, held mass meetings to demand the extension of parliamentary franchise and a degree of social recognition which they did not yet receive. Lord Byron, a central figure in the Regency, flouting conventions of society both in his personal conduct and in his verse, set new norms of libertarian thought; then went too far for public opinion, and left England for ever, to create in exile in *Don Juan* an unforgettable picture of a 'tight little island' lacking essential freedoms.

So oppressive was the experience of working in the rapidly growing towns and cities of Britain that many of those who no longer lived in the countryside turned for solace to nature poetry and to landscape painting, both of which flourished in the Regency as never before. Others sought escape from the pressures of the time in fiction, and especially in the novels of Sir Walter Scott, which, because they took their themes from history, seemed to hold out the promise of release from a problem-ridden present. But it was an era of travel in reality as well as of visionary journeys in the imagination. Improved communications within Britain, largely the work of two skilled road-makers, Telford and McAdam, allowed far more people to explore their own country (discovering, among other regions, the Scottish Borders and Highlands already made popular by Scott) than at any previous point in history. A generation which had been starved of foreign travel during the Napoleonic Wars took to visiting

European countries, and especially France, in the years after Waterloo to such an extent that the exercise of this new liberty became
known as 'the British mania'.

This book describes and attempts to account for the Regency cult
of freedom as it is revealed both in life and literature. It differs from
earlier studies of the period in treating the contemporary written
word of journalists, poets, and novelists as providing some of the
truest evidence on which to base a historical view — truest, because it
reflects most fully the actual human response of imaginative men
and women who were caught up in unprecedented stresses and
excitements. The title, from Coleridge's poem published in 1816
(although written in an earlier revolutionary decade, the 1790s),
emphasizes the artistic splendour of the Regency. Even if, as this
book shows, there existed 'caves of ice', it was nevertheless a time of
triumph and of confident creation.

What follows is not intended to be a comprehensive history. It
does not deal at any length, for example, with religion or education,
with Regency advances in medical and scientific knowledge which
made possible a new degree of freedom from disease, or with the
story of Britain's sometimes illiberal, sometimes far-sighted relations
with her vast and scattered overseas empire in the early nineteenth
century. The reader must look elsewhere for a detailed account of
such events as that bizarre episode in the history of Anglo-American
affairs, the naval war of 1812. Inevitably, a great deal which belongs
to the complete record of Regency Britain has had to be left out; the
Book List at the end of this book contains suggestions for further
reading. If *That Sunny Dome* whets the reader's appetite and leads
him or her to construct another, and perhaps very different interpretation of the Regency, it will have served its purpose, for as
Hazlitt wrote, 'the truth is not one, but many'.

Chronological Table

Edmund Kean's début as Shylock at Drury Lane
M.C.C. first play cricket on present Lord's Ground

1815   Napoleon escapes from Elba; his 'Hundred Days' (20 March–29 June); Wellington and Blücher defeat him at Waterloo (18 June); he is banished to St Helena (17 August)

Congress of Vienna redraws the map of Europe

Passing of the Corn Law, resulting in high food prices in Britain

Apothecaries Act in Britain forbids unqualified doctors to practise medicine

Sir Humphry Davy invents miner's safety lamp

1816   Distress and poverty lead to large-scale emigration to Canada and U.S.A.

Spa Fields Riots take place when crowd, which assembles to hear demands for political reform, marches on London

Byron leaves England

Elgin Marbles bought by British Museum

William Cobbett's *Political Register*, published at 2d, the first cheap periodical

1817   Political unrest in Britain

Prince Regent is fired at on return from opening Parliament

Death of Princess Charlotte

James Monroe President of U.S.A.

Coleridge, *Biographia Literaria*

Constable, 'Flatford Mill'

Opening of John Rennie's Waterloo Bridge

1818   Allied troops leave France

Frontier between U.S.A. and Canada defined as the 49th Parallel

John Nash's Indian dome at the Royal Pavilion, Brighton

Mary Shelley, *Frankenstein*

1819   The 'Peterloo Massacre' at Manchester

Government bring in Six Acts to preserve public order, including measures to curtail the right to hold public meetings, and to impose stiffer penalties for seditious libel

Working day for children in cotton factories limited to 12 hours

First ship fitted with steam engine crosses the Atlantic, in 26 days

Thomas Telford begins Menai Suspension Bridge (1819-21)

Byron, *Don Juan*, Cantos 1 and 2

1820   Death of George III and accession of George IV

Trial of Queen Caroline

Cato Street Conspiracy to assassinate the Cabinet

First iron steamship is launched

André Ampère's laws of electro-dynamic action

John Clare, *Poems Descriptive of Rural Life and Scenery*

Keats, *Lamia and Other Poems*

[1]

The Regent and the Regency

If one asked a group of people chosen at random what associations the phrases 'The Regency' and 'Regency Britain' held for them, their answers would almost certainly include at some point 'The Battle of Waterloo', 'Brighton Pavilion', and 'stage-coaches', and two key ideas: a way of living which, if somewhat raffish and not always very moral, was unmistakably elegant, and a particular style of furniture and of interior decoration. It is immediately arresting that while these two last ideas are quite distinct from each other, the first having to do with the social conduct of a nation, or of part of it, and the second with material objects for the home, they have one thing in common — the perception of a certain aesthetic 'style'. This fact becomes all the more impressive when one takes into account that whereas specialists in the history of furniture use the term 'Regency' for a period lasting from about 1800 until 1830, it is possible to define the rather wild, yet poised, mood of the Regency much more narrowly, either within the years when the Prince of Wales was Regent (1811 to 1820), or as a specifically post-war phenomenon, something which came into being after Waterloo as a reaction to too much fighting and after a few years burned itself out, like the Jazz Age in the 1920s. It makes little difference whether the focus is on culture as a living process or on culture as artefacts, on thirty years or on five: Regency Britain possessed a creative flair peculiar to itself.

This book is not about furniture, but (in the strict chronological sense) about Regency Britain and its way of life. And straightaway a number of questions suggest themselves. What manner of man was the eldest son of George III who at the age of forty-nine at last found himself King in all but name of the British people? To what degree

1

did the Regency receive its general tone of *brio*, and its exceptional artistic confidence, from the Regent himself? How much, on the other hand, came about despite, or independently of, his influence? Equally important, how truly does a view of the Regency decade based on the social exploits and varied aesthetic achievements of a few of its outstanding citizens represent the experience of the majority? Is 'the real Regency' and its way of life rather to be sought elsewhere, in the statistics of the early Industrial Revolution, or in the simple annals of the poor?

*　　*　　*

Historians of the British monarchy are fond of pointing out that at no stage in history has the Crown been in lower repute than during the Regency and the reign of George IV. Had it not been for the long, popular and respectable reign of Queen Victoria, they argue, the institution of monarchy might never have recovered its prestige in Britain. Whatever the truth of this hypothesis, it is undeniably true that the fourth George was not the kind of scion of a royal house whom the nation was willing to love. 'Respectable' — an epithet which could have been applied to his father no less than to Queen Victoria — was the very thing that he was not. He was by contrast like a spoiled boy whose development had been arrested at the very point of his most outrageous misbehaviour; or so it appeared to his contemporaries. Shockingly extravagant, too fat, a womanizer who had an absurd preference for mistresses older than himself so that they could mother him the more effectively when he felt unhappy — such was the common view of him both during the Regency and his subsequent spell on the throne. As will emerge in due course, this view by no means does justice to a man of very real talents; but it was certainly not without foundation.

As Prince of Wales he had spent a great deal of his life since the 1780s in pestering the King and Parliament for pocket money.[1] His debts amounted to nearly £270,000 when he was only twenty-four. The Government tried every method to restrain him, but like his

---

[1] Contemporary accounts show that he spent twenty pounds a week on perfumed toiletries; the rest of his spending was on the same scale.

waistline, the sums he asked for kept growing. Sometimes when he sought more thousands 'to maintain the royal establishment' (a phrase which was accurately interpreted as referring to gambling debts and race-horses, as well as to necessary costs), remorse and princely courtesy tempered his request. But he resented his role of dependant, and at other times his manner was petulant, expressing aggrieved pride. By 1812 he owed more than £550,000 and took it for granted that because he was now Regent he was entitled to spend more freely: petty wrangling over money should have stopped long ago. He had tried his father's patience so often that some believed the main cause of the King's madness lay here, in his eldest son's forty-year record as a financial delinquent who had forever been promising to turn over a new leaf but who had scarcely once done so. In contrast to such traditional explanations of George III's 'madness', it has recently been persuasively argued by Ida Macalpine and Richard Hunter that he suffered from acute porphyria, an inherited physical illness capable of producing symptoms of severe mental disturbance. Whatever the truth of this matter, the King had been incapacitated since 2 November 1810 when as a result of his raving and sometimes violent behaviour he had been placed in a strait-jacket. The Regency Bill of January 1811 had granted the Prince of Wales monarchical powers with a number of restrictions, and these restrictions had been removed in 1812.

During the Regency particular criticism was directed towards the Regent's behaviour to his wife, who became the darling of the people precisely because it was known that the two had fallen out. The Regent loved many women in his time, but it is doubtful if he ever felt love for Caroline of Brunswick. His reason for getting married in 1795 was that his debts had got out of hand; he needed to please his father and win a larger allowance. 'Undoubtedly she is the person who naturally must be most agreeable to *me*', George III wrote to Pitt after the Prince told him about Caroline, who happened to be available and less plain than some other girls of better reputation. The Queen, however, was apprehensive, writing to her brother, 'There is a woman I do not recommend at all.' The wedding itself had been a kind of tragic farce. Lord Melbourne, who was in waiting, noted that

> the Prince was like a man doing a thing in desperation; it was like Macheath going to execution; and he was quite drunk.

3

The Prince further insulted his bride by looking too often at Lady Jersey, his then mistress, a well-preserved grandmother. Nevertheless, for a short time after what Byron called the 'treaclemoon', the couple had lived together amicably enough, and a daughter, Charlotte, had been born in January 1796. But Lady Jersey was said to have her bed in the Prince's dressing-room at the Pavilion in Brighton, and Caroline's patience ran out. Before the end of that year, she and her husband had separated. Caroline's behaviour was as erratic after her fashion as the Prince's. She was fond of feckless men, laughed loudly at risqué jokes in public when as a princess and a lady she was expected not to, and took pleasure in ignoring other rules of social decorum because the Prince (who would one day be called 'the First Gentleman of Europe') attached great importance to etiquette. In time, she took lovers, an Italian among them, yet her promiscuity never matched that of her husband in his youth.

The people, who knew from the Press all about the separation, although not about Caroline's indiscretions, took her side early on, during the 'reign' of Lady Jersey, and scarcely once wavered in her support. But the Prince as Regent did not propose to allow Caroline to become Queen, and since to divorce her he needed proof of her adultery, there began in 1814 an inquiry on the part of the Crown into Caroline's behaviour. (It was not the first of its kind, for the so-called 'Delicate Investigation' had taken place in 1806, after the royal family had expressed alarm at rumours of Caroline's misconduct. While the findings of that shady government inquiry had been inconclusive, the Princess had been banished from royal society as a result of its criticism of her 'indecorous' conversation and actions.) Much of the evidence was collected in Italy, where Caroline now went to live for several years. George III died in January 1820, and that summer, with popular feeling in Britain running strongly against his son and the 'Milan Commission', a trial was held: Italian waiters and other unexpected witnesses were produced to speak for and against Caroline's conduct. Before a verdict was reached, Caroline herself appeared in Britain, to the delight of the London crowd. The Duke of Wellington told one group of demonstrators, 'Well, gentlemen, since you will have it so, God save the Queen — and may all your wives be like her!' Then the Divorce Bill was dropped, she failed in her attempt to gatecrash the Coronation, and went away, relieving the Crown and Parliament of further embarrassment.

Not only did the man in the street know that the Regent had behaved abominably towards his wife; there was, too, a widespread belief that he had bullied his daughter Charlotte, who was — partly for this reason — even better liked than her mother. The Regent had done his utmost to keep mother and daughter apart, and was reported on good authority to have stormed at Charlotte when, after the royal advisers had gone to a great deal of trouble in arranging an engagement, she refused to marry the lack-lustre Prince William of Orange. Charlotte married for love in 1816, the man of her choice being Prince Leopold of Saxe-Coburg-Sallfeld. When she died in childbirth the next year, the whole country mourned her.

The Regent was not simply disliked by the working people of London; they actually hated him, and frequently took the opportunity to hiss at his carriage in the streets. At times this was extremely embarrassing. In 1814, when Napoleon was on Elba and fighting seemed to be over, the Regent acted as host to the monarchs who had triumphed in the war, among them the Tsar Alexander and his ally, the King of Prussia. Prince Metternich of Austria and the conquering Field Marshall von Blücher came also — it is hardly surprising that this was remembered as 'The Year of the Sovereigns'. Here, surely, was a chance for the Regent to be cheered by a happy crowd, welcomed as a victor among victors. But the British people shouted their approval of the foreign visitors, and hissed their stand-in ruler. More humiliating still, they cheered his estranged wife, who had chosen this of all times to reappear in London society. One night the Regent went with the brilliant foreigners and with Lord Castlereagh, the Foreign Secretary, to the opera at the Haymarket Theatre. The Regent was seen to look nervously at an empty box in the otherwise packed building. As the second act began, the Princess noisily entered this box, heavily rouged, and curtsied to the Emperor of Russia in the royal box. Because the Tsar bowed in acknowledgment, the Regent had to do the same. Wild cheering broke out, and afterwards a mob surrounded Caroline's carriage, offering to burn down Carlton House, the Regent's home. Nor did his nightmarish experiences among the crowned kings end there. When he tried to introduce the Marchioness of Hertford, his current matronly paramour, to the Tsar at a reception, Alexander bowed but did not speak. 'This is my Lady Hertford', said the Regent loudly, thinking he had not heard. Still there was silence.

Such evidence as this, of family quarrels, a pattern of self-centred living, and extreme unpopularity, might make it appear on the face of it unlikely, to say the least, that the Regent helped to set the tone of the Regency, let alone inspire its creative activities. Paradoxically, however, he did both, and in the course of indulging his own tastes made what J. H. Plumb has called 'the greatest contribution by an English monarch to the enduring beauty of his country'. The key lies in the word 'tastes' — he had a cultivated mind, and was genuinely interested in the arts, especially literature, painting, and architecture. The Regent liked good conversation, and was responsible for introducing some of the most brilliant people of the time. Parties which he gave in Carlton House, at Brighton, and elsewhere did more than encourage others to play host or hostess in their turn. They sparked off an active interest in ideas, and especially in artistic ideas, first of all in southern English society, and then, by a process of interaction and imitation, in other parts of Britain.

The Regent saw nothing odd about caring equally for race-horses and for beautiful paintings, and if this produced a materialistic, connoisseur's outlook, it was on the other hand largely thanks to his example that the arts were accepted as part of everyday living in the Regency: he resisted that tendency, present in every period, to separate aesthetic pursuits from the rest of life. Whenever he had the chance to help writers whose work he admired, he took it. Royal interest of a discriminating nature in such matters had been lacking before — George III was unlettered in comparison. Lord Byron was astonished on meeting the Regent to discover how much he knew about contemporary poetry. His tastes were indeed catholic, for he went out of his way to praise Jane Austen, then a little-known novelist who wrote about an entirely different part of society from that in which the Regent and Lord Byron moved: feeling obliged to acknowledge the favour he had shown her, she dedicated her next novel, *Emma*, an eminently proper and moral tale, to this Prince who was notorious for his loose conduct.

Royal patronage of authors was no longer a necessity as once it had been. The men who controlled the fortunes of authorship in the early nineteenth century were now 'the booksellers' or publisher-booksellers, driving, ambitious businessmen like Constable, Longman and Murray. Money apart, it is probable that the best writers of the age would have produced their masterpieces even if the

Regent had taken no notice of them. Nevertheless, it made a difference to the social and intellectual climate that the Regent was as
ready to talk with poets as with statesmen, and to confer a baronetcy
on Walter Scott; in this way writers were made to feel that they
counted for something in society.[1]

Exactly the same is true of painters of the period, but in their case
not only the Regent's intelligent interest but his patronage also was
crucially important. In comparison with the highly organized world
of London publishing, the means by which promising young artists
could hope to find sponsorship were drastically limited. Either their
work was accepted for exhibition by one of the two groups which
controlled their destinies, the Royal Academy and the British Institution, or the likelihood was that they would remain unknown.
There was only one other possibility for a painter seeking to gain a
reputation, and that was to receive commissions directly from
wealthy individuals. The Prince Regent regularly spent part of the
money he extracted from the Cabinet on commissioning portraits by
such artists as Thomas Lawrence (knighted by him in 1815), who
had a gift for representing accurately the appearance of his sitters
while also flattering them by his subtle use of paint. During the visit
of the crowned heads of Europe and illustrious generals of the
victorious allied countries in 1814, for instance, Lawrence had
orders to paint the Tsar of Russia, the King of Prussia, Blücher and a
number of others 'in a manner that might not only commemorate
their visit, but transmit the state of British art to future generations'.
It has to be said that portrait painters stood to gain more from the
Regent than their colleagues in other genres which lacked the
immediate social interest — and the appeal to vanity — of por-
traiture. However, the lead which he gave made the wealthy and
high-born up and down the country eager to have dealings with
painters. While most commissioned family portraits, others asked
for landscape paintings of their estates, for sporting scenes, or for
pictures celebrating Britain's recent naval and military victories.

The Regent's overriding ambition was to create around himself a
pleasing aesthetic environment. He was therefore always on the
lookout for good paintings from the past; and if he spent very large

[1] He subscribed regularly to The Literary Fund, a society for the relief of distress
among authors, and in 1818 obtained for it the right to use his crest; the Royal
Literary Fund still exists.

sums in acquiring these old masters, it can be said on the other side that the Royal Art Collection is now the envy of the rest of the world, containing what are today priceless treasures, and that the Prince Regent did more than anyone else to build it up. Famous works of art came on the market more frequently in the early nineteenth century than in most other periods, because the war in Europe had led to the dispersal and sale of a number of distinguished collections, both private and public. The Regent saw to it that few major buying opportunities of this kind were missed. Such was his reputation as an avid collector that not long after Waterloo Pope Pius VII offered him classical sculpture which Napoleon had taken from Rome to the Louvre, including the Apollo Belvedere; it was going to cost the Vatican too much to transport everything back south of the Alps. But even though they would have brought him much pleasure, the Regent preferred on this occasion not to acquire further master-pieces, for he recognized that what had been created in a Mediter-ranean country should remain there. Graciously declining the Pope's offer, he helped the Royal Academy to obtain casts of the sculpture, then paid for its return to Italy.

Paintings formed only one small part of his definition of a congenial environment. He was equally ready to lavish resources on buildings and streets, with perhaps even more significant results. The area to the north of Westminster where once there had been royal parks and residences had become the fashionable 'West End', and it was here that the Prince of Wales lived while in London. In 1787 Carlton House, originally a plain brick building, had been brilliantly redesigned for him by Henry Holland. Its interior came to excel in splendour every private house in Britain (as well as the rather dowdy palaces occupied by George III), while its assured neo-classical façade lent distinction to the entire West End. The royal occupant of Carlton House noticed, however, that its surroundings left much to be desired: opening off the favoured enclaves of Pall Mall, St James's Street, Piccadilly and Bond Street, were mean and cramped alleys and acres of buildings, and it was a problem to find one's way from one island of good architecture to another. Beau Brummell might jest to Sheridan on meeting him in the Strand that he had got lost by straying so far east of Piccadilly, but the Prince was not amused by the 'unimproved' appearance of so much of the only part of London he knew well and really cared about. When he became Regent he decided that something must be done about it, and on a large scale.

Instinctively, he turned to John Nash.[1] Nash was almost sixty, with a successful career as a country-house architect behind him, but instead of thinking of retirement, he was looking for some new and challenging task. This 'clever, odd, amusing man, with a face like a monkey's but civil and good humoured to the greatest degree', had brilliance, unfulfilled ambitions and prodigious energy. He wanted to succeed where he had failed once before, for as a young man he had been made bankrupt by speculating unwisely in a house-building venture in Bloomsbury, and the memory had never been erased. A psychologist might claim that he was still compensating for the early disappointment at the end of his life when he rebuilt Buckingham House as Buckingham Palace.

In 1811, Marylebone Park, which had originally been a hunting park of Henry VIII but which had in recent times been leased as farmland, reverted to the Crown. The previous Surveyor General to His Majesty's Revenues, John Fordyce, had been a man of great vision who understood the need to develop part of the Park without spoiling the scene; he wanted if possible to improve access to it from the West End by widening the congested streets between the Oxford Road and the Marylebone-Euston Road further north, which had recently become the effective boundary for upper-class residential building. Fordyce had written four reports on Marylebone Park, the last in 1809, and a competition had been held for officially employed architects to submit plans for development. Easily the best plan came from Nash. What he proposed was the application of updated landscape design principles in an exclusive, self-contained residential estate. The main feature was to be an artificial lake with three serpentine loops. In the central area of the Park there would be a double circus with a 'national Valhalla' on rising ground; nearby, the Prince would have his own *guingette* or pleasure pavilion. There were to be handsome terraces close to the Outer Circle, the Park perimeter, and some forty or fifty villas were to be set in their own grounds within, in such a way that 'no Villa should see any other, but

---

[1] As early as 1798 Nash exhibited in the Royal Academy a drawing of 'A Conservatory for H.R.H. the Prince of Wales'. Piquancy is added to the tale of his association with royalty by the fact that Mary Anne Bradley, a coalmaster's lusty daughter twenty years his junior whom he married in this same year, is said to have been at one time a mistress of the Prince.

each should appear to possess the whole of the Park'. This planned
development, in Nash's view, would greatly increase the royal
revenues, but it must not take place at the expense of natural
amenities which alone made possible his creation of *rus in urbe*. Nash
sought to add to the Park's beauty, not to lay it waste, and therefore
urged that

> the attraction of open Space, free air and the scenery of Nature, with the
> means and invitation of exercise on horseback, on foot and in Carriages,
> shall be preserved or created in Mary-le-bone Park, as allurements or
> motives for the wealthy part of the Public to establish themselves there.

It took many years before the money was raised to lay out the
Park and erect buildings to meet Nash's specifications. He was not
able to carry out every part of the original plan as some ideas proved
too expensive; for instance, he had to drop the notion of a national
Valhalla and princely *guingette*. But the essential concept was realized before 1825, and what was achieved followed his principles of
planning. Regent's Park triumphantly reconciled the demands of
conservation and development. Rich men bought houses, while
visitors to London wrote glowing descriptions of the transformed
scene. James Elmes communicated the sense of wonder people felt
in his *Metropolitan Improvements*, published in 1827. There he
compares Regency London to Pericles' Athens and Louis XIV's
Paris, and writes of Nash's achievements, 'which have metamor-
phosed Mary-le-bone Park and its cow-sheds into a rural city of
almost eastern magnificence'. The supreme merit of it all, in Elmes's
opinion, was that 'the elegancies of the town and the beauties of the
country are co-mingled'.

Planning the Park was one thing, building 'The New Street' quite
another; yet the execution of Nash's plan for the Park depended
upon his successfully completing the task of linking Portland Place
with the West End, which entailed making more than a mile of new
highway through a built-up area, in addition to widening existing
roads. Otherwise, why should men of substance, including M.P.s
with duties at Westminster, choose to live so far from the centre of
things as the Park? It was in the years of frustration which preceded
and accompanied the creation of the new road, with Crown Commissioners waiting to attack Nash when he took controversial decisions, but no central authority which could give him financial
support, that the Regent's backing counted for most. Some funds

were available to recompense individuals whose houses were re-moved, and to pay for improvements in the Park, but the main burden of expense had to be met privately, by Nash, and by those builders he could persuade to join him in the speculation. The 'New Street' was the biggest gamble of its kind of the entire Regency, a period of high inflation (brought about by the transition from a war to a peace economy, by inequalities of overseas trade, and by an excessive supply of paper currency). Beside it, most other risky ventures of the time (there were dozens of private ones like Sir Walter Scott's building of Abbotsford in the Scottish Borders) pale into insignificance. Nash himself not only had to design and build the Quadrant north of Piccadilly as a solution to the problem of changing the axis of the street; he had to advance more than £60,000 of his own money to get the job done. Then there were the many builders, to whom parts of the street had been contracted out, to be encouraged and supervised. Only Nash could ensure that all the different sections had unity.

Throughout the Regency he was severely criticized for daring to interfere with the layout of London's streets. There were objections, too, on grounds of risk to health. Another generation was to pass before much was done about sanitation for ordinary people in British cities, but well-to-do Londoners were already concerned about the districts in which they lived themselves. Nash therefore had to submit his street plans for the approval of several groups of 'experts'. All this meant delay, and cost him the promised invest-ment of a number of builders and house-buyers. But Nash was indestructibly resilient. He believed in what he was doing with the kind of passionate commitment that I. K. Brunel was to display as an engineer in the early Victorian age.

And through it all, the Regent never wavered in his support. He understood from the beginning what the scoffers reluctantly grasped as the street neared completion in 1823. Nash's New Street was one of the truly great streets in Europe, long enough and broad enough for processions, but also varied and free from monotony, its shop-fronts and houses graced with colonnades, its classical straightness relieved by magnificently confident curves. The Regent could privately smile — as Nash no doubt did himself — at the *Quarterly Review*'s jibe at the use of so much of the Rev. Parker's 'Roman cement', stucco:

11

> Augustus at Rome was for building renown'd,
> And of marble he left what of brick he had found;
> But is not our Nash, too, a very great master? —
> He finds us all brick and he leaves us all plaster.

But the Regent's faith in his own aesthetic taste survived this and many similar jokes. It was to be vindicated in a few years' time when Henry Crabb Robinson wrote in his diary after riding through the Park in a gig:

> I really think this enclosure, with the new street leading to it from Carlton House, will give a sort of glory to the Regent's Government, which will be more felt by posterity than the victories of Trafalgar and Waterloo, glorious as they are.

The names Regent's Park and Regent's Street did not come into use until after the Regency was over. But they were deserved, because the Regent had fought hard to make each of Nash's 'metropolitan improvements' possible.

There was, however, a disturbing side to all this new magnificence. Regent Street owed its existence to a planning philosophy so anti-democratic as to amount to a kind of urban apartheid. Nash had got the plan for the New Street accepted by emphasizing that it would effectively divide off the homes of the London ruling classes from their poorer neighbours. In his own words, the idea was to

> make a complete separation between the Streets and Squares occupied by the Nobility and Gentry, and the narrow Streets and meaner Houses occupied by mechanics and the trading part of the community.

Neither the Regent nor his architect worried about leaving the many to fend for themselves while spending large sums to create a pleasing environment for the lucky few. The supreme illustration of this kind of cavalier disregard for the needs of the majority of the population is Brighton Pavilion, the 'sunny dome' itself, which cost the nation half a million pounds by the time George IV died. It was one man's personal plaything, an aesthete's palace of art.

The Prince seems to have recognized the potential of Brighton as a place 'to get away from it all' as early as 1783, when he first went there to try a sea-water cure for swollen glands. At that time Brighthelmstone was little more than a large village. The Prince rented a small farmhouse on the Steine, a broad strip of lawn that ran down towards the sea. In the summer of 1787 Henry Holland, fresh from planning the reconstruction of Carlton House, built for the

Prince on his Brighton land a bow-fronted house in the classical manner, topped by a shallow dome. Even in this early, restrained form, the building was known as 'The Prince of Wales's Marine Pavilion'. With each royal visit, the Pavilion seemed to grow in size and fame; and Brighton grew with it. An apologist for the Prince might truthfully claim that he created Brighton's appeal as a place to live in or visit, and hence gave jobs to many people. The number of houses there more than doubled in the last part of the eighteenth century and had almost trebled itself again by 1820. Brighton acquired a reputation as a leading centre of fashionable life. In the eyes of the young and daring, it was more exciting than Bath. 'A visit to Brighton', sighed Lydia Bennett in *Pride and Prejudice* (1813), 'comprised every possibility of earthly happiness.'

As the Prince frequently longed to escape into privacy, the rapid growth of the town did not altogether suit him. Yet he enjoyed being, for a change, truly at the centre of things. His attitude towards people who flocked after him in Brighton (the undesirables armed with opera-glasses and the boldest of all with naval telescopes) was tolerant, whereas he hated a London mob. On this marine strand an attendant crowd, usually deferential if not obsequious, encouraged pleasurable role-playing. The phrase 'alternative life-style' might have been coined with the Master of the Pavilion in mind. Every extravagance, every gesture of largesse, contrasted with his father's dullness and frugality. At Brighton the Prince was nothing less than a monarch in exile, a make-believe King.

Even his horses were grandly accommodated. The stables with their massive dome designed by William Porden were worthy of an emperor of the East; and at the beginning of the century oriental ideas ran much in the Prince's mind. Indeed, he thought of enclosing the entire Pavilion in the structure of a Chinese pagoda, until it was pointed out to him that this building style could not easily be reconciled with Holland's English classicism. Acutely disappointed — already he had ordered a gallery to be specially constructed in the north wing to use up a gift of Chinese wallpaper — the Prince had to content himself for the time being with introducing Chinese motifs throughout the furnishings and bric-à-brac of the house. His taste for *chinoiserie* differed from that enthusiasm for delicate shades and fragile objects of beauty which had swept the country in the 1770s and which periodically recurs as a fashion. He surrounded himself

13

with florid colours, wrathful shapes. It appeared to some visitors that a large part of the angriest art of imperial China had found a home, quite inappropriately, beside the English Channel.

Then the Prince 'discovered' India. Here was a manner which combined grace and lightness with the monumental dignity appropriate to majesty. Stimulated by the excellent engravings of pavilions, mausoleums, and onion-dome temples in Thomas and William Daniell's *Views of Oriental Scenery,* he commissioned Humphry Repton to design a new exterior for the Brighton complex. Repton knew that whatever style seemed to have a regal and exotic flavour appealed to his patron. The Indian taste now dominated, but earlier sources of fantasy — Gothic, Moorish, Chinese — had not been banished forever. The Chinese rooms must remain. All the same, recognizing a shift in taste, he took up and developed a theme initiated in Porden's Moorish stable-dome, and proposed in his expensively produced *Designs for the Pavilion at Brighton* (1808) an entire series of Indian apartments crowned by gleaming domes. So bold was his idea, so skilled his hand, that in his drawings the luminous Indian domes seemed to float majestically on air. The Prince was bowled over. His praise was generous to the point of being fulsome. 'Mr Repton', he wrote,

> I consider the whole of this work as perfect, and will have my part carried into immediate execution; not a tittle shall be altered — even you yourself shall not admit any improvement.

But this was to reckon without the stubborn reality of the war against Napoleon. Money was not available to let the Prince build as he wanted at Brighton. Years passed by. The battles rolled from Austria to Spain and Russia, and while the Peninsular War dragged on and Napoleon retreated from Moscow, John Nash was proving himself in London as the most gifted architect of the age. The Prince, who had not abandoned his dream of an Indian Pavilion, asked Nash to take over the planning of the royal works at Brighton. He did not mean this as a slight to Repton, although sadly he was no longer a fit man. Characteristically, the Prince had simply forgotten the promise in his own letter. Nash was now instructed to design a number of rooms which would be suitable for entertaining foreign ambassadors and visiting princes. Brighton Pavilion must become the most commanding and at the same time the most elegant palace in Europe. The Regent made it very clear that its existing rooms were too small

14

and unimpressive to match the demands of playing Royal Host on the nation's behalf.

No architect had ever carried out his client's wishes more dramatically than Nash proceeded to do at Brighton. Making use of Repton's plan, but subordinating it to his own sweeping conception of the whole, he added a great Indian dome in 1818, and two years later this was flanked by two other domes over a large and sumptuously decorated banqueting-room and a music-room of similar costliness and elegance. The Regent's mother, Queen Charlotte, who normally disapproved strongly of his expensive schemes of renovation, was so pleased with the large, up-to-date, well-equipped kitchens in the Pavilion that in 1817 she gave £50,000 towards the cost of the work still in progress. The next year the Regent held a splendid supper party especially for the domestic staff in the new kitchens. The *Sussex Weekly Advertiser* described how

> A scarlet cloth was thrown over the pavement, a splendid repast was provided, and the good-humoured Prince sat down with a select party of his friends and spent a joyous hour. The whole of the servants, particularly the female portion, are delighted at this mark of Royal condescension.

Such an episode immediately provoked satirical comment in London. Within a few days of the party George Cruikshank had produced a cartoon showing 'High Life Below Stairs' as another form of absurd play-acting by the Regent. But the Regent's pride in the Pavilion and in its distinctive social life was genuine. He believed that the nation needed to maintain a reputation for excellence in cuisine, as in the arts, and that Brighton symbolized this special social and cultural awareness. There was also a very practical side to his thought on the subject. In 1818, when gas was only beginning to be used for lighting, he saw to it that the Pavilion was brilliantly illuminated by gas lights. Those who were invited to one of the numerous dinners held at Brighton were treated to this display, and went away talking appreciatively of the wonders of modern science as well as of a building unlike any they had previously seen, a strange and beautiful pleasure dome.

* * *

The Duke of Buckingham was certainly well justified in his declaration that

> The Prince Regent, as the sovereign *de facto*, is exercising a beneficial influence in various directions, particularly in the cultivation of the Arts and Sciences.

Not only did the Regent interest himself in a wide range of cultural activities, in this way helping to mould the ethos of the time; he also took a leading part in supporting what was almost certainly the most brilliant architectural achievement in London since the work of Wren in the seventeenth century, and was responsible for the creation at Brighton of a marine Pavilion which has recently been described as 'the most magical building in England'. However, during his lifetime few thought of what he had accomplished at Brighton and elsewhere in these terms. The Pavilion was regarded by many of those who came to look at it as a symbol of expensive bad taste rather than of elegance. 'It looks as if St Paul's Cathedral has come down to Brighton and pupped', was the much-quoted comment of Sydney Smith, a prominent divine and wit — not for him the subtleties of the Indo-Chinese Picturesque. William Hone's satirical verses 'The Joss And His Folly' belong to the tradition of popular radicalism, which had for so long found in the Prince of Wales a figure to mock:

> — The queerest of all the queer sights
>   I've set sights on; —
> Is the *what d'ye-call't thing*, here,
>   The Folly at Brighton
>
> The outside — huge teapots,
>   all drill'd round with holes,
> Relieved by extinguishers,
>   sticking on poles;
>
> The inside — all tea-things,
>   and dragons, and bells,
> The show-rooms — *all* show,
>   the sleeping rooms — cells.
>
> But the *grand* Curiosity
>   's not to be seen —
> The owner himself —
>   an old fat Mandarin.

Scarcely more respectful than Hone was William Hazlitt, a man well known for his strong likes and dislikes in aesthetic matters, who wrote,

16

> The Pavilion at Brighton is like a collection of stone pumpkins and pepper boxes. It seems as if the genius of architecture had at once dropsy and the megrims.

It became something of a game, in fact, to suggest similes or nicknames sufficiently outrageous to apply to the Regent's favourite residence. William Cobbett's choice was more exotic than Hazlitt's. 'The Kremlin', he wrote dismissively, 'has long been the subject of laughter all over the country.'

*   *   *

Cobbett summed up here very accurately how part of the nation turned the 'Folly' at Brighton into a joke, even while resenting its expense. Yet for every person who laughed or criticized there must have been ten who scarcely knew of the existence of the Royal Pavilion. A large part of the population had never been to London, let alone Brighton. In the new industrial towns of the Midlands, in rural Scotland, and elsewhere in the United Kingdom, the Regent and his entourage were unknown. He belonged, quite simply, to another world. They lived out their lives, for the most part laboriously and unspectacularly, and the behaviour of the ruler of the land impinged upon them neither for good nor for ill. So far as they were concerned, he might as well not have existed.

What impinged upon the lives of everyone, rich and poor alike, was the conduct of the war and of the Government. Britain had been at war with France for almost twenty years when the Regency opened. This, and not the bizarre lifestyle of one man, was the most significant factor affecting British attitudes in the years 1811 to 1820: indeed, the Regent's own actions can be seen to have been in part a response to it. There was in the first part of the period an overwhelming longing for a return to peace. In time of war, it is natural to see peace not merely as a means of restoring social normality, but as the key to nearly every kind of problem; expectations accumulate in direct relation to the degree of frustration war has caused. The war against Napoleon had led to many restrictions — for example, travel in Europe, international trade, and political activity aimed at bringing about a reform of the British Parliamentary system (which some believed was essential for the country's good) were all severely curtailed. Above all, people had become

17

bored with a situation which had dominated their consciousness for as long as many of them could remember. They envisaged peace as bringing freedom: freedom from fear and boredom, and freedom to travel, engage in overseas trade, disturb the political status quo, or simply seek pleasure. The story of the Regency is that of a headlong pursuit of freedom by a people harassed by too much waiting and suffering.

It was not easy in 1811 to see how ultimate victory over the French could be attained. Nelson's famous sequence of triumphant naval engagements at Cape St Vincent (1797), the Nile (1798) and Trafalgar (1805) had ensured that Britain and her allies were supreme at sea. There was therefore no fear of invasion from France as once there had been. Admiral Collingwood had more ships of the line than his enemies, and although it was necessary to keep a constant watch off Antwerp, Brest, Rochefort, and Toulon, in case the French fleet should receive orders to sail, few doubted that any French initiative could be countered swiftly and effectively. But on land, where Napoleon's military brilliance had proved more than a match for his adversaries, things were very different. No sooner had Nelson tilted the war in Britain's favour at Trafalgar than Napoleon had inflicted an equally decisive defeat on the Austrians at Austerlitz. This had been followed in 1806 by the Battle of Jena, where it had been the turn of the Prussians to lose; and the seal had been set on the series of French triumphs by their humiliation of Russia at Friedland in 1807, followed by the Treaty of Tilsit, made on a raft in the Niemen, at which Napoleon persuaded the young Tsar Alexander to become his ally. The French–Russian partnership made it practically impossible for British ships to police enemy coasts, and so gave Napoleon the means of answering Britain's control of the Western Mediterranean: by his Berlin and Milan Decrees allies of France and neutral countries alike were forbidden to trade with Britain or with any of her colonies. These measures, which threatened the very survival of the British as a mercantile power, forced them to take extreme action in return. All Napoleonic Europe was subjected to blockade – in theory at least – by increasingly stringent Orders in Council of 1807 and 1812. These Orders, giving the captains of British vessels the right to search ships belonging to neutral powers, interfered with the European trade enjoyed up to this time by neutrals who were not involved in the war. The result was nearly disastrous, for in June 1812 the United States, as the neutral country most directly involved because of her cotton and tobacco trade, declared war on the British.

Clearly, this was an event with very serious implications. The logistics of fighting a war 3,000 miles away from home had proved too much for Britain during the American struggle for independence. Their former colony had now become a powerful nation capable of waging war both on land and sea. In London, Government Ministers and Chiefs of Staff, regretting that they had not listened to leaders of the trading community who had warned them against provoking the United States, decided to seek an early end to hostilities with the Americans, for they knew that any other course of action would give Napoleon the chance to attack for which he had been waiting. Fortunately, the United States had no interest in pursuing the quarrel with Britain beyond its natural limits as a clash over the right of all nations to sail the seas and trade freely. Contrary to the fears and suspicions of commentators in Britain, including political cartoonists, the new enemy did not join forces with France and Russia. Instead, apart from two episodes which were to take their place in the history of the United States — the burning of the Capitol in Washington by a British squadron, and Andrew Jackson's successful defence of New Orleans against a force which lost two generals and two thousand men — the Anglo-American War was largely restricted to a series of naval skirmishes fought off the coasts of the United States and Great Britain and elsewhere in the Atlantic.[1]

British ships came off worse in a number of these encounters with American privateers. This was a blow to national pride, and it marked the end of an era in which the Navy, as the consistently victorious force, had been much more popular than the Army. (Not only had the Army failed to bring the French to heel, their very existence had been resented in some quarters as a threat to the liberty of the British people, whereas it was absurd to see in the Navy a threat to anyone except the nation's foes in war.) The nation now looked to its soldiers for deeds of heroism, and especially to the

[1] Fighting at sea went on for two years, a treaty being signed between Britain and the United States in 1814. The Anglo-American War was quickly forgotten by the British, preoccupied with European affairs, but would be remembered for a long time in North America.

Duke of Wellington, the old Etonian son of an Irish aristocratic family, who was serving in Spain. For several years everyone interested in military affairs had been anxiously watching the course of the war on the Iberian Peninsula, where a British force of some 30,000 men under the command of Sir John Moore and more recently of Wellington had been attempting to relieve first Portugal and then Spain from the effects of a massive French invasion. Adopting a policy of attrition (Napoleon's army, under Massena, at one point numbered 300,000 men), Wellington finally succeeded in 1813 in winning an important victory at Victoria and driving Massena and his demoralized force close to the Spanish-French border. Sustaining the pressure, Wellington crossed the Pyrenees and entered France early in 1814.

He had earned his victorious progress by a combination of exceptional military skill and discipline, but he was ready to admit that he had been helped in 1812 by the withdrawal from Spain of large numbers of French soldiers. This turn of events was brought about by a rebellion against Napoleon by his allies in distant Russia, where the imposition of the Emperor's decrees had become an intolerable hindrance to trade. Napoleon was furious, not least because news of the Russian defection encouraged Germany, which had also become increasingly restive under French supervision of trade, to follow suit. Accordingly, he gathered a huge army, recruiting for the purpose men under and over normal military age — for France's manpower had been reduced by all his campaigning in the past fifteen years — as well as recalling some of Massena's best troops from Spain, and set out for Moscow. At first all went well, and the morale of his men was high; but Napoleon had reckoned without the terrible, destructive power of a Russian winter and the skill of experienced Russian generals in exploiting this. The retreat from Moscow in the winter of 1812-13 brought unspeakable hardship to the French Army. A lesser general than Napoleon would have capitulated to his enemies at once. As it was, Napoleon with his depleted forces suffered the first major defeat of his career at the Battle of the Nations at Leipzig in 1813, and the next year Austrians, Prussians and Russians followed Wellington's example and entered France.

Despite the potency of Napoleon's reputation, most people now believed that the strength of the greatest military genius of modern times had been tamed; it was simply a matter of waiting for the end.

This seemed to be confirmed in April 1814 when Napoleon abdicated and left for the island of Elba. The allied leaders decided that France should keep her boundaries of 1792, it was agreed that the social changes which had resulted from the Revolution should remain intact, and Louis XVIII was reinstated as King — everything appeared to be firmly under the control of the new authorities. Then, as suddenly as he had left the scene, Napoleon reappeared on French soil, and with his former soldiers flocking to his standard and Louis XVIII making a hasty escape, marched once more to take possession of Paris. As always, Napoleon sought the advantage of surprise in military and political affairs. The Russians had left western Europe, while already the armies of the other allied powers had begun to disperse. Britain declared war at once, and at the beginning of April 1815 Wellington was sent over with orders to defend the Low Countries along with Prussian troops under the command of Blücher until the arrival of a larger army from the east.

Wellington disliked his situation, 'neither at war nor at peace, unable on that account to reconnoitre the enemy and ascertain his position by view', but set about planning a combined invasion of France by the three allied armies, for it seemed to him unlikely that Napoleon would attack the British and Prussians; on 13 June he wrote to a colleague, 'I think we are now too strong for him here.' Only five days later, however, Napoleon led the French assault on Waterloo. He had conceived the daring plan of driving his army like a wedge between the right flank of the Prussians and left of the British and then dealing in turn with each adversary. The battle lasted from eleven-thirty in the morning until the late evening, when, in a final attempt to break the resistance of the British contingent, who had held out alone for several hours before being relieved by the Prussians, Napoleon launched against them the crack troops of his Imperial Guard. They were driven back, and Wellington gave the signal to advance on the retreating French. By the end of the day there were some 44,000 dead and wounded on the French side, and 22,000 on that of the allies. 'It has been a damned nice thing,' said Wellington, 'the nearest run thing you ever saw in your life.'

News of the victory reached London on 23 June, and people were to remember for the rest of their lives what they were doing when they received word of Wellington's achievement, so great was the elation — and surprise — of the moment. Someone who by chance became involved in the process of spreading the news was the painter Benjamin Haydon, who had spent the evening of the 23rd in the Edgware Road . . .

> I had stayed rather late, and was coming home to Great Marlborough Street, when in crossing Portman Square a messenger from the Foreign Office came right up to me and said, 'Which is Lord Harrowby's?[1] The Duke has beat Napoleon, taken one hundred and fifty pieces of cannon, and is marching to Paris.' 'Is it true?' said I, quite bewildered. 'True!' said he; 'which is Lord Harrowby's?' Forgetting in my joy this was not Grosvenor Square, I said: 'There', pointing to the same point in Portman Square as Lord Harrowby's house occupies in Grosvenor Square, which happened to be Mrs Boehm's where there was actually a rout. In rushed the messenger through servants and all, and I ran back again to Scott's. They were gone to bed but I knocked them up and said: 'The Duke has beat Napoleon, taken one hundred and fifty pieces of cannon, and is marching to Paris.' Scott began to ask questions. I said: 'None of your questions; it's a fact,' and both of us said 'Huzza!'

Mrs Boehm's rout no doubt celebrated straightaway in a manner which matched or heightened their mood of euphoria. The overwhelming majority of the British people followed suit within the next few days. (The exceptions were those individuals like William Hazlitt who had seen in Napoleon a kind of god, and who found it almost impossible to accept that he had been beaten on the battlefield and would command the loyalty of Europe no longer.) The Poet Laureate, Robert Southey, was quickly ordered to commemorate the battle, and responded by producing 'A Poet's Pilgrimage to Waterloo'. Meanwhile, hundreds of Britons who did not have Southey's official pretext for doing so made plans to visit Belgium and see for themselves the meadows close to La Haye Sainte where the fighting had taken place; villagers and city-dwellers alike considered how best to honour the victors, especially Wellington; Waterloo medals were struck, statues were erected, streets and public buildings were renamed. From every quarter, Wellington found himself showered with gifts, tributes and invitations. It was in vain that he tried to explain to non-combatants that the loss of so many lives at Waterloo had filled him with sadness: 'nothing except a battle lost', he remarked, 'can be half so melancholy as a battle won'. Not since John Churchill's military victories in the early eighteenth

---

[1] As Lord President of the Council, the Earl of Harrowby was a member of the Cabinet.

century had a British commander been so feted, and Wellington's well-wishers belonged to every country in Europe.

So intense was patriotic feeling in Britain that one Englishwoman, believing retribution would strike the nation, commented, 'Like the frog in the fable, we shall all burst with national pride.' She was right to think that many people had allowed their natural delight at the outcome of events to blind them to the actual situation in which they were placed. Because the nation had won a great victory, the British now looked for the realization of all those hopes and dreams which had sustained them during the war; everyone wanted everything to happen at once, indeed assumed that they had a right to expect it to happen. For example, soldiers who had been through the Peninsular War and the recent campaign in Belgium expected jobs when they returned home — secure employment, not medals was their idea of a just reward for their sacrifice. Housewives who had skimped and done without essential foodstuffs for years 'because of the war' quite naturally believed that things would surely now be plentiful again in the shops. Merchants who had seen their livelihood diminished and threatened by the Orders in Council of their own government welcomed the dawn of what they hoped would be a new era of prosperity. Citizens who had to put up with an electoral system which was clearly in need of change — some large towns could not yet return a single Member of Parliament, while a number of villages boasted two — reasoned that because France had been defeated, the Government no longer had any excuse for failing to bring in immediate reforms.

Not one of these expectations was fulfilled with the speed and completeness for which men and women hoped. There was rising unemployment after the war; even without the extra pool of labour created by demobilization, there would not have been enough jobs to go round. (This state of affairs was due partly to a sharp increase in population since the late eighteenth century and partly to the fact that manufacturing processes which previously had required manual operation had been mechanized at an increasing rate during the period when thousands of men were abroad serving in the Army and Navy.) A succession of very poor harvests forced up the price of bread, making the housewife's dream of an age of plenty for her family rapidly fade, and at the same time creating bad feeling between those who owned large farms and had enjoyed good rents throughout the war, and the poor. Overseas trade would take a long time to recover, as the enforcement of sanctions over many years had turned some of Britain's potential trading partners into embittered rivals. Finally, so far from meeting popular demands for the reform of Parliament, the Government appeared determined to carry on behaving as though such views (which in reality were supported by many people of moderate opinions) belonged only to 'unprincipled Radicals' whose ambition was to destroy the country's constitution. This anti-democratic attitude on the part of men in power, coupled with the economic distress of a large part of the population, made the first few years after Waterloo a time of acute social tension and widespread disillusionment.

The Tory Prime Minister, Lord Liverpool, had taken office in 1812 after his predecessor, Spencer Perceval, had been shot while in the House of Commons.[1] He was an astute party manager, and was able to claim that he and his colleagues, who included most notably Lord Castlereagh at the Foreign Office, had 'won the war' . . . a claim which was to help him remain in his post without a break until 1827. On the Opposition side, the Whigs were in disarray: they felt that the Prince Regent, at one time a close friend of their former leader, Charles James Fox (who had died in 1806), had let them down by not asking them to form a government, and moreover they were not now allowed to forget that they had for a long time wanted to make peace with Napoleon rather than fight to a finish. Their nominal head was Earl Grey, but they were split into three factions.

The Tories failed to use their strong position as the party established with a clear majority in office to come to terms with the forces which were threatening to polarize British society after the war. The Cabinet, with a background in the land-owning gentry rather than in small tenant-farming or in industry, seldom understood the problems of homelessness, population 'drift', and unemployment associated with the accelerating Agricultural and Industrial Revolutions, and when it did understand, failed to communicate with the people directly affected. Indeed, for all the attention paid to them, those who suffered most from the major changes brought by the nine-

---

[1] The information that Perceval's assassin was deranged, with no political motive for his action, was received sceptically by politicians who had been inclined ever since 1789 to suspect that one day the common people of Britain would follow the French example and seize power by violence.

teenth century might as well not have been there at all. Eighteenth-
century Britain, with its agrarian-based economy and strictly
stratified society, had gone for ever, but the men of property from
the apex of that pyramid who still controlled the country's fortunes
were wedded to an eighteenth-century view of things.

Completely outside their experience was the kind of life —
insecure, badly housed, overshadowed by the fear of suddenly being
put out of work — led by thousands of men, women, and children in
the Midlands and the North of England, in the Welsh valleys, and in
the industrial heartland of Scotland. These people were in many
cases first or second generation migrants from the countryside,
forced to move by enclosures which effectively concentrated lands
in the hands of the few, and now living in villages, small towns, and
larger centres of population in the hope of finding steady work in
domestic service (still, with agricultural labour, the largest source of
employment in Britain) and in such growth industries as cotton
manufacture. The adjustment they had to make from an age-old
rural to a new urban pattern of living was interrupted first by the
war, from which many seamen and private soldiers failed to return,
and then by large-scale unemployment. When they fell on evil days,
the State as such did nothing to help them, for there was as yet a
complete lack of nationally organized welfare. Assistance came
either from a system of Poor Relief at parish level, or from private
individuals; or else they fell upon the doubtful charity of the
workhouse, dreaded by the poor as equivalent to being incarcerated
in prison. Similarly, the conditions of employment which dominated the lives of the cotton-workers depended almost entirely upon
the character of individual employers; there was very little legislation governing these matters.

A few humane employers stand out as men of vision who
responded to a crying social need by working to improve the lot of
those under their control. Most remarkable of all was Robert Owen,
author in 1813 of *A New View of Society*, a Welshman who showed
at New Lanark in Scotland that it was perfectly possible to achieve
good results in the cotton industry while bearing the costs of housing
and educating a large workforce. The general record, however, was
bleak. In 1819, after lengthy debates at Westminster, an Act was
passed which forbade the employment in cotton mills of children
under the age of nine, and limited the hours to be worked by those

aged between nine and sixteen to twelve hours a day. No inspectors were appointed to enforce the Act, however, with the result that employers could easily evade it; and nothing was done about the hours of work of adults, or about the employment of children elsewhere than in cotton mills, although both were subjects requiring action.

The working people of Britain, in other words, lacked basic rights or freedoms, and had to put up with much misery. In a later chapter the story is told of how a minority of them — the so-called Luddites — took to smashing machines which they feared would remove their livelihood, of how a larger number sought redress at mass meetings such a 'Peterloo' in Manchester in 1819, and of how crofters were driven off their land to make way for sheep in the Sutherland Clearances. All this is part of the social pattern of Regency Britain. In the middle and upper classes, the disillusionment which succeeded the dizzy raptures of Waterloo expressed itself in other forms. One very common reaction to the end of the war — it could be argued, to the fact of war itself — was a plunge into hedonism and the pursuit of pleasure. Regency London was never short of 'bucks', 'dandies' and 'exquisites', pleasure-loving young men who attached a great deal of attention to appearances, shrinking from contact with ordinary people as though they were contaminated. The most famous of the dandies was Beau Brummell, for a time a boon companion of the Prince Regent himself, and long celebrated for his question to a mutual acquaintance on seeing the Regent after they had fallen out — 'Who's your fat friend?' Brummell, in turn, came to be replaced as a possible hero in the minds of the young by Lord Byron, who was at once a hedonist and a political idealist outraged by the conduct of the British Government and of the allies at the 1815 Congress of Vienna.

In many ways, Byron is the central figure of Regency Britain, an influential poet who also set social trends, an enthusiast for the liberation of Greece and Italy, an idol of society who ended up as a witty iconoclast mocking in exile at the superficiality of the Regency code, the exemplar of a people's search for different kinds of freedom. Yet no single individual can represent the age in all its aspects, for the very time when Byron was cutting a dash in the West End saw an upsurge of puritanism and of the 'evangelical revival'; the fathers and mothers of the Victorians were already on the scene, distributing tracts, visiting the poor, preaching against such ungodly poems as *Childe Harold's Pilgrimage*, which had made Byron's name. Their activity, too, was a bid to achieve freedom — from the world and its deceptive standards. How some of these groups and individuals clashed, interacted, and contradicted each other is explored in the pages which follow.

[2]

The Public Prints

In his persistent search at Brighton for his own highly distinctive kind of personal freedom, and in prizing his right to do exactly as he chose, the Prince Regent was true to his age and to one view of royal privilege. But this did not mean that he was treated with the respect to which he felt entitled by the British Press. Many newspapers dared to criticize his expensive tastes; others laughed at his physical appearance; still others printed the names of his mistresses and gambling companions. The truth is that the Prince and his doings were a godsend to the Press. In Carlton House it was always the silly season — or so they made out in Fleet Street. The Prince had been good for miles of copy for a quarter of a century before he became Regent, and now this was more than ever the case.

True, in attacking the Prince, as distinct from reporting his actions, some newspapers were guilty of hypocrisy, of adding to what Byron was to call 'cant', but the Press reflects public opinion, and there is no doubt that a majority of Britons, of all ages, thought the Prince fair game for criticism. More seriously, however, journalists — or at any rate the radicals among them — had a particular axe to grind. They keenly resented that one man should enjoy such excessive freedom when the Press was denied a number of basic liberties.

The position of the Press was paradoxical. Milton and other campaigners had long ago won for it considerable exemption from direct censorship. Even with the nation's survival at stake during the Napoleonic Wars, a certain degree of freedom to report and comment on public events and personalities was assured. Foreign observers like Louis Simond were astonished, indeed, by the amount of licence allowed to the British periodical Press and to the caricaturists — this was the age of George Cruikshank, James Gillray and Thomas Rowlandson — who engraved satirical prints.[1]

But it was one thing to publish remarks critical of, say, the current war policy, in a newspaper, another altogether for its owner to sell enough copies of that paper to live on. When the Regency opened, there was no such thing as a cheap newspaper. Duty had to be paid on newsprint; there was a heavy tax on advertisements; most damaging of all, the cost of an official 'Stamp', required by law, was threepence halfpenny on every copy of each paper. This figure went up to fourpence in 1815. As an inevitable result of these charges, the lowest possible cost of a daily newspaper from the newsvendor was well beyond the pockets of most middle-class and of all working-class readers. This of course prevented newspapers from selling widely and thus spreading subversive ideas among the people.

In the eyes of successive early nineteenth-century British governments *all* newspapers were untrustworthy. Experience had proved, however, that most proprietors and editors had their price. The Treasury regularly paid secret subsidies to journals which backed official policy. The Whig opposition in the Regency did the same for its sector of journalism. This was simply accepted as part of the shabby legacy of undercover dealings between political parties and newspapers which had existed in Britain since at least the time of Walpole eighty years before. Journalism, naturally enough, was thought of by many people — however avidly they read newspapers — as a contemptible, venal occupation. The provincial Press might sometimes be free of taint, but a London morning or evening paper, or a Sunday paper, was an ungentlemanly thing. 'Nothing but a thorough-going blackguard ought to attempt the daily Press', Scott

---

[1] Simond wrote, 'Foot-passengers walk on with ease and security along the smooth flag-stones of the side pavement. Their eyes, mine at least, are irresistibly attracted by the allurements of the shops, particularly printshops; not that they always exhibit those specimens of the art so justly admired all over Europe, but oftener caricatures of all sorts. My countrymen [Simond had been born in France], whenever introduced in them, never fail to be represented as diminutive, starved beings, of monkey-mien, strutting about in huge hats, narrow coats, and great sabres; an overgrown awkward Englishman crushes half a dozen of these pygmies at one squeeze. It must be owned, however, that the English do not spare themselves; their princes, their statesmen, and churchmen, are thus exhibited and hung up to ridicule, often with cleverness and humour, and a coarse sort of practical wit.' *An American In Regency England*, ed. Christopher Hibbert, 1968, p. 28.

wrote in his Journal in 1829, 'unless it is some quiet, country diurnal.'

Part of the interest in going through Regency newspapers lies here, in trying to decide how 'blackguardly' particular editors were, or, to put it another way, with what kind of determination they reacted to the powerful economic and social pressures to which their job exposed them. Then, as now, some people were in journalism for money and little else. Sex and violence as staple ingredients of Sunday papers are by no means new. 'Honest Confessions', showing the influence on the Press of broadsides and chapbooks, detailed reports of criminal and divorce proceedings from the law-courts, and columns of society news were already popular in the late eighteenth century.

For a Sunday newspaper editor the most profitable approach was to concentrate on the sensational story. A daily paper, on the other hand, was more likely to balance political news with many columns of advertisements, reviews of drama and the arts, and market statistics. The temptation facing the man who edited a daily was not so much sheer sensationalism as compromise with political agents, or, in some cases, with booksellers or theatre managers. Certain editors were willing, for instance, to 'puff' books and plays in return for advertising.

Of course, the basic pattern of spicy Sunday papers and apparently respectable dailies which were in reality nothing of the sort was subject to as many variations as there were non-conformist journalists. Different degrees of compromise can be identified, some more honourable than others. In 1814, James Perry's *Morning Chronicle* was criticized by Henry Brougham because, so far from reporting that the Prince Regent was hissed in the London streets when his foreign visitors were cheered, it credited him with the crowd's 'applause'. The distortion of fact in this case occurred in a pro-Whig but notably independent paper edited by a man in late middle age who had when younger raised the standard of parliamentary reporting by the use of new techniques. Perry was no hireling of party or of Carlton House (though such existed), but rather an editor mellowed by long success, who made it a policy not to give unnecessary offence. His paper's mistakes were real enough, but Perry is to be sharply distinguished from Grub Street's true descendants in the Regency, journalists whose entire selection and presentation of news was designed to please their political paymasters.

Perry was the best known of many Scots employed in London journalism in his time. (Scotland, with lots of good schools and four universities to England's two, gave a useful general education but had fewer jobs for ambitious journalists.) He had a born editor's flair for organizing news-reporting. This was demonstrated most vividly when he created the first parliamentary press corps in newspaper history — his successor on *The Chronicle*, John Black, was to employ Dickens as a parliamentary reporter — and again when he decided that the best way to cover the French Revolution was to live in Paris for a year and build up a team of capable writers on the spot who would continue to supply news once he was back in London. In each case, his example challenged his competitors to review the haphazard and unsystematic methods by which they ran their papers. It was no longer enough to rely on an individual's phenomenal but fallible memory for news of the House of Commons, or on sporadic reports from abroad to supplement the translated extracts from foreign newspapers with which the Post Office supplied them at a cost of a hundred guineas a year. The future lay, as Perry well understood, with teams of reporters trained to note down in shorthand each word of debates at Westminster, and with permanent representatives in overseas capitals sending dispatches home by the swiftest and most reliable means.

The war with France created a study public demand for military and diplomatic news. This underlined the importance of Perry's idea of specialist 'foreign correspondents'. But there were many difficulties in the way of newspaper editors trying to gain news of events abroad within a few days, or sometimes even within a week, of their occurrence. Here editors were largely at the mercy of the Post Office, whose senior civil servants, the 'clerks of the road', had instructions to deliver no mail to newspaper offices until they had safely delivered everything addressed to Cabinet Ministers and to Foreign Ambassadors. This rule was usually observed; but a well-placed bribe could result in one newspaper receiving its packets well before the others did. Corruption was widespread in a system which gave so much scope to Post Office staff.

As if bribery in the Post Office were not enough, some editors suffered from political discrimination. Francis Freeling, Secretary to the Post Office, was a zealous supporter of the Government, who kept up a secret surveillance of correspondence and newspapers. His agents thoughout the country regularly wrote to him about the use of the post for purposes of 'sedition', whereupon he would inform the Home Secretary. It was possible for his clerks of the road to hold up for several days reports from abroad addressed to editors known to be critical of Government policy, which of course gave the advantage of first publication to their political opponents. John Walter II, who owned *The Times*, was forced to resort to a complicated system of subterfuge, whereby reports intended for *The Times* were addressed to a number of mercantile houses and to private addresses, with constantly changing symbols to show the recipients what they were. But it obviously sometimes happened that Whig readers had to wait longer for their news than Tories.

Then there were the special problems posed by Napoleon's habit of fighting on two or three fronts at once, several hundred miles apart (most wars in the previous century had been easier to report because they were fought on a smaller scale and in limited areas), and by the blockades of his 'Continental System'. Lines of communication from northern Europe were particularly hard to protect in the period 1809 to 1813. The Harwich packet-boats could no longer reach Dutch ports in 1809, and the following year the only ports open to British ships, those on the north-west coast of Germany, were under the control of Louis Napoleon. How was news to be brought to London?

The answer was found in the use of smugglers, who knew all the secret coasts and forgotten sea-lanes, and who were ready to carry French newspapers (and sometimes no doubt intelligence reports) along with brandy and other luxuries. Receiving the contraband newspapers did not worry the Post Office. As the official history of *The Times* puts it, 'With the sanction of the Postmaster-General, Stanhope's Foreign Post Office staff secured, at intervals, the Paris papers.' When the Admiralty seized a smuggler's boat carrying news and other articles in April 1811, the Comptroller of the Foreign Post Office protested that the Government needed 'a channel by which Intelligence may occasionally be obtained', only to be informed that their Lordships of the Admiralty could not 'interfere in the case of smugglers'. This left only the possibility of news being smuggled by private blockade runners who were not carrying forbidden goods.

John Walter II put the idea to John Wilson Croker, Secretary to the Admiralty, and an old friend of his father's, in a letter which reveals above all his instinct for getting news:

> The difficulty of obtaining French papers has increased lately to an extraordinary degree — to overcome which a plan has been proposed to the following effect. It is pretty certain that no French journals whatever can be procured but by the means of smugglers — a person of this description, who is in collusion with a French officer near a certain port is willing to exchange contraband traffic in which he has been hitherto engaged, for one, which is perfectly innocent with respect to its operation on the public revenue, namely the conveyance of French papers only to England. He feels disposed to engage in this traffic if he could be well assured of certain facilities, which seem to be necessary to the execution of the scheme. Government will I apprehend be no less desirous than myself of obtaining the information contained in these papers . . .

He added that, if Croker allowed him to go ahead, he would send on the papers received 'with all possible expedition'.

The notion of having information first for a change, rather than depending upon the whim of the Post Office, must have greatly appealed to Walter. No reply from Croker survives, but the scheme was put into practice, with Government agents keeping a close watch on the vessels involved. By using his wits, Walter had put his paper in a very strong position in the continuing competition for foreign news. *The Times* was looked to for early reports from all over Europe. This is illustrated by a note from an under-Secretary at the Foreign Office to Walter, dated September 1813:

> Mr Hamilton presents his compliments to Mr Walter, and is directed by Lord Castlereagh to request he will have the goodness to tell him if he has received any Intelligence of the reported defeat of the French near Dresden which is now in Circulation.

The problem of producing newspapers quickly enough, like that of obtaining news from abroad, was experienced most acutely in the offices of the dailies. It did not matter very much if a weekly failed to report the latest incidents in Spain. The editor made a digest of information in the daily and foreign Press, and gave much more space to comment and political leaders than the dailies could. Further, he had a margin of time in which to print the paper. Certain pages could be prepared in the first half of the week — just as, today, the weekend colour supplements are printed in advance — thus reducing the pressures of work on Friday and Saturday. But no respite was enjoyed by the staff of the *Morning Chronicle, Morning Post,* and *The Times,* or by those equally hard-pressed journalists and printers who produced such leading London evening papers as *The Courier* and *The Sun*.

In 1810 all printing, whether of books or newspapers, was still done by hand. No more than 250 copies of a newspaper could be printed in an hour; an edition of 4,000 copies entailed continuous printing for sixteen hours. Most people who controlled newspapers were resigned to this cumbersome process, and dismissed as a waste of money the proposals which inventors put forward every now and then for harnessing the production of newspapers to steam-power. James Perry was no exception. When in 1813 Frederick Koenig, a highly skilled inventor from Saxony, demonstrated to the trade his cylinder-machine for steam printing, Perry 'declined to disturb himself with a visit' to see how it worked. He believed that the actual printing of his newspaper did not justify large-scale capital outlay, and preferred to use his profits to attract gifted writers, like Sheridan, Coleridge and the economist Ricardo.

At Printing House Square, John Walter II took a different view. *The Times* was only one important part of the printing business he had inherited. He understood clearly that technical improvements would benefit both the newspaper and the general printing works which he owned. After going into the subject closely, he agreed to buy two machines from Koenig, at a cost of £1,100 each, and for a further £500, 'two Steam Engines of Two Horse Power each to work the said machines'. Walter ordered Koenig to assemble the machines in complete secrecy in a private room in Printing House Square. He feared that his compositors, recognizing the challenge to their jobs inherent in the new technology, might destroy the Press. (It was a time of intense anxiety for many employers, as the example of the Luddite frame-breakers in the Midlands could lead to violence on the part of other groups of workers whose livelihood was threatened by new machines.) One morning before six, Walter went into the press-room and astonished the men there by saying to them: '*The Times* is already printed — by steam.' The *fait accompli* worked. A number of compositors lost their jobs as a result of the change, but Walter prevented serious reprisals by promising to continue their wages until they were re-employed, and by pointing out that 'if any violence was attempted there was a force ready to suppress it'.

Koenig's machines printed over 1,000 copies of the paper in an hour, four times as many as the old method. On 29 November 1814 anyone scanning *The Times*'s first leader would have read:

> Our Journal of this day presents to the public the practical result of the
> greatest improvement connected with printing, since the discovery of the
> art itself. The reader of this paragraph now holds in his hand one of the
> many thousand impressions of *The Times* newspaper, which were taken
> off last night by a mechanical apparatus. A system of machinery almost
> organic has been devised and arranged, which, while it relieves the human
> frame of its most laborious efforts in printing far exceeds all human
> powers in rapidity and despatch.

The 'system of machinery almost organic' underwent many
improvements, until in 1827 Walter's office brought out a new
'multiple' machine with four cylinders which could print 4,000
sheets in an hour. But the crucial innovation belongs to the Regency.
This was the first in a series of changes in the application of
technology to newspaper production which is still a matter of vital
concern today. In the 1830s, steam began to be used for printing
books as well as periodicals. Walter did not exaggerate in claiming for
Koenig's invention an importance in the history of printing second
only to Gutenberg's original use of movable type almost 400 years
before. Steam made possible the mass production of the printed
word.

John Walter II now had a clear advantage over other newspapers.
He added to it by appointing as editor of *The Times* Thomas Barnes,
who combined a confident understanding of public opinion as a
force in politics with the integrity needed to keep clear of the kinds
of party connection which had demeaned journalism for too long.
These were exactly the qualities to make people read *The Times* in a
period of mounting agitation for reform.

Barnes was certainly not a dandy, but he was in some respects a
Regency buck, handy with his fists and a lover of town pleasures.
While an undergraduate at Cambridge, he told an earlier editor of
The Times

> . . . having had lessons from a boxer, he gave himself airs, and meeting
> with a fellow sitting on a stile in a field, who did not make way for him as
> he expected, and as he thought due to a gownsman, he asked him what he
> meant, and said he had a great mind to thrash him, 'The man smiled', said
> Barnes, 'put his hand on my shoulder, and said, "Young man, I'm Cribb". I
> was delighted; gave him my hand; took him to my room, where I had a
> wine party, and he was the lion.'

This incident brings together the greatest pugilist of the age and an
unknown student one day to be described by the Lord Chancellor as

'the most powerful man in England'. Already, Barnes's pugnacity was tempered with realism. Between this incident and the time when he became editor of *The Times* in 1817 he studied law at Lincoln's Inn, and wrote much dramatic and literary criticism for his old school-fellow Leigh Hunt's *Examiner* and for another prominent liberal weekly paper, John Scott's *Champion*. His style gained in edge and authority as a result.

Now, however, it was no longer possible for him to rely on the method by which, 'after several complaints of his irregularity', he had met the deadlines for his series 'Portraits of Authors' in *The Champion*: during that phase, according to Horace Smith,

> at his customary hour he retired to rest, sober or not, as the case might be, leaving orders to be called at four o'clock in the morning, when he arose with a bright, clear, and vigorous intellect, and immediately applying himself to his task, achieved it with a completeness and rapidity that few could equal, and which none, perhaps, could have surpassed.

He soon found that to edit a daily he had to work at full stretch, writing articles himself, organizing contributions from his staff, seeing people from whom he wanted information.

Barnes sought a reputation for *The Times,* not for himself. He avoided personal publicity throughout his career, as did John Walter II. These two were mainly responsible for creating the very strong tradition of anonymity in the columns of *The Times,* which lasted into the 1960s. In Barnes's judgment, the intrusion of a writer's identity lessened his freedom to be critical, objective, and detached. Issues, not personalities, were the true concern of journalism. He carried this principle to the point of being at times a remote, mysterious figure. As an editor, he was the very reverse of the sycophants which so many others in his age allowed themselves to become. In due time, statesmen consulted Barnes, not their under-secretaries. His contemporary, the poet Praed, summed up his power thus:

> He breathes his spell in a dark dark den,
> The Chancellor well knows where;
> His servants are devils, his wand is a pen,
> And his circle is Printing House Square.

Among many other journalistic achievements Barnes was the only editor of a national daily with a reporter on 'Orator' Hunt's platform at the time of the charge at Peterloo (see Chapter 3). The authorities made the mistake of arresting him. His editor then described him as 'about as much a Jacobin, or friend of the Jacobins, as is Lord Liverpool himself'. *The Times*'s reports of the incidents in St Peter's Fields were copied by newspapers and magazines throughout the land, and made many readers very critical both of the behaviour of the militia and of the Government's attitude.

John Walter II and Barnes made *The Times* the most authoritative and influential newspaper in Britain — 'The Thunderer'. It took coolness and political consistency to do so. But in the eyes of one man whose flair for journalism equalled that of Barnes, *The Times* was guilty of 'trimming' for the sake of popularity. William Cobbett remembered the harshly reactionary line on many domestic and foreign issues taken by *The Times* under Dr John Stoddart, editor for a short while before Barnes. When Barnes showed a keen interest in the movement for reform, and then picked up a large readership by following Cobbett's own lead in supporting Queen Caroline during her trial in 1820, Cobbett saw red. In characteristic fashion he described *The Times* in *The Political Register* as 'The Turnabout', 'that cunning old trout'.

Cobbett's anger was understandable. In 1816-17, the period of Stoddart's control, *The Times* had led a campaign by pro-Government newspapers to 'write him down', and had sold specially printed anti-Cobbett leaflets. It had not hidden its glee when he had been forced to flee the country in 1817 and edit *The Political Register* from America. Yet he, and not *The Times* or any other newspaper, had created the strongest public interest in journalism since the decade (1762-72) of John Wilkes's attacks on Lord Bute's government in *The North Briton* and of *The Public Advertiser*'s anti-ministerial 'Letters of Junius'. It was he who deserved to prosper, Cobbet believed, not *The Times*!

Cobbett was nearly always indignant about something. Scarcely a week passed when he did not roundly condemn prominent politicians of the time in *The Political Register*. His direct communication of his anger to his readers was one reason for his immense popular appeal. To read his invective is to become involved in an intensely personal drama. He expresses naked contempt and hatred for all those people — Cabinet Ministers included — whom he identifies as enemies of social justice. Many journalists since have tried to cultivate the same wrathfulness, knowing that it sells papers.

But Cobbett's anger was genuine, not faked. There have been very few men since who have equalled his ability to write about politics with sustained animosity and at the same time with simplicity and clarity.

Like Byron, Cobbett was 'born for opposition'. As a young man he enlisted in the Army in 1784, served in Nova Scotia, and became a sergeant-major. He liked the life and the rank but soon detected corruption of a serious kind among the officers of his regiment, and, when his attempts to have the matter investigated were ignored, left the Army. After a short period in France, he settled in America. It was during the years which he and his growing family spent in America, from 1792 to 1800, that Cobbett was first drawn into political controversy. Before leaving England, he had read and admired the republican writings of Tom Paine, but now his political feelings were aroused by the anti-British rhetoric of many Americans who sympathized with France in the early stages of the Revolutionary War. As 'Peter Porcupine' he became a fearless and widely influential publicist for the British cause, and a denouncer of every kind of revolutionary impulse. Typical of his behaviour was the defiance with which he hung up in the windows of his shop in Philadelphia portraits of the British royal family, along with

> all the English Ministry; several of the Bishops and Judges; and, in short, every picture that I thought likely to excite rage in the enemies of Great Britain.

The young North American republic did not share his sense of humour. He lost a lot of money in a lawsuit for libel brought by one of his political opponents, a 'noted bleeding physician' whom he had described as 'a quack', and decided that it was time to go home.

Government politicians gave him the kind of welcome usually reserved at that time for naval heroes. Within days of arriving in London, he was dining with Pitt at the house of the Secretary for War, William Windham, and was directly invited to edit a Government daily newspaper. He was given the chance to do this with 'property, office, types, lease of houses, and all'. The offer was worth several thousand pounds, and would have brought security to his family. But Cobbett was his own man. He felt nothing but contempt for writers who allowed themselves to be bought, thus giving up their freedom to express what they believed. One such journalist tried to explain to him that this was the normal practice:

I tell you what, Cobbett, we have only two ways here; we must either kiss
their ——, or kick them: and you must make your choice at once.

Cobbett made his choice, and started his own daily, *The Porcupine*; when it failed after six months he began *The Political Register*.
He saw himself as a spokesman for the great inarticulate majority of
the population, and especially for country workers, whose values he
believed were being trampled underfoot by politicians and the new
moneyed classes. 'I set out', he wrote later, 'as a sort of self-depen-
dent politician. My opinions were my own. I dashed at all prejudices.' In 1804, believing that the words of those who governed
should be open for inspection by anyone, he began serial publication
of *Parliamentary Debates*, which grew into today's *Hansard*, the
official report of the proceedings and debates of Parliament. By
1807, he had seen enough of 'The Pitt System' or 'The Thing' — his
terms for the unethical alliance of men of property, law, and politics
by which he believed the nation was controlled — to have become a
pungent critic of the Government. The committed Tory was now a
committed radical.

This maddened Westminster, confused Cobbett's old admirers,
and gave an opening to those who wished him ill. But his change of
heart was sincere and, in one sense, proof of consistency. He was
always inspired by his memory of the pastoral beauty and satisfying
way of life round Farnham in Surrey where he grew up. As he now
saw it, the only way to keep alive the England of his atavistic rural
imagination was to become a tribune of the people. For, 'The Crown
had one party in *possession* and another party in *expectancy, while
the people had no party at all.*'

Ironically, many of the poor who had Cobbett as their self-
appointed leader in the next twenty years knew no life but that of
the towns where they grew up, worked, and died. Topics which
interested him deeply, like 'driving the small birds from the turnip
seed, and the rooks from the peas', held no associations for them.
For all that, Cobbett the countryman came closer to understanding
their political desires and frustrations than anyone else in public life.
A man's basic need to have work that will produce enough food for
his family and himself to live on does not vary very much from town
to country; nor does his wish to have a say in the running of his own
affairs. These things, having much to do with survival and self-
respect, were Cobbett's constant themes.

The Regency was a time of raging inflation, like the 1970s. Land values had climbed steadily during the war, which meant that the rich were very rich, but for the greater part of the population the cost of living was now a nagging daily worry. Various sophisticated economic remedies were put forward and tested, none with immediate success. Meanwhile, unemployment mounted, and with it, Cobbett's anger. He remembered the days when men traded in real money, gold and silver, not 'THE PAPER CURRENCY'. Wanting 'to get back to the gold standard', he tirelessly preached the case for doing away, step by step, with a false currency system, one which caused prices to soar because it was based on promissory notes and expected future wealth, rather than on actual earnings. Not even Milton Friedman in our own time has been so scathing in his criticism of fashionable economics as Cobbett:

> At first there were no bank-notes under 20 pounds; next they came to 15 pounds; next to 10 pounds; at the beginning of the last war, they came down to 5 pounds; and before the end of it they came down to 3 and to 1 pounds.

In Kent, notes circulated worth as little as seven shillings. Where was it all to end?

His own career had nearly ended, his enemies thought, when he was sent to prison in 1810 for publishing an article condemning the practice of disciplinary flogging in the British Army. Like Leigh Hunt, however, he turned the two-year sentence to his advantage by continuing to edit his journal, and by making the most of the alleged unfairness of the authorities in choosing to prosecute *The Political Register*. By the time the war ended, he was already the best-known popular journalist in the country, and the most vigorous defender since Tom Paine of the rights of the common man. *The Political Register* was bought by groups of labourers clubbing together, by subscription libraries and by public houses. To that extent, the high price of a shilling and a halfpenny — made necessary by the Stamp Tax, by the absence of Government advertising, and by Cobbett's costs — was offset by the ingenuity of an enthusiastic reading public.

After a while, however, Cobbett began to receive reports that the publicans who took in *The Political Register* were being threatened with the loss of their licences. He responded by producing, in addition to the usual *Register*, a *Weekly Political Pamphlet* which did not contain news as such and was not subject to the Stamp Tax.

The price was twopence, which he calculated would allow three or four working-men to buy the paper for themselves. As the un-stamped pamphlet could not be sent by post, he invited shopkeepers and others all over the country to become newsvendors and offered a modest commission on sales. Parcels of *Pamphlets* were sent by coach to these agents, who readily sold large numbers to the public with the incentive of Cobbett's scheme, and hired sub-agents to sell the rest in outlying districts.

The first number, dated 2 November 1816, was an 'Address to the Journeymen and Labourers', in which Cobbett stated his case for a redistribution of political power. He wrote as though speaking at an electoral meeting. 'Friends and fellow-countrymen', he began,

> Whatever the Pride of rank, of riches or of scholarship may have induced some men to believe, or to affect to believe, the real strength and all the resources of a country, ever have sprung and ever must spring, from the *labour* of its people.

Contemporary Britain was no exception to this truth. In fact, the splendour of the Regency would prove his point exactly:

> Elegant dresses, superb furniture, stately buildings, fine roads and canals, fleet horses and carriages, numerous and stout ships, warehouses teeming with goods; all these . . . spring from *labour*.

The central part of Cobbett's argument was equally direct, a call to action and self-protection:

> As it is the labour of those who toil which makes a country abound in resources, so it is the same class of men, who must, by their arms, secure its safety and uphold its fame. . .
>
> With this correct idea of your own worth in your minds, with what indignation must you hear yourselves called the Populace, the Rabble, the Mob, the Swinish multitude; and with what greater indignation, if possible, must you hear the projects of those cool and cruel and insolent men. . .

The 'cheap edition' of *The Political Register* ranks with John Walter II's investment in steam printing as a landmark in the history of journalism. By evading the Stamp Tax and thus slashing the retail cost of his publication, Cobbett had dramatically enlarged the public for political journalism. Whereas no newspaper in 1816 sold more than 5,000 copies, the weekly sales of the twopenny *Register* were 40,000 or more.

Cobbett was always very much a family man. He knew that in some homes the head of the household could not read, but this, too, could be overcome:

> The *children* will also have an opportunity of reading. The expense of
> other books will be saved by those who have this resource. The wife can
> sometimes read, if the husband cannot.

The effect of his 'Address to the Journeymen and Labourers' on the
kind of man for whom he wrote it, he recalled later,

> was like what might be expected to be produced on the eyes of one bred
> up in the dark, and brought out, all of a sudden, into broad daylight. In
> town and country, there were, in two months, more than two hundred
> thousand of this one Number printed and sold; and this, too, in spite of all
> the means which the Government, the Church, the Military, the Naval
> Half-Pay, and all the innumerable swarm of Tax-Gatherers and Tax-
> Eaters, were able to do to check the circulation.

It was a sign of his success, not of weakness, when Castlereagh
christened the new journal 'Cobbett's Twopenny Trash'. Returning
patrician contempt with gleeful impudence, he decided to make use
of the title himself in the future.

Early in 1817, however, the Cabinet suspended the Habeas
Corpus Act, thus making it possible for them to detain indefinitely
those suspected of subversive activities. Cobbett felt himself to be
vulnerable, because Sidmouth, the Home Secretary, stated in the
House of Lords that the Power of Imprisonment Bill would enable
law-officers of the Crown to seize, without immediately bringing to
trial, persons suspected of seditious publication. Cobbett's decision
to leave the country was taken on the spur of the moment. 'One of
my sons', he was to explain,

> brought me, from the House of Lords, an account of this speech of
> Sidmouth. 'Oh! then', said I, 'we must strike our tent and be off.'

He crossed the Atlantic, and although branded as a runaway by
Tories and by less successful anti-Government writers alike, somehow continued to edit *The Political Register* from Long Island. In
the summer of 1819 he decided just as suddenly to return, having
read with delight that a Bill of Peel's for gold repayments (which he
had been recommending for years) had been made law.

If the Government had been jittery when he left, they were
consumed by anxiety now. Cobbett landed at Liverpool on 20
November 1819, three months after Peterloo. There were, he soon
discovered, less congenial measures on the statute book than Peel's
Act for restoring gold to its rightful place in the economy. The 'Six

Acts', passed in the wake of Peterloo, were in process of becoming law. Among them was the Newspaper Stamp Duties Act, and it was aimed specifically against Cobbett's twopenny *Pamphlet* and all the other radical twopennies founded in imitation. As Lord Ellenborough put it in the Lords, this Act, which compelled payment of the fourpenny stamp duty on all pamphlets (except those of a religious nature) published at intervals not exceeding twenty-six days and costing less than sixpence, was directed

> not against the respectable Press . . . but against a pauper Press, which, administering to the prejudice and the passions of a mob, was converted to the basest purposes . . . such that it threatened the most material injury to the best interests of the country, unless some means were devised of stemming its torrent.

Undaunted, Cobbett raised the price of the *Pamphlet* to sixpence, and began to concentrate on whipping up sympathy for Queen Caroline and ill-feeling against the Ministers who had so oppressed the people. He had established a point of principle. The Stamp Tax, which prevented countless thousands from reading what they wanted to read, would one day be abolished. Cobbett did not live to see it done away with, but he inspired a whole generation of journalists to carry on the 'War of the Unstamped' against 'Taxes on Knowledge'.

Cobbett was a pioneer in introducing the debate about reform into cheap periodicals which could be bought and read by working men. It is hard to exaggerate his importance: the periodical reading public was greatly expanded as a result of the *Political Register,* and has remained so to this day. It would never again be possible for British politicians to pretend that the argument about national policy and the distribution of wealth could be restricted to the well-to-do.

Nevertheless, during the Regency itself the circulation of most periodicals which dealt with political affairs was limited to the upper and middle classes. 'Top people' in 1815 did not yet necessarily take *The Times* — the *Morning Chronicle* was probably in the leading position — but they did make a point of reading, according to their political bias, the Whig *Edinburgh Review*, which had been appearing since 1802, or the Tory *Quarterly Review*, founded seven years later on the initiative of Walter Scott.

These were the intellectual heavyweights of the time, book-length quarterlies which made no concessions to their readers but instead assumed that they would give both time and intelligence to the study of contemporary events. Both contained long reviews of books, on every kind of subject from travel and scientific discovery to poetry and fiction, this breadth of scope reflecting the Scottish Enlightenment education of Francis Jeffrey, the Edinburgh lawyer who edited the *Edinburgh Review,* and of Scott, whose interests influenced the *Quarterly*: wide curiosity was prized far more highly than specialization in one corner of literature. A good review in the *Edinburgh* or *Quarterly* was enough to make an author's name, so great was their prestige among the educated. Conversely, it was hard to survive a hostile one. Keats, for instance, who was unsympathetically reviewed in the *Quarterly,* had to summon up all his artistic courage to produce his third and best book, *Lamia and other Poems* (1820).

But it was current affairs, rather than 'belles lettres', which mattered most to the staff of the leading periodicals of the Regency. 'The right leg' of the *Edinburgh Review,* Jeffrey reminded Scott, 'is politics.' First principles of the social and political contract were continually being invoked. When asked to review a book on some recent episode in British or European history, prolific contributors to the *Edinburgh* or *Quarterly* — men like Henry Brougham, Francis Horner, Sir James MacIntosh, Robert Southey, J. W. Croker — would nearly always take the chance to develop a close and sustained political analysis relating to the issues of the day. They saw themselves, indeed, as engaged in a battle over the present and future nature of British society. Fundamental divisions existed between the parties, despite the social privileges which Whigs shared with their Tory adversaries. As the Whigs saw it, the Government must stop behaving as if all political change were necessarily evil. There existed a crying need for rational and progressive reform of national institutions, beginning with Parliament itself and in particular with methods of election to Parliament. But electoral reform, in many Tory eyes, was a step on the slippery slope towards social anarchy. Would Britain, the Tories anxiously wondered, seek to go the way of France, choosing a disastrously egalitarian philosophy and so running the risk of future dictatorship?

Nearly every word in the *Edinburgh* and *Quarterly* reviews during the Regency was coloured by the French Revolution and the war. The generation now in its thirties and early forties had grown up in the 1790s. This is the key to a great deal in the period. Henry Cockburn, a schoolfellow of both Jeffrey and Scott, and like them a distinguished lawyer, wrote in his *Memorials* of life in Edinburgh in that decade of divisive argument when all three had passed through university and then qualified as advocates:

> Everything rung, and was connected with the Revolution in France; which, for above twenty years, was, or was made, the all in all. Everything, not this or that thing, but literally everything, was soaked in this one event.

Not only the great reviews, but many of the monthly magazines, produced to entertain as much as to inform, showed strong political loyalties. An example is *Blackwood's Edinburgh Magazine*, which was begun in 1817 as a general-interest periodical publishing a wide range of feature articles, poems, and fiction. *Blackwood's*, like many other magazines, belonged to an enterprising bookseller-publisher who wanted to get his imprint known. William Blackwood and his two unofficial editors, Scott's son-in-law J. G. Lockhart and John Wilson, a professor of philosophy, had an anti-Whig bias; they had grown up, after all, in the shadow of Jeffrey. They encouraged contributors to 'dish the Whigs' both in hard-hitting columns of social gossip and in book reviews. These appeared under a bewildering variety of initials and pseudonyms so that it was seldom possible to identify the writer with certainty. The *Blackwood's* style of literary entertainment was undeniably livelier than that of old-established rivals like *The Gentleman's Magazine*. *Blackwood's* still survives, but it has lost the refreshing vigour and impudence of its early years, and become staid and respectable.

Inevitably, such a publication provokes lawsuits. Several aggrieved individuals sued *Blackwood's* between 1817 and 1825, and there were a number of settlements out of court. But one episode stands out as a reminder that in the early nineteenth century the 'code of honour' — the duelling code — still challenged the rule of law. John Scott, the brilliant editor of a rival to *Blackwood's*, *Baldwin's London Magazine*, which from its inception in 1820 had contributions from both Hazlitt and Lamb, took issue with Blackwood's helpers, and especially with Lockhart, over what he judged to be their disgraceful literary ethics. He published several very stinging articles, hot words were spoken, and in the end he was called on to fight a duel with J. H. Christie, who was acting for Lockhart.

The affair was seriously mismanaged, and Scott was fatally wounded. As was customary, the others escaped to the Continent for a time, although Christie was eventually cleared at the ensuing coroner's inquest and trial.

In 1821, when this took place, the overwhelming majority of Britons would have condemned duelling as a barbarous relic of a bygone age. But 'the honour of a gentleman' mattered very much indeed, and many quarrels were settled with bare fists. The period from 1814 to about 1825 was the 'golden age of pugilism' in Britain. The sport produced its own racy and colourful literature — much of it published serially, or in periodicals — which in turn added to the intense public interest in every major contest. Pierce Egan, the creator of much of this literature, was very widely read. If Cobbett ruled supreme among popular writers on politics, Egan was master when it came to sport and entertainment. Not only did he report all the big fights, making Cribb, Belcher, Scroggins, Molyneux and Mendoza household names, he composed the words of popular songs, and was the author of *Life in London or The Day and Night Scenes of Jerry Hawthorn, Esq. and his Elegant Friend, Corinthian Tom in their Rambles and Sprees through the Metropolis*. The three principal characters in this work, Tom, Jerry and their friend Bob Logic, immediately caught on with the public to a greater degree than any other fictional heroes of the age, the Waverley novels included. Parents were even to name their children 'Tom' and 'Jerry'.

Boxing is a kind of mimic warfare. It is not hard to understand why it flourished in Britain as never before or since in the years immediately after Waterloo, although, curiously, the subject has been neglected by social historians. The nation was proud of victory and convinced that physical combat was a real test of character. Fist-fighting was encouraged in every rank of society: Byron learned to box at Harrow, and then took lessons, along with other young noblemen, from 'Gentleman' Jackson, a former champion of All England who did much to give the sport rules. What better way, Pierce Egan asked, to ensure that Britain should remain the land of the free than by promoting a love of this manly sport? If those who criticized prize-fighting were heeded, he warned, 'the English character may get too *refined* and the *thoroughbred* bull-dog degenerate into the *whining* puppy'.

46

Egan himself was a small, tough, and cheerful Irishman who had lived all his days in and around London. He knew the book trade and journalism through a long and varied apprenticeship before making his mark in 1816 as the boxing reporter of Bell's *Weekly Dispatch*. In 1814, for example, he had published a thinly disguised satire — one of several of the time — concerning the Regent's love for an actress, Miss Robinson. The style of *The Mistress of Royalty, or The Loves of Florizel and Perdita, Portrayed in the Amatory Epistles between an Illustrious Personage and a Distinguished Female* was not perhaps highly original. . .

> Perdita to Florizel:
> I cannot, my much admired Florizel, reply in your strain; as well might an Arne attempt to surpass an Handel. They were both great masters in the art, the science of music; but never reached you, in the art and science of love.
>> Accept this from
>> Perdita.

Yet there was evidence here of Egan's ability to amuse his readers. Once he found his subject, boxing, he never looked back. His reports, whether published in the *Weekly Dispatch* or in his seemingly endless serial history, *Boxiana,* are detailed and very often make use of italicized words and of slang expressions. He was, in fact, to become an authority on slang, and publish a revised edition of Francis Grose's famous *Dictionary of the Vulgar Tongue*. Egan's technique is to draw the reader in to the secrets of 'The Fancy' (those who love the sport) by persuading him to share the special language of the ring, and its values. He sketches in the lightweight master, Ned Scroggins, in a typical passage:

> His appearance, when stripped, is not unlike the stump of a large tree; and, from his loins upwards, he looks like a man of fourteen stone. He stands firm upon his legs. His frame is round, hardy, and capable of great exertions, either in *giving* or receiving the blow, accompanied with a *nob*, which seems laughing at all opposition. A projecting forehead too, which, in a great degree, protects his *peepers* from being easily measured for a *suit of mourning*. . .

But, like every good sporting journalist, Egan is happiest in describing action. When he comes to write of a contest between Jack Martin, the baker, known as 'The Master of the Rolls', and six dandies who had pestered a young married woman, his pleasure in the event is infectious:

> He *let fly* with his right hand on the *nob* of the first that approached him, and the Dandy went down as if he had been *shot*; the second shared the same fate; the third was no better off; the fourth came in for *pepper*; the fifth got a severe *quitting*; and the sixth received for his *insolence* so strong a blow on his mouth as to dislodge some of his *ivory*. It was truly laughable to see the ridiculous way in which the *Dandies* appeared — the *claret* trickling down their cheeks, and holding their hands up to their heads; but when the *Swell* observed, 'JACK MARTIN, give it them', the name operated like a shock of thunder upon their nerves, and they all *bolted* like *racehorses*, or rather after the manner of the French *sauve qui peut*.

He makes Martin's fighting thoroughly heroic, but without losing his freedom to throw in a pun or an outrageous sequence of slang terms when he chooses. In celebrating brave deeds by boxers, Egan is never solemn.

It is a tribute to his skill that two of the most gifted prose writers of the age, J. H. Reynolds, and William Hazlitt, should have written on the subject of boxing and brought in terms from the language of 'The Fancy'. Hazlitt's single essay 'The Fight', with its exciting opening sentences

> *Where there's a will, there's a way.* — I said so to myself, as I walked down Chancery lane, about half-past six o'clock on Monday the 10th of December, to inquire at Jack Randall's where the fight the next day was to be; and I found 'the proverb' nothing 'musty' in the present instance. I was determined to see this fight, come what may, and see it I did, in great style

has been much anthologized. It should be read not in isolation from its original context, but along with 'The Fancy' by Reynolds and the best of Egan's writings on Regency pugilism.

Egan admired above all other qualities 'bottom' or courage, which requires '*wind* and *spirit* or *heart*'. His main characters in *Life in London* get into all kinds of scrapes. Not all of them are entirely creditable, for the book is in the tradition of *The London Spy*, introducing Egan's readers to the pleasure of 'slumming' or mixing in low society. Tom and Jerry sometimes break the law, as when they tip over a 'Charley' or watchman's box (subject of a famous cartoon by Cruikshank, who worked with Egan on the book). But they consistently show 'bottom', and their attitude to the poor and down-and-out is never patronizing. Egan despised the exclusive spirit of the dandies. Corinthian Tom is an idler or 'swell', which means that he likes dressing well and enjoying himself in town; however, he is in no sense a snob. One reason for the great success of *Life in*

London with all classes was probably Egan's genuine interest in every kind of popular entertainment, from a pub sing-song to a day's outing to see a fight. Whatever the pockets of despair in London, poor people were still capable of communal pleasure:

> It is ... the Lower Orders of Society who really *enjoy* themselves ... Their minds are daily occupied with work, which they quit with the intention of *enjoying* themselves, and *enjoyment* is the result.

Egan's genial writings undoubtedly helped to make the upper and middle classes in Regency Britain better disposed towards 'the lower orders of society'. This by-product of his wish to be entertaining was of some importance, for as the next chapter will show, Tom's and Jerry's fellow countrymen were faced with a situation which threatened social disunity and even held the possibility of class war.

[3]

The Dispossessed

From the moment when the Prime Minister, Spencer Perceval, was killed by an assassin's bullet in the House of Commons, to the discovery in 1820 of an entirely serious if ill-thought-out plan by Arthur Thistlewood and his associates to murder the entire Cabinet while they were dining, violence, riot and destruction of property were ever-present dangers throughout the Regency. There was a general fear of some kind of revolution on the British mainland, in comparison with which the Jacobite Rebellion of 1745 would dwindle into insignificance. Thoughts turned obsessively to France in 1789, and memories of more recent events closer to home, including the Irish Rebellion of 1798, were very much alive. In retrospect, this period may seem to have been an 'age of elegance', but many of those who lived through it were racked by anxiety.

John Bellingham, who shot 'Little P', as Spencer Perceval was nicknamed, had no political motive for doing so — he was simply deranged. Thistlewood, on the other hand, wanted to see a complete redistribution of land and wealth. He belonged to the extremist remnant of Spencean agitators, so named after Thomas Spence (1750-1815), who had combined a passion for the reform of spelling with equally strong views on land-tenure. In this chance difference between two men of violence there is a clue to a more general social change during the Regency. Between 1812 and 1820 protest directed against authority, whether peaceful or otherwise, increasingly became politicized. Individuals with grievances joined larger groups seeking retribution. Class interests assumed increasing importance.

At the beginning of the Regency there was a series of very bad harvests. This alone was enough to send the price of bread beyond the means of poor families. Moreover, from 1812 overseas trade, which was already difficult, became all but impossible: not only was Napoleon's 'Continental System' operative, denying Britain much of her normal European commerce, but the country was also at war with America, her chief alternative trading partner. The main cause of disaffection can be summed up in one word, distress. 'A hungry man is an angry man.' No period in British history illustrates the truth of this saying more vividly than the years which stretch from Bellingham's crime to the conspiracy of Thistlewood. Children were starving, and, as it must have seemed to their parents, they were starving in a land of plenty. Why should there be one law for the rich, and another for the poor? When the crops failed, the landowners never seemed to go short. Nor for that matter did the millowners and their kind.

Hunger not only made men angry; it made them bitter. When, in May 1812, news of the assassination of Perceval spread through the country, working men who would in ordinary times have been expected to react with shock or dismay seemed to take leave of their senses. At Bolton, according to a certain Colonel Fletcher, 'the Mob expressed *Joy*'. Somewhere in the Potteries,

> A man came running down the street, leaping into the air, waving his hat round his head, and shouting with frantic joy, 'Perceval is shot, hurrah! Perceval is shot, hurrah!'

There was a similar response in Nottingham, where the crowd 'paraded the town with drums beating and flags flying in triumph'. Most shocking of all was the behaviour of Londoners, who cried 'God bless him' as Bellingham was led to the scaffold. The poet Coleridge chanced to be present at the scene, and heard someone shout a threat, 'This is only the beginning.' Perceval was not given a public funeral. The risk of serious rioting was thought to be too great.

Lord Sidmouth and his staff at the Home Office knew better than to given any opportunity to the London mob to create a disturbance. Since the late eighteenth century the streets of the capital had been taken over on many occasions by a lawless rabble whose only purpose was to loot or destroy what did not belong to them. This was part of the price the country paid for not yet having a regular police force. During the Gordon Riots in 1780, when street fighting had become endemic in London, nobody dared to venture out of doors for days for fear of attack. One slogan heard in the Gordon Riots, 'No Popery', was still enough to cause a riot;[1] and whenever there was a parliamentary election, particularly in radical Westminster, hooligans gathered, looking for free drink and a prolonged brawl. Only when loyal troops were available to carry out duties in London could the Government dare to provide any occasion for demonstrations there.

In May 1812 nearly all the nation's soldiers were deployed elsewhere. A very large contingent was serving in the Peninsular War, but it is a clear sign of how worried the Government was about unrest at home that Wellington's army contained no more British soldiers than had recently been sent to the Midlands to put down the Luddites.[2] In Nottingham General Dyott commanded 800 cavalry and 1,000 infantry. As was stated in the House of Commons on 14 February 1812, this in itself was

> a larger force than had ever been found necessary in any period in our history to be employed in the quelling of a local disturbance.

The Nottingham force was merely one part of a far mightier body of soldiers now charged with keeping the peace among the people of the Midlands and the north. Derbyshire, Leicestershire, Yorkshire, Lancashire, Cheshire ... each of these counties had been stocked with trained fighting men. In the Manchester to Liverpool area alone, to take another example, there were gathered eight regiments of regular militia, containing seventy-one companies of infantry, and three cavalry regiments made up of twenty-seven troops of Horse Guards and Dragoons. In addition to the regulars, large numbers of special constables and volunteers had been enrolled in the operation. On 1 May the Home Office received a note from Lancashire stating that 1,500 special constables had been enlisted in the Salford Hundred, a number equal to 10 per cent of the adult males and 2 per cent of the entire population.

Not only the large textile towns, but outlying villages also, had troop concentrations. However remote the situation, it was no

---

[1] Catholic Emancipation remained a live issue throughout the Regency, especially in Ireland. By the Roman Catholic Emancipation Act of 1829, Catholics became eligible to stand for Parliament and to hold almost any public office in the British Isles.

[2] Followers of 'Ned Ludd' or 'General Ludd', a mythical figure probably named after a young lunatic machine-breaker in eighteenth-century Leicestershire.

longer possible to go into an inn anywhere in the region without coming across at least a few soldiers. Many of the men involved in the exercise were billeted in inns, not only because it was hard to find enough accommodation for them elsewhere, but also because the Home Office had decided that the surest way to control the population was by preventing groups of potential rioters from coming together to discuss plans. 'Divide and conquer' became the official, though unstated, policy. The malcontents of different counties must at all events be stopped from combining in a united rebellion.

It is easy to claim with the benefit of hindsight that the Government had no need to act as it did. Sidmouth, some historians have argued, grossly over-reacted to what were no more than local outbursts of indignation against hosier-masters and frame-owners guilty of malpractices against their employees. The danger of concerted political action by the Luddites, or of widespread rioting was small. Certainly, there is a great deal of evidence to suggest that very few of the Luddite leaders were seeking more than redress for what they suffered through loss of work or through being paid inadequately for very long hours of work. The followers of 'General Ludd' in Nottinghamshire, where it all began, were industrial demonstrators; and machine-breaking, while obviously an extreme and dramatic measure, had a history which went back for more than a century. This, however, is to overlook the degree of alarm which Luddism caused in the population at large. Moreover it might well be argued that the rioting would not have come to an end as it did had there not been large army detachments at hand to enforce the law. To make frame-breaking a capital offence was clearly an unjustified panic reaction. But the decision to send in more troops than were in Spain may conceivably have been correct, given the circumstances of 1811 to 1812. It was at any rate natural to assume that a force which caused havoc as purposefully and effectively as did the rioters who terrorized Nottinghamshire and Yorkshire would be capable of other kinds of subversive activity.

When the true Luddites — as distinct from mere petty thieves and hooligans — made their early raids, magistrates and government agents who reported on the situation in the provinces to the Home Office were appalled by their strength of will. Not even the death of their own followers deterred them. This had been shown during an attack on the stocking frames of Edward Hollingsworth in the small

town of Bulwell in Nottinghamshire in November 1811. Marching
under cover of darkness, seventy men had advanced on a frameshop
they knew to be guarded. Hollingsworth, a bold-minded and prosperous hosier, had positioned defenders with firearms at various
strategic points on his property. Shots were fired on both sides.
When one of the attackers, a man from nearby Westby called Arnold,
was killed, it brought only a momentary pause in hostilities while his
fellow Luddites carried away his body. The rioters, who had previously swung great hammers and axes at the doors of Hollingsworth's frameshop, surged forward again. Entering the building,
they broke the frames they had set out to break, then retreated into
the night.

The pattern of this raid was repeated many times in the north-
western district of Nottinghamshire. There was system, as well as
hatred, in these sudden unwelcome visits at night. The groups of
assailants were nearly always well led. They knew exactly what they
wanted to do, and everyone had a particular task assigned to him.
Men with hammers and muskets went in front, breaking down doors
and smashing frames. Meanwhile, lookouts made sure that the
militia were not at hand. Householders were left unmolested under
temporary guard unless they offered physical resistance.

The thrust of Luddism was directed not against all machines, but
against wide stocking frames, and, further north, against cropping
and shearing machines because these spelled the end of a specialist
occupation in the cloth-making trade. Apart from the owners of
such machines only those hosiers who paid low wages, or 'truck'
(goods instead of wages), or who otherwise operated dishonestly in
the eyes of the workforce by producing 'cutups' — cheap stocking
material which devalued traditional skills — were selected as victims.
There was undoubtedly an instinctive feeling against technology, a
sometimes blind fury at new-fangled ways which put men out of
work or forced them and their wives and children to slave for sixteen
hours a day in order to survive. But Luddism was essentially an
attempt through direct action to protect the interests of particular
groups of workers who wanted above all to stop their wages from
being further eroded, not a sinister plot to throw a spanner in the
works of the entire Industrial Revolution. Its aims are summed up in
'General Ludd's triumph', a set of verses which found their way from
the Midlands to the Home Office:

The Guilty may fear but no vengeance he aims
At the honest man's life or Estate,
His wrath is entirely confined to wide frames
And those that old prices abate.
These Engines of mischief were sentenced to die
By unanimous vote of the Trade
And Ludd who can all opposition defy
Was the Grand Executioner made.

Let the wise and the great lend their aid and advice
Nor e'er their assistance withdraw
Till full fashioned work at the old fashioned price
Is established by custom and law.
Then the Trade when this arduous contest is o'er
Shall raise in full splendour its head
And colting and cutting and squatting no more
Shall deprive honest workmen of bread.

What worried the Government most about the Luddite disturbances was that popular sympathy in the Midlands was almost unanimously with the rioters. Here, rather than in the separate incidents themselves, lay the major danger of disaffection. 'Ludd' in the Midlands rhymes with 'Hood'. The 'General' and his men were quick to exploit the legend of Sherwood Forest, where in fact many of the Luddite gatherings met. There is a controlled impudence which seems to carry an echo of Robin Hood in the threatening notes sent out to framework knitters who had been slow to support the rioters' cause:

> Gentlemen all, Ned Ludd's Compliments and hopes you will give a trifle towards supporting his Army as he well understands the Art of breaking obnoxious Frames. If you comply with this it will be well, if not I shall call upon you myself. Edward Ludd.

Leaving this aside, fair-minded observers of all classes could see that checks must be imposed on the introduction of new methods of cloth production if the result was not to be utter wretchedness for many and large profits for a few. The angry workers in Nottinghamshire were supported by many of their neighbours in the community not out of romantic admiration for the outlaw or because they made use of intimidation, but from an instinctive sense of social justice.

In Yorkshire, too, the machine-breakers had the backing of the people. 'Cropping', which involved a finishing process in the making of woollen cloth, raising the 'nap' or fluff on the surface and then shearing it, had traditionally been done by hand. For as long as men could remember, the croppers had been looked on as among the most highly skilled workers in the trade, and for that reason they were a group who did not take kindly to any reduction in their earnings and status. Now they saw themselves facing ruin. Since the beginning of the century a machine had existed which could do much of their work for them. Consisting merely of a double pair of shears working on a frame, it was simple to operate. Nobody could claim that the shearing-machine finished the cloth as smoothly as a cropper; but understandably the men who owned cropping-shops around Leeds were not all ready to forego profit for the sake of quality and good labour relations.

In the spring of 1812, the atmosphere in the Yorkshire cropping villages was charged with tension. The hated shearing machines had recently been installed in many places in the neighbourhood of Leeds and Huddersfield, and the Luddites had made a number of completely successful raids, which had been highly publicized. Now, they were surrounded by troops on every side, and there was great danger in further sorties. Yet as they saw it they had to venture out again and take action against certain very determined and hostile individuals who had persisted with the machines; otherwise, their aim of banning the new methods could not possibly be realized.

On 9 April, for example, an armed band of rioters, numbering several hundred men, attacked the house and workshops of a Mr Foster, a manufacturer who lived at Horbury near Wakefield. When they found they could not easily get into the workshops, they dragged Foster's three sons out of their beds and marched them out of doors, making them open the adjoining buildings at pistol point. Shivering and terrified, the proprietor's sons stood by helplessly in their nightshirts as the destruction got under way. The rioters shouted out 'Enoch' as they battered the shearing machines, because the firm which had become notorious for making the equipment was that of Messrs Enoch and J. Taylor of Marsden. Not content with putting the machines out of order, the Luddites burned the cloth which had been made on them and set fire to the workshop itself. None of the Fosters was injured in any way; but their family business was ruined.

Two nights later, however, the Yorkshire Luddites ran into trouble. The object of their fury this time was the mill of William Cartwright at Rawfolds, one of the largest in the county. Cartwright had made no secret of the fact that he intended to guard what he owned, come hell or high water. His family shared his spirit, and he had hired men with guns from Huddersfield to add strength to their joint resolve. Towards midnight on this Saturday, the watch-dog gave the alarm, barking at the approach of strangers. Led by George Mellor, a young cropper from a small finishing shop at Longroyd Bridge outside Huddersfield, a small army of 150 Luddites moved forward towards the mill. As they did so, Cartwright gave the order to fire. Two men were shot and badly wounded. This threw the raiders into a state of confusion; it was said afterwards that they had expected to be joined by other groups from Leeds and Halifax, who failed to turn up; in any case, nobody had been shot before this in the Yorkshire troubles. Mellor tried to rally his men. The familiar sound of hammer blows was heard above the shouts and the dog's terrified barking. But Cartwright's preparations had been well made. Try as they might, the Luddites could not break into the mill. In the end they went away, leaving bloody tracks and broken windows. Mellor himself, it was said, stayed to the bitter end, like a captain reluctant to abandon a doomed ship.[1]

The Rawfolds episode marks a turning-point in the history of Yorkshire Luddism. On the one hand, Cartwright's defiance made him a hero of the property-owning middle class, one who would be spoken of for years in the same breath as Wellington. He had dared to stand up to the menace, and his machines had survived. Charlotte Brontë would later base part of her novel *Shirley* upon this affair as she heard it described at Haworth Parsonage, Cartwright becoming the strong figure of Gérard Moore, and his friend the Reverend Hammond Robertson being aptly renamed as Helpstone, the military parson. The common people, on the other hand, saw Cartwright as a symbol of all that they most disliked. They refused to pass on the rioters' names to what they now identified as members of an enemy class, leaving the magistrates to rely on paid informers and on what they could piece together from other sources.

A no less disquieting result was that the Luddites began to plan

---

[1] An incident which took place in the small hours of the Sunday morning reveals how the Luddites hated 'spies'. The seriously wounded had been taken to an inn, where one of Cartwright's friends, a parson called Hammond Robertson, was present. Seeing Robertson trying to extract information from his colleagues, a tanner's apprentice called John Booth summoned Robertson to his side and asked, 'Can you keep a secret?' 'I can', came the eager reply. 'So can I', said Booth, and with that he turned over and died.

and carry out acts of violence against selected millowners. They wanted revenge, and the failure at Rawfolds had made them desperate. An attempt to assassinate Cartwright misfired, producing only an increased determination on the part of the authorities to bring the lawless men to justice. Less fortunate, however, than Cartwright, who seemed to live a charmed life, was John Horsfall of Ottiwells, one of the leaders of the Huddersfield Committee for the suppression of the disturbances. Every Tuesday he attended the Huddersfield Exchange, where, for months past, he had been heard to say that he would one day 'ride up to his saddle girths' in Luddite blood. On his way home from the Exchange on 27 April he was ambushed and murdered. Relentlessly, the forces of order reasserted themselves. Government troops, magistrates, constables, and Home Office 'spies' (or semi-official detectives whose job it was to infiltrate and then report upon meetings of the disaffected) all set to work to find out who was responsible for the outrages. In the end, Benjamin Walker, who had been an accomplice of George Mellor and of two other croppers from Liversedge in planning the death of Horsfall, decided to save his own skin by supplying the names of his colleagues — 'turning King's Evidence'. There followed a great round-up of men from the cropping villages all over the Yorkshire Dales.

When sixty-four men were accused and brought to trial in York Castle in January 1813 a formidable number of soldiers were on duty to protect the court and the town. Despite this menacing presence, popular unrest continued until all the verdicts were announced. Only then were the people of the North stunned into recognizing the risks they had been running. It had naturally been expected that Mellor, with his accomplices Thorpe and Smith, would be sentenced to death for the murder of Horsfall; and there had been rumours that some of those who had taken a leading part in the destruction of private property would be sent to Botany Bay. But few could have anticipated the savagery of the actual sentences which were meted out. Seven men were to be deported for seven years for taking illegal oaths — in the eyes of the governing class a sinister, treasonable crime — while no fewer than seventeen were to be executed. Five received the death penalty for machine breaking at Rawfolds, three for stealing arms, and seven for ordinary robberies committed in the name of Ludd.

In the event, sixteen out of the seventeen were hanged at York early in 1813. Large and sullen crowds watched them die. The message could not be plainer: machines had come to stay. There could be no stopping Cartwright and his admirers now. The way of life enjoyed by generations of croppers had come to an end, and those who could bring themselves to do it must learn to accept change. Even then, they had no assurance of steady or profitable work. Everyone else faced certain starvation. No pity would be shown by the well-to-do.

In the course of the Luddite disturbances, squires and millowners, who previously had tended to despise each other, had drawn closer together; inevitably, they discovered a common enemy in the frightening mob. A new alliance of propertied interests was formed which was to influence the development of society throughout the textile counties. But no less significant was the growth in solidarity, and in radicalism, which took place among working people during and after the troubles. If the Government had succeeded in stamping out Luddism, it had done so at a cost which it did not fully understand. Men and women who hitherto had been politically unaware were now alerted to the fact that working people formed a distinct part — or class — of the population, just as the wealthy did. They must look to their own. Their future, and their children's future, depended upon the degree to which they could change the bias of the system. Not only the symbols of injustice at work must be attacked, but the root causes. If they held together and formed a union or unions of workers in the trades, then one day they might win. Others, understandably, felt nothing but anger and despair. Given the chance, it seemed likely that they would act no less violently than Mellor, Smith, and Thorpe had done.

The reports of Home Office spies sounded a constant note of alarm. They made England north of the Trent seem like a hostile colony, alien and incomprehensible, requiring to be subjugated. Given the norms of Government thinking, this is not surprising. The Midlands were very different indeed from the peaceful Thames valley. Not that the area was predominantly one of large factories — as yet, only Manchester, Stockport, and a few other cotton towns were major urban factory centres, and most people still worked at home or in small forges, loomshops, or mills in their villages. But their outlook was distinctively that of a region undergoing a quite new kind of transition and social stress, associated with the continuing movement away from agriculture to industry in a time of rapid population increase. Preoccupied with other things, and in any case largely indifferent to the needs of the northern workforce, the Home Secretary and his Cabinet colleagues were reluctant to turn their minds to the problem.

The end of the war complicated matters further. Thousands of soldiers returned from the Continent looking for work. They found none, or where they did, it was often at the expense of already desperate unemployed men. The year 1815-16, which ought to have been a time of celebration, was experienced by a sizable part of the population as a year of unprecedented poverty. The outdated English Poor Law was not enough to deal with the cases of homelessness and malnutrition which occurred; and conditions were scarcely less bad in Wales and Scotland. One stop-gap solution to the problem of unemployment was to set squads of labourers, to construct monuments to Britain's victory. Towers, arches, and memorials to the fallen were erected by public subscription or on the impulse of mighty landowners; but although this went a little way to alleviate suffering locally, it did nothing to remove the underlying causes of the nation's plight. There was still a dearth of overseas trade and a surplus of labour. It would take Britain many years to recover from the dislocating effects of war.

No occupation was harder hit than that of the agricultural labourers. Disturbing tales of lawlessness and disorder began to come in from traditionally quiet and settled parts of the country. In 1816 unemployed labourers in East Anglia went on the rampage, stealing, burning, committing assault. So great was the panic which this caused over a wide area that the university authorities in Cambridge issued undergraduates with heavy sticks. The 'Fen Tigers' eventually split up and either went home or walked in search of work to the heartland of England, but not before they had caused acute worry in London. If East Anglian labourers could make so much trouble, what might not be expected from the unruly cloth and iron workers of Lancashire? Norwich, it was noted, was a centre of dissidence, probably because like Westminster its electoral basis was unusually open – in the eyes of the Government, far too open. Manchester, by contrast, did not yet have a single Member of Parliament. But then, as everyone knew, it *ought* to be represented in the Commons because it now had a population of over 100,000. For how much longer would the people of Manchester be willing to tolerate this state of affairs?[1] Lancashire had its share of unemployment. What form would the protests of its discontented men and women take?

Manchester resembled Glasgow in being at the centre of uncontrolled forces of social and industrial change, and while it had fewer immigrant families than Liverpool or Glasgow, its population had still grown quite dramatically within the past two generations. Cotton manufacture was the outstanding growth industry of the new age, and Manchester was a cotton city without rival. Inevitably, the dispossessed poor from neighbouring and indeed from distant parts of England tended to think there would be work for them in southern Lancashire. But the spinning and weaving of cotton, silk, and the other fabrics in which the area specialized were subject to sudden alterations in the overseas market. Sometimes, when the textile masters took on new workers in their hundreds to cope with all the raw material they had imported, a period of hectic activity led to gross overproduction. Then the looms both of urban workers and of those in outlying districts fell silent. Large numbers found themselves 'laid off' as abruptly as they had been employed, and large-scale unemployment became the lot of the people.

Even when there was plenty of work, it was very poorly paid. The typical Lancashire lad and his lass could only survive by developing a wry attitude towards 'King' Cotton and the frequently harsh cotton masters. The outlook of the workers is clearly reflected in the ballads of the northwest, and especially in a group of songs linked with the name of 'Jone o' Grinfilt'. At the end of the war, people were singing in the pubs round Manchester 'Jone o' Grinfilt Junior', which expressed the disillusionment felt by very many of them. Only a traditional singer could bring out all the pain and anger in these verses in dialect, but the expression of unhappiness cannot be missed:

> Aw'm a poor cotton-wayver, as mony a one knaws,
> Aw've nowt t'ate i' th'heawse, un' aw've worn eawt my cloas,
> Yo'd hardly gie sixpence fur o' aw've got on,
> Meh clogs ur' boath baws'n, un' stockins aw've none;

---

[1] Like Birmingham and a number of other large English cities and towns, Manchester gained two parliamentary seats by the Reform Act of 1832.

> You'd think it wur hard, to be sent into th'warld
> To clem[1] un' do best 'oot yo' can.

Significantly, the next stanza reveals that John has a bone to pick with his local parson. Although himself a complete stranger to manual work, the parson has repeatedly urged his poorer parishioners to endure adversity in silence in the expectation of a change for the better...

> Eawr parish-church pa'son's kept tellin' us lung,
> We'st see better toimes, if aw'd but howd my tung;
> Aw've howden my tung, toll aw con hardly draw breoth,
> Aw think he lives weel, wi backbitin' the de'il,
> But he never pick'd o'er in his loife.

(It would of course be nonsense to deduce from this that all the clergy in the region sought to use their influence to suppress protest. But at least one Church of England parson, the Rev. W. R. Hay, was already well known and would soon be notorious for his efforts to suppress disaffection in every way he could. He was Chairman of the Manchester and Salford Bench of Magistrates, and the Home Office had no more persistent correspondent and friend in northern England.) The ballad goes on to describe how John and his wife live for a time on nettles, come to think of 'Waterloo porridge' (porridge made with water?) as a rare treat, and finally have their furniture removed by the bailiff. The bailiff's action is the straw that breaks the camel's back. Despairingly, John goes again to the warehouse where he has been employed in the past, only to find no work, and Margaret his wife bursts out that if he had clothes on his back he would make the journey to London and confront the King, even if this should mean fighting in blood up to the eyes. 'Hoo's nout agen th'king but hoo loikes a fair thing.'

Margaret's wild talk of petitioning the King and of violent action shows both how confused and how strongly committed to protest events had made the working people of Manchester. Their burning sense of injustice was not confined for long to ballads. The weavers, and with them other disadvantaged sections of the population, soon ran out of patience. Some took to carrying banners and attending open-air meetings held for the purpose of demanding annual parliaments and universal suffrage. There were many admirers of Major John Cartwright (1740-1824), the veteran campaigner for parlia-

[1] Clem: starve.

mentary reform, whose Midland tours in recent years had led to the setting up of local 'Hampden Clubs' in imitation of the London Hampden Club to which, with Sir Francis Burdett, Lord Byron and other radically minded aristocrats, he belonged. Cartwright was strictly a non-violent political thinker, whose watchword was 'Hold fast by the laws'. 'English gentlemen', he had written

> are perpetually travelling. . . Some go to see lakes and mountains. Were it not allowable to travel for seeing the actual conditions of a starving people?

Like Don Quixote, he had brought with him a long-suffering steed and high ideals. The starving people of 'the labouring classes' took him to their hearts because he so clearly cared about their condition. Most were in full agreement with his law-abiding philosophy.

One of Cartwright's Lancashire followers was Samuel Bamford, a young silk-weaver from Middleton, near Manchester. Bamford was intelligent, self-confident, at times impetuous. There was a rebellious strain in his family history, for his grandfather had joined the Jacobites during their ill-fated journey through northern England in 1745. Bamford was brought up in poverty, and when he had a chance of going on to 'the Latin class' at school, his father would not hear of the idea but instead insisted that he should become a weaver like himself. Although he would have preferred to stay on at school and perhaps go to university, the young Bamford duly served his apprenticeship in the trade, and after spending some years at sea returned to it. But he remained a keen reader, and on coming across a copy of the poems and songs of Robert Burns, began to write verses. For a time, Bamford carried his admiration for Burns to the point of copying his unruly life-style. As a result, he acquired a liking for drink, and later blamed on Burns the fact that at one point he was served with an 'affiliation order' or paternity warrant. Luckily, he had learned other lessons from the Ayrshire ploughman's works: to take pride as a writer in his own dialect, and to ask defiantly,

> Is there for honest poverty
> That hangs his head an' a' that?

He was to place these lines from the Scottish poet on the title-page of his autobiography. His own gift, however, was for prose, not verse.

Through Bamford's eyes, it is possible to watch the drama of Regency troubles in Lancashire unfold and come to its climax.

Passages in the Life of a Radical, published in Middleton in 1834-41 as a kind of primer for Chartists (supporters of the movement for parliamentary and social reform), describes in vivid detail his political education as Secretary of the Middleton Hampden Club, the prominent local and national personalities he met, and the sudden twist events took towards nightmare in 1819. (The book has been described by E. P. Thomson in *The Making of the English Working Class*, 1963, as 'essential reading for any Englishman'.) Part of its interest lies in the evidence Bamford offers of the activities of Government 'spies'. Those like himself who were working for peaceful change were under surveillance for much of the time. They never knew whether a stranger coming into their midst could be trusted. 'Oliver', the most feared of all the spies, taught his colleagues how to pass for members of Hampden Clubs in other parts of the land or at least as plausible sympathizers with the aims of the Lancastrian reformers. Skilled agents knew how to work on the anger of those amongst whom they had come so as to make them give up details of their plans. This made it difficult for Bamford and his friends to hold discussions with outside groups, even when they shared political beliefs. Nor was that all. The authorities made use of whatever information they received from spies, accurate or not, to harass and intimidate. Nadin, the very active Deputy Constable of Manchester, had singled out Bamford as a dangerous figure. More than once, the silk-weaver was dragged out of bed in the middle of the night by the sound of heavy knocking on the door. He enjoyed recalling that on such occasions he had shown little respect for his unwanted callers until they identified themselves:

> Bang! bang! came the blows on the door.
> 'Hallo! who's makin that din at this time o' neet?'. . .
> 'Open the door', said a voice, authoritatively.
> 'Open the door' — imitating the voice, 'an hooa arto, at I should oppen my dur to thee? Theawrt sum drunken eawl or other, or elze theaw wud no' come i' that way.'. . .
> 'Will you open the door, man?' said another voice.
> 'Well, but hooa ar yo' an wot dun yo' want? for thurs moor nor won, I say.'
> 'We are constables, and we want you', was the reply.
> 'Oh! that's a different thing quite: iv yoar constables yo' shane com in by o' myens. Why didno yo' tell me so at forst?'
> By this time, both my wife and myself were decently attired; and advancing to the door, I took away the prop, and shot the bar, and bid them come in; and not soil the silk work in the looms.

1 The Prince Regent in Profile (c. 1814) by Sir Thomas Lawrence. *National Portrait Gallery*

2 'By Royal Authority' (1816), cartoon showing the Prince Regent mounting his horse. *Royal Pavilion, Brighton*

BY ROYAL AUTHORITY.

A New way of mounting your Horse in spite of the GOUT!! *Dedicated to all fashionable Equestrians afflicted with Gout.*

3 'New Baubles for the Chinese Temple' (March 1820), cartoon showing George IV and the Prime Minister, Lord Liverpool, arguing about the cost to the nation of Brighton Pavilion. *Royal Pavilion, Brighton*

4 'The Yankey Torpedo' (1 November 1813), published by T. Tegg. *British Museum*

5 *Left:* Princess Charlotte Augusta of Wales (1813) by Thomas Heaphy. *National Portrait Gallery*
6 William Cobbett by an unknown artist. *National Portrait Gallery*

7 Henry 'Orator' Hunt by Adam Buck. *National Portrait Gallery*

8 'Massacre at St Peter's or "BRITONS STRIKE HOME"!!!' (16 August 1819), published by T. Tegg. *British Museum*

Massacre at St Peters or "BRITONS STRIKE HOME"!!!

THE BRITISH ATLAS, or John Bull supporting the Peace Establishment.

9 'The British Atlas, or John Bull supporting the Peace Establishment.' *British Museum*

10 'Sun rising through Vapour: Fishermen cleaning and selling Fish' by J. M. W. Turner.
Reproduced by courtesy of the Trustees, the National Gallery, London

Yet, as this passage makes clear, there were real terrors in such an experience. Bamford's wife was in tears as she listened apprehensively to the knocking, knowing that another period of separation and distress lay ahead. To play any part in the movement agitating for parliamentary reform and for better conditions of employment required steady nerves. As a member of the Female Reformers' Union in her district (one of the earliest groups of women in Britain to press for political change), Mrs Bamford was every bit as resolute as her husband.

A great many of the working people of Manchester were to show that they possessed similar qualities of patience and determination when things finally came to a head at St Peter's Fields on the afternoon of Monday 16 August 1819. By one o'clock that day, some thirty-five thousand men and women were gathered together in the open air, in an area measuring about 100 by 160 metres. (This was one of several large open air meetings in the summer of 1819.) They had come to hear Henry Hunt speak to them about the inequalities of the current system of parliamentary representation. Many of them carried banners daubed with slogans: UNITY AND STRENGTH, LIBERTY AND FRATERNITY, PARLIAMENTS ANNUAL, SUFFRAGE UNIVERSAL. Some had branches of laurel, 'token', in Bamford's account, 'of amity and peace'. The presence of infants in arms and of small children was a further sign of their peaceful intentions. 'Orator' Hunt was the William Cobbett of the spoken work, a Wiltshire farmer with a showman's presence and a national reputation as an effective publicist for radical politics. A great cheer went up when his white top-hat came into view. He had a very loud voice, but had some difficulty making himself heard as, from his position on a platform erected between two large carts, he attempted to call the crowd to order. A wind was blowing against him which prevented his first words from carrying, and his huge audience had been made restless by the approach of a mounted detachment of the Manchester and Salford Yeomanry. What orders, they asked each other, had been given to these unpopular, poorly trained creatures?

According to the reporter from *The Times*, who was on the platform beside him, Hunt managed after a few minutes to produce 'a dead silence'. He did so by telling all who could hear him that it was their duty to pass back the request to be quiet and listen; if they failed to do so, the day would be wasted as far as reform was concerned. But when this tactic had worked upon the good temper of the company to achieve the desired result and Hunt was beginning to deliver the speech he had prepared, Tyas of *The Times* spotted a sudden movement on the edge of the crowd. The horsemen of the Yeomanry were riding in among the people, and seemed to be trying to reach the place where the hustings had been erected. To the minds of those on the platform, it must have appeared that the city magistrates, who had been watching proceedings all this while from a house adjoining St Peter's Fields, had decided to arrest Hunt while he was speaking: many had been surprised that he had not been arrested in the week before the meeting. Hunt turned and said something to those close to him, but it was lost in the hubbub of noise which broke out. People shouted; there was the sound of horses whinnying in fear as they were ridden into the throng and found themselves shut in and jostled by humans on every side. A woman's scream pierced the air.

Understandably, a part of the crowd panicked straightaway, and tried to turn and get away from the scene. But their panic was mild in comparison with that of William Hulton and his fellow-magistrates, who had sent in the Yeomanry. What happened now would have been farcical, were it not for the cost in human life. Troops of the 15th Hussars, wearing their Waterloo medals, were at hand. They were appalled to see what was taking place. As one of them, Lieutenant Jolliffe, put it afterwards,

> [The Yeomanry] were scattered singly or in small groups over the greater part of the Field, literally hemmed up and hedged into the mob so that they were powerless either to make an impression or to escape; in fact, they were in the power of those whom they were designed to overawe, and it required only a glance to discover their helpless position, and the necessity of our being brought to their rescue.

Colonel Guy L'Estrange, who was in charge of the Hussars, looked up inquiringly to the window of the house where the representatives of civil authority were sitting. He needed their instructions before he could act. 'Good God, sir!', Hulton called down to him, 'do you not see how they are attacking the Yeomanry? Disperse the crowd.' L'Estrange at once ordered his men to advance. Hulton, meanwhile, turned his head away, not wanting 'to see any advance of the military' — even though he was the man who had just demanded that it take place. The Hussars were commanded to drive the people forward with the flat of their swords. Their job was to reach and protect as quickly as possible the Yeomanry, some of whom were even now being assaulted by the angry demonstrators as local men who had taken up arms in a treacherous cause against their own people. The need for urgency, rather than humane considerations, governed the Hussars' actions in the next two or three minutes. Despite their orders, 'sometimes', Lieutenant Jolliffe was later to admit, 'as is almost invariably the case when men are placed in such situations, *the edge was used*'. Jolliffe was bound to speak up for his regiment. To defend them from wider criticism he explained that 'the greater amount of injuries were from the pressure of the routed multitude'.

This was indeed true, although a large number of sabre wounds were inflicted also. People were trodden down right, left and centre. So vast a host could not be expected to break up quickly without serious injury; many stumbled and fell as they tried to escape. By the time Hunt made his way through a hail of blows about the head and shoulders from constables to give himself up to the magistrates, the ground was littered with corpses and with the bodies of the injured.

What did it feel like to be present in Manchester that day? Mima Bamford was to supply her account in *Passages in the Life of a Radical*. She had come to St Peter's Fields largely because she feared for her husband's safety. It had been the talk of the region for weeks past that 'if the country people went with their caps of liberty, and their banners, and music, the soldiers would be brought to them'. She wanted to keep an eye on her Samuel.

> I accordingly, he having consented after much persuasion, gave my little girl something to please her, and promising more on my return, I left her with a careful neighbour woman, and joined some other married females at the head of the procession.

The Middleton contingent reached the meeting-place in the middle of the day, and at this point her husband's very serious expression filled her with a sense of foreboding that something untoward was going to happen. 'My husband got on the stage, but when afterwards I saw him leap down, and lost sight of him, I began to be unhappy.' It was a very hot afternoon. Mrs Bamford felt sick shortly after taking up a position in the crowd. Deciding to leave, she heard men on either side of her say 'make way, she's sick, she's sick, let her go out'.

She found shade inside the front door of a house in Windmill Street where nobody objected to her resting, and anxiously looked over the meeting she had left. There was no sign of her husband, but she could see soldiers on horseback riding among the people and striking them with their swords. A man passed wiping blood from his head, 'and it ran down his arm in a great stream'. She crept into a cellar, hoping to escape from the horrid noise and to be hidden from the soldiers, and sat down trembling on some firewood. Then the body of a middle-aged woman was carried into the cellar by a number of men.

> I thought they were going to put her beside me, and was about to scream, but they took her forward, and deposited her in some premises at the back of the house.

Eventually, the noise of weeping and the general commotion outside dropped away. Someone in the house above took pity on her when she was heard to repeat several times 'My lad, my poor lad!' She was asked where she came from, and what was her husband's name. 'Middleton', she replied to the first question, but gave no answer to the second. Then the people of the house asked a constable to take her to Market Street, which he did with courtesy, escorting her over the now 'almost deserted field'. Everywhere she looked, she expected to see her husband lying dead. On catching sight of one of the people who had come that morning from Middleton, she took her leave of the constable and asked if there was any word of her husband. This man told her he had heard that Bamford had been killed. A little later someone else from her villaged joined them and said he was in the infirmary, then another person denied that report and declared he was in prison. None of these rumours was correct, as it happened, and Mrs Bamford was soon to be reunited with her husband; but only for a short time, because Bamford, in common with Henry Hunt and numerous other leaders of the people, was arrested and prosecuted for treason, spending several months under lock and key before being acquitted.

Within a few days of the Manchester meeting, all Britain was talking about what had happened. Eye-witness reports which appeared in the *Manchester Gazette* and in *The Times* were reprinted in daily and weekly newspapers throughout the land. The correspondent of *The Times*, who had been hand-picked for the assignment, enjoyed a major 'scoop'. His vivid account of the afternoon's events included details of how the men sent in to overawe the crowd had committed acts of physical brutality and victimization. He described, for example, the narrow escape from death of a Press colleague:

> A person of the name of SAXTON, who is, we believe, Editor of the Manchester Observer, was standing in the cart. Two privates rode up to him. 'There', said one of them, 'is that villain SAXTON; do you run him through the body.' 'No,' replied the other, 'I had rather not — I leave it to you.' The man immediately made a lunge at SAXTON, and it was only by slipping aside that the blow missed his life. As it was, it cut his coat and waistcoat, but fortunately did him no injury. A man within five yards of us, in another direction, had his nose completely taken off by a blow of a sabre.

According to the *Times* journalist, who had been arrested along with Henry Hunt shortly after this incident took place, there was no room for doubt that a significant number of those representing authority had behaved vindictively at St Peter's Fields. It was with contempt that he recalled their lack of self-discipline at the worst moments of the affair:

> The constables, who suffered nearly as much as the rest of the multitude, from a perfect want of system and plan, showed in many instances a savage spirit of malice and revenge.

His next sentence was dignified with italics when reprinted in a front page article, 'The Proceedings at Manchester', in *The Scotsman*, The Edinburgh Opposition weekly, on 28 August. Already, the St Peter's Fields 'massacre' had been nicknamed 'Peterloo'. It seems certain that one reason for this fiercely ironical way of regarding it lay in the stupidity of a certain Manchester constable. . .

> Some of them were seen beating with their staves those who had fallen, and one of them, in the drunken delirium of triumph, brandished his baton, and exclaimed, 'Here is our field of Waterloo.'

The Scotsman on 28 August gave the number of dead as five. But the true total of men, women, and children killed was eleven, while at least four hundred people had been injured, many of them seriously. There was no precedent for so terrible a day in recent British history. 'If such proceedings meet with any countenance,' argued the editor of *The Scotsman*, 'it is almost tantamount to telling the lower class that they are out of the protection of the law.' He concluded ominously, 'Make the case but a little more general, and the country is in the flames of a civil war.'

Unfortunately, it was possible to share the fear of civil war without understanding the need for conciliation. The Prince Regent and the Home Secretary had both been quick to send messages congratulating the forces of law and order on their 'decisive' conduct. Now the Government proceeded to take action which exalted social insensitivity into new laws. Given the disturbed state of the country, three of the 'Six Acts' rushed through Parliament late in 1819 were perhaps not unreasonable; these gave wider powers of search for arms to magistrates, prohibited citizens from meeting for the purpose of military training, and reduced delays in the process by which suspected law-breakers could be brought to trial. But the other measures were much more controversial, being deliberately designed to prevent people from holding public meetings like the one at Manchester (any meeting for the drawing up of petitions was to be narrowly limited to residents of the parish in which it was held), to restrict the circulation of cheap newspapers and journals, and to make the publication of 'blasphemous and seditious libels' punishable by stiffer penalties than in the past, including transportation. About the same time the standing army was increased by 10,000 men. These actions — the short-term results of 'Peterloo' — meant that certain traditional individual and group liberties were, for the time being, taken away. Not since the iron rule of Cromwell had the British people been so cribbed and confined. The winter of 1819 to 1820, which happened to be particularly cold, was bleak indeed for supporters of parliamentary and social reform. The Government, so far from seeking to understand and communicate with distressed working people, chose simply to ignore their existence.

Sensing this, the poet Shelley, who had rejected many of the social and political assumptions of the aristocracy into which he had been born, wrote a sonnet describing the unhappy state of 'England in 1819':

An old, mad, blind, despised, and dying king, —
Princes, the dregs of their dull race, who flow
Through public scorn, — mud from a muddy spring, —
Rulers who neither see, nor feel, nor know,
But leech-like to their fainting country cling,
Till they drop, blind in blood, without a blow, —
A people starved and stabbed in the untilled field . . .

And in 'The Mask of Anarchy, written on the occasion of the Massacre at Manchester', he deplored the fact that Cabinet Ministers were implicated in the 'ghastly masquerade' of Peterloo, and urged his fellow countrymen to break free from the condition of 'slavery' which oppressed them:

> Rise like Lions after slumber . . .
> Ye are many — they are few.

Shelley's vision of radical change in society remained unfulfilled in his lifetime, but the long-term results of the Manchester affair were significant, nevertheless. People in the middle and upper classes who read newspapers such as *The Times* and *The Scotsman* were horrified at the attitude of the Government in the dark days of 1819-20, and found themselves siding with, and in some cases publicly supporting, the working-class reformers: parliamentary reform ceased to be a sectional and instead became a national movement with very wide backing. Try as it might, the Government could not wish such a concerted campaign away, and as the 1820s went on the pressure increased. The scandal of a single afternoon in Manchester would never be forgotten. In the words of Asa Briggs, 'the memory of it remained vividly alive for generations to come, and inspired hundreds of new reformers'. Thus not only the First Reform Act of 1832, but a whole series of subsequent changes in the system of national and local government were connected with and influenced by what had taken place in the north of England at the end of the Regency.

*   *   *

Tragically, for a very long time no such beneficial legislation was to result from an event which in its own way was no less shocking than 'Peterloo' — the violent eviction of crofting families from their homes in Strathnaver in the remote and beautiful Scottish county of Sutherland in the summer of 1814. (Many crofters returning to Sutherland after fighting in the war found that their families had been evicted during their absence.) This, the most callous of the early Highland 'Clearances', was the work of Patrick Sellar, principal factor on the Countess of Sutherland's huge estates, who had recently become tenant in Strathnaver (the crofters were his sub-tenants). In common with his employers, Sellar was committed to a policy of 'improvement', by which he understood doing away with unprofitable smallholdings and instead using the land to support large numbers of Cheviot sheep, the wool of which was in far greater demand than any other product of the region. It has recently been calculated that in the period from 1808 to 1821 between 5,000 and 10,000 Sutherland crofting folk were expelled from their homes, many of which were on land where their forbears had lived from time immemorial, in order to create 'sheepwalks'. In 1811 the Sutherland factors explained their policy in response to an inquiry from the Board of Agriculture:

> Sheep-farms are paying well on the Sutherland estates. The number of Cheviots are now about 15,000. More ground will be laid off for the same mode of husbandry, without decreasing the population. Situations in various ways will be fixed on for the people. Fishing stations, in which mechanics will be settled; inland villages, with carding machines; moors and detached spots calculated for the purpose will be found, but the people must work. The industrious will be encouraged and protected, but the slothful must remove or starve, as man was not born to be idle, but to gain his bread by the sweat of his brow.

It did not matter that the crofters had little inclination to become fishermen round Scotland's dangerous northern coasts, or that the Countess of Sutherland and her husband the Marquis of Stafford were among the wealthiest people in Britain.[1] Calvinist and economic doctrine were at one; 'man was not born to be idle'. Where Sellar differed from his colleagues was in the degree of insensitivity with which he carried out this coldly logical, anti-social programme. Sutherland has very few trees, and at this time the roof-beams of crofters' houses were among their most precious possessions. Normally, evicted crofters were allowed to take their roof-beams with them when they tried to set up a new home on the coastal strip. Not only did Sellar prevent those Strathnaver tenants who have been slow to obey his orders from doing this: he burned their roofs over their heads. In Sutherland, 1814, known to some in the south as 'the year of the Sovereigns', was to be remembered as 'the year of the Burnings'. A sixteen-year-old girl, Betsy MacKay, described a typical incident long afterwards:

---

[1] 'Agricultural Sir John' Sinclair of Ulbster, an improver who had introduced Cheviots to Caithness in 1790, recognized the need for change to be slow and gradual, and a few years later proposed that northern Scottish crofters and their landlords should turn sheep-farming to everyone's advantage by running joint-farm cooperatives; but nobody with capital listened to him.

Our family was very reluctant to leave, and stayed for some time, but the burning party came round and set fire to our house at both ends, reducing to ashes whatever remained within the walls. The people had to escape for their lives, some of them losing all their clothes except what they had on their backs. The people were told they could go where they liked, provided they did not encumber the land that was by rights their own. The people were driven away like dogs who deserved no better, and that, too, without any reason in the world.

Someone who was present at the pulling down and burning of a house at Badinloskin in Strathnaver was Donald Macleod, a stone-mason. According to Macleod, the only person in the house was a bed-ridden woman almost a hundred years old. When the factor approached, Macleod pointed out to him that the woman's illness and great age made it impossible to move her without endangering her life. Sellar, however, had lost control of his temper because of all the resistance he had already met with, and he replied 'Let her burn'. . .

Fire was immediately set to the house and the blankets in which she was carried were in flames before she could be got out. She was placed in a little shed, and it was with great difficulty they were prevented from firing it also. The old woman's daughter arrived while the house was on fire, and assisted the neighbours in removing her mother out of the flames and the smoke, presenting a picture of horror which I shall never forget, but cannot attempt to describe. She died within five days.

There were other scarcely less horrifying incidents, as when, for instance, a pregnant woman climbed on to the roof of her cottage in an attempt to defy Sellar's men, and they promptly responded by putting flame to the thatch beneath her feet.

The Sheriff-Substitute of Sutherland, Robert MacKid, egged on by various interested individuals, gathered as much evidence as he could about the Strathnaver Clearance, and in 1816 Sellar was brought to trial in Inverness. (He was charged with 'culpable homicide, oppression and real injury', and with 'wickedly and maliciously setting fire and burning'.) The jury of fifteen, however, included two merchants, a lawyer, and no fewer than eight local landed proprietors. It is likely that they listened apprehensively when Sellar's counsel, James Gordon, warned them that,

The question at issue involves the future fate and progress of agricultural and even moral improvement in the county of Sutherland ... it is in substance and in fact, a trial of strength between the abettors of anarchy and misrule, and the magistracy as well as the laws of this country.

Despite the inaccuracy of this claim, and despite the well-attested stories of burning and summary eviction, Sellar was acquitted, and in due course successfully brought an action against the unfortunate MacKid. No single episode illustrates more clearly than Sellar's trial how firmly the propertied class in the Regency closed ranks against the poor when they felt their essential interests to be at stake.

A perceptive contemporary comment on the Sutherland Clearances is that of Robert Southey, the Poet Laureate, who accompanied Thomas Telford through the Highlands in 1819. 'There is at this time a considerable ferment in the country', he wrote,

> concerning the management of the M[arquis] of Stafford's estates: they comprise nearly two-fifths of the county of Sutherland, and the process of converting them into extensive sheep-farms is being carried on. A political economist has no hesitation concerning the fitness of the end in view, and little scruple as to the means. Leave these bleak regions, he says, for cattle to breed in, and let men remove to situations where they can exert themselves and thrive.

Southey conceded that a traveller looking 'only at the outside of things' might accept this line of reasoning, for the appearance of the crofters' houses was unprepossessing in the extreme. (He wrote, 'I have never — not even in Galicia — seen any human habitations so bad as the Highland *black-houses*.') But then he went on to state the other side of the argument:

> Here you have a quiet, thoughtful, contented, religious people, susceptible of improvement, and willing to be improved. To transplant these people from their native mountain glens to the sea coast, and require them to become some cultivators, others fishermen, occupations to which they have never been accustomed — to expect a sudden and total change of habits in the existing generation, instead of gradually producing it in their children; to expel them by process of law from their black-houses, and if they demur in obeying the ejectment, to oust them by setting fire to these combustible tenements — this surely is as little defensible on the score of policy as of morals.

The important truth in the last phrase of this summing-up was to go unheeded for half a century. The Clearances continued, not only in Sutherland but elsewhere in the Highlands and Islands, and if nobody burned down houses in the manner of Sellar, there were to be countless other cases of enforced destitution and emigration. For too long, the Highlander's only form of redress was to pass on to his children the tale of the Year of the Burnings and of similar outrages; but as a result resentment against the landowner and the Great Sheep did not die, and the way was prepared for the Crofters' Act of 1886, which belatedly gave security of tenure and set up a commission to fix fair rents.

Thus Strathnaver, as well as Peterloo, helped — with a legacy of bitterness and indignation — to produce a different kind of society. The concept of 'improvement' or planned progress, which in the early part of the nineteenth century had been applied ruthlessly, and without regard for the feelings of the people most directly concerned, to the socio-economic problems of the Highlands, was gradually tempered and strengthened until a point was reached when it was no longer thought adequate to take decisions solely on the basis of economic calculation; then at last the practice of clearing men from land where their forefathers had lived came to an end. The various stages of this process of social change and education could not have been guessed at in the later Regency, when class antagonisms flared into violence in the north of England, and Patrick Sellar gained notoriety in Scotland. But what people did recognize at that time was that the sense of national unity which had been present in Britain during the struggle against Napoleon had been scattered to the four winds. During the winter of 1819-20 it was no doubt with nostalgia that many people thought back to the days of the war.

[4]

Brummell or Byron?
The Search for a Hero

I want a hero, an uncommon want,
When every year and month sends forth a new one (Byron, *Don Juan*)

At the time when the Regency opened, the whole of British society
had been united in the war effort against Napoleon. Just as they were
to do in two world wars more than a hundred years later, people
from many different walks of life worked together with a common
purpose. The shared aim of national victory triumphed over class
divisions; it was strong enough for the time being to counteract,
although not to reconcile, the separate interests of particular social
groups which were to become so apparent in the later years of the
decade, and to prevent any one group from seeking too much for
itself. Those who wanted to see changes in the political system
would have to wait till the war was won. National survival came first.

The young must have found this argument depressing, even dis-
honest. The war, after all, was not of their creating. It belonged to
their parents' generation, and seemed now to be dragging on inter-
minably. True, there had been some fine naval victories years ago,
and it had been exciting to hear from one's elder brother about the
great Lord Nelson, in whose navy he served. But Nelson was ancient
history now. There was little really dramatic news from Spain, only
stories of near-victories, near-defeats: an interminable series of
skirmishes. Anyway, why should those in their twenties be denied
the chance to travel and have fun which their parents had enjoyed
when the war was still young and not yet as firmly established as the
Church of England? In such a situation it would not be surprising if
ideas of republics and revolutions should have found some favour.
They were at least different from the same old status quo in Britain.

76

To have expressed such thoughts openly would have been unthinkable. Young Britain in 1811 was not young America, sick of the Vietnam War, of the 1960s. It can even be doubted if more than a small proportion of the population consciously formulated to themselves their private objections to the war. Patriotism, for most, had only one possible meaning: beating the French. Nevertheless, feelings of disillusionment existed. They were experienced acutely, and not to be able to talk freely about their cause made the situation worse. A source of intense frustration was the realization that power lay with men whose vision of the nation's future was limited to such a degree by *idées fixes* inherited from a shabby and no longer relevant past. The Prime Minister of the day was dull, the Regent anything but inspiring. Britain lacked a hero. Those under thirty, idealistic and at the same time naturally rebellious, were tinder ready to catch fire.

Some turned to Beau Brummell, and sought to join the ranks of the dandies. The military metaphor may seem out of place; but the phenomenon of the dandy at this time is surely best explained as a make-believe officer about town, wearing his own special uniform and devoting a gentlemanly degree of care to its appearance. Brummell himself had served in a real army, which is one clue to his unchallenged leadership of the dandies. To be a dandy was to belong to an exclusive social set without the risks or responsibilities of naval or military men. The dandy was detached from the vulgar concerns of the day. He was a bachelor, a leader of fashion, and — in some few instances — a wit. He surveyed the world coldly from his club in St James's, spent his evenings gambling or preening himself among the *ton*, and pretended not to notice when inferior mortals laughed at him. He was, in Carlyle's phrase, 'a Clothes-Wearing Man, a Man whose trade, office, and existence consists in the wearing of Clothes'.

Brummell stood out in Regency circles both as clothes-wearing man and as wit, hence his social prestige in war-weary London. His mother came from a well-connected family, and his father had been private secretary to Lord North, enjoying various sinecures, for example as Receiver of the Duties on Uninhabited Houses in Middlesex. Brummell went to Eton and Oxford, but left university at the age of sixteen when on his father's death he inherited some £15,000. The regiment in which he served briefly as a captain, the 10th

Hussars, was known as 'The Elegant Extracts': already, his preference for leisured ease was declaring itself. He became friendly with
the Prince of Wales, formed part of the escort for Caroline of
Brunswick when she first arrived in England, and later was present at
their wedding.

In 1798, Brummell came out of his regiment and bought a house
in London. Almost at once he was made a member of White's, '*the*
club from which people have died of exclusion', and of the no less
highly select Brooks's, across the street. But for Brummell it was not
enough to be admitted to these places: he wished to be seen to
command them. He sought to do this by setting new standards of
personal elegance, and in this he began with a big advantage. In the
time before his 'reign' began men had dressed casually, and frequently avoided soap and water. It was therefore a simple thing to
cultivate a reputation for taking care over one's appearance. Scrupulously clean at all times, Brummell had the habit of scrubbing his
face with a flesh-brush until he 'looked very much like a man in the
scarlet fever'. That high-coloured look became fashionable, although
it must have been a painful process to restore the salmon glow each
morning. In that sense, at least, Brummell earned his fame the hard
way.

The sartorial example which he set was essentially simple rather
than flamboyant: it was the very high stiff collar, an innovation later
in the Regency, which made for an absurd effect. Brummell himself
favoured lightly-boned high lapels on his blue woollen coat, but
avoided extremes of dress. This coat was worn outside a buff
waistcoat and spotless white cravat. 'Fine linen, plenty of it, and
country washing' was his prescription for a gentleman's cravat. The
coat was buttoned tightly over the waist, and its tails were tucked
into shining black Hessian boots. The buttons on his coat were of
brass, while two links of a heavy gold watchchain could be seen in
front of his waistcoat. His evening dress was also straightforward: a
blue coat, white waistcoat, and black pantaloons buttoning tight
over the ankles, with striped silk stockings and oval-toed pumps.

Although the style was simple, Brummell insisted on correctness;
he made its rules indispensable to the definition of taste at Brooks's.
It was all very well for his admirers to claim that 'his chief aim was to
avoid being marked', or to note that 'the severest mortification
which a gentleman could incur, was to attract observation in the

street by his outward appearance', but Brummell was a master of discreet publicity. It was *known* that he spent hours knotting his cravat so that the appearance would be exactly right (a friend calling at his house in Chesterfield Street one morning passed his valet coming out of his dressing-room with a dozen or more pieces of crumpled muslin over his arm, which he described as 'our failures'), and that the Regent asked to be with him while he was doing so in order to learn the proper technique. Would-be disciples heard, and if they were fortunate saw, that he blacked the soles as well as the uppers of his shoes. They were uneasily aware that from his bow window in White's he observed every detail of what they wore, and that those who did not conform must expect to be 'cut'.

Brummell once told Lady Hester Stanhope that he had chosen the only course which would 'separate himself from the society of the ordinary herd of men, whom he held in considerable contempt'. From 1800 to 1810 he enjoyed unquestioned supremacy as arbiter of male fashion in London. His remarks on everything relating to the style in which a gentleman should live were heeded; indeed, they seemed at times to have the force of corporate authority. But his admirers also treasured his laconic *mots* on other matters. Brummell became, in Hazlitt's phrase, 'the greatest of small wits'. Asked to dine in Bloomsbury, he inquired if he would have to change post-horses en route. This remark characteristically emphasized the exclusiveness of the dandy world. He was similarly particular about what he ate. When a society hostess anxiously put to him the question, 'Mr Brummell, do you *never* eat vegetables?', he replied after a suitable pause, 'Madam, I once ate a pea.'

The secret lay in making little things seem significant, and in ignoring whatever was unpleasant. The ever-present problem of ready cash fell into this latter category, but Brummell's credit at his Old Bond Street tailor's was excellent, because he brought so much custom. Elsewhere, he could disregard embarrassing requests for money because he was a close associate of the Prince of Wales — not that *he* was quick to pay his debts. So potent was Brummell's influence, in fact, that he even appeared to survive without loss of face a breach with the Prince in 1811. (It may be that the Prince saw in Brummell a rival to himself.) 'I made him what he is,' Brummell is reported to have said, 'and I can unmake him.'

To exclude the Regent, however, was to become an over-reacher.

Brummell was a victim of his own hubris in forgetting that 'Poodle' Byng and his kind, the habitués of White's, Brooks's, and of Watier's, the gambling club which he now increasingly patronized, were conformists before they learned to conform to his personal code. The Regent might be a laughable fellow, but Carlton House still issued invitations which gentlemen could not ignore. Sooner or later, the word went round, and sooner rather than later now that he had quarrelled with his royal patron, Brummell's debts must catch up with him. After all, he had for many years spent £8,000 every year: he must owe at least £50,000. Like rats leaving a sinking ship, the dandies began to desert their hero.

Brummell ended his reign with cool dignity when eventually the time came. On the evening of 16 May 1816 he dined quietly as usual with one or two friends at his club. No sign was given that the evening was to be different from any other. He went to the opera, then drove straight from the Haymarket Theatre in a private carriage to Dover. The next day, he crossed to Calais. His arrangements had been made with care. No creditors could hope to sue him successfully now that he was out of the country; but he would have to stay abroad, a permanent exile. A few days later, handbills appeared in his old haunts, advertising

> The genuine property of
> A MAN OF FASHION
> Gone to the Continent.

Among the snuff-boxes included in this sale of Brummell's effects was one with a note saying it had been intended for the Regent 'if he had conducted himself with more propriety toward me'.

Brummell soon became a notable tourist attraction in Calais. However, when the Regent had become King, and as George IV passed through the town in 1821, he made a point of commenting, 'I leave Calais, and have not seen Brummell.' And indeed, Brummell in exile was a broken man. The remainder of his life was anti-climax. He lived on until 1840, latterly an alcoholic with no pride left in his appearance.

Brummell and his satellites — men like 'King' Allen, 'Silent' Hare, 'Apollo' Raikes, and 'Kangaroo' Cooke, a military dandy who complained to the Duke of York that he could find no food in the Peninsula except kangaroo — enjoyed for a time a social prestige strongly tinged with ambiguity. By their every gesture, the dandies revealed contempt for the levelling process which had been taking place in modern society. They were visibly gentlemen, aristocrats of *ton*, and in this sense, their life-style was part of the continuing conservative reaction to the threat posed by the French Revolution. At the same time, the fact that they remained aloof from serious public affairs allowed them to take a sardonic view of *all* politics. To a generation which had grown up in the shadow of war abroad and political stalemate at home, they stood for welcome frivolity.

Dandyism was a product of *ennui*, and by its very nature its appeal was bound to be limited. Leaving aside the dandies' total lack of commitment to any generous social ideal, Brummell was noticeably cold towards women. This produced among the dandies a faintly ridiculous anti-romantic pose, which, coupled with their extreme fastidiousness over dress, caused many people to link the word 'dandy' with homosexuality. Whatever the degree of truth in this favourite Regency jest, women did not like to be ignored. And for their part, few men cared to lead so restricted a life as Brummell's régime made fashionable. Some of the best-known dandies literally did nothing but dress, eat, parade, and gamble.

It was in March 1812 that Regency society found a more dashing hero than Beau Brummell. This was Lord Byron, the twenty-five year old author of *Childe Harold's Pilgrimage*, a poem in two Cantos newly published by John Murray. An aristocrat, single, strikingly good-looking and very widely travelled, Byron had just made his maiden speech in the House of Lords, a very daring one, it was said, which had shocked and set him apart from the traditionally conservative majority of the members. Mystery surrounded his personality and background — he had spent so long out of the country, exploring the Near East — but it was known at least that he differed from Brummell in one important respect. He liked the company of pretty women. Indeed, some chaperones had been heard to hint darkly that he liked women only too well. Behind him, it was whispered, lay a trail of broken hearts. But then, if one were to believe everything spoken by one's chaperone, no man under forty-five was to be trusted. It sounded as if Lord Byron might be that most exciting of all creatures, an eligible aristocratic rebel, with dark secrets waiting to be shared, like Montoni in Mrs Radcliffe's best Gothic novel, *Udolpho*. What could be more desirable than to find out more about him?

If marriageable girls and apparently staid matrons reasoned in this way, men were scarcely less impressed. Byron wrote like somebody who thought for himself. His recent Tour had taken him to places his contemporaries would have given their back teeth to see. He was no respecter of persons and certainly not a pedant. Clearly, here was someone to watch, a refreshingly independent and original observer. Moreover, *Childe Harold's Pilgrimage* differed from every other work, whether verse or prose, known to the public. Attractive and detailed descriptions of exotic places were combined with eloquent support for the political struggles of small nations. And that was not all. There was also the intriguing figure of Childe Harold himself, whose moody, sometimes misanthropic musings gave the work a powerful subjective character: presumably, Childe Harold and Lord Byron were alike in feeling haunted by a sense of sin and of the world's ills.

The descriptive writing and liberal politics of *Childe Harold's Pilgrimage* would have been enough in themselves to ensure the poem's success. Childe Harold's travels took him from England to Portugal, and from there, via Spain, to the Mediterranean. There were extensive descriptions of Albania — scarcely known to Western travellers at this period — and also of Greece and of parts of Asia Minor. But for the creator of Childe Harold it was not enough to record in memorable verse the visual impressions made by these countries. He also wanted to express strong views on contemporary international politics. Passages evoking the beauty of the countryside are followed, characteristically, by a call to political action.

Initially, his observations on the Iberian Peninsula are in the aesthetic tradition of the Picturesque. He appreciates, for instance, the appearance (technically 'sublime' rather than 'picturesque') of a mountainside near Lisbon:

> The horrid crags, by toppling convent crown'd,
> The cork-trees hoar that clothe the shaggy steep,
> The mountain-moss by scorching skies imbrown'd,
> The sunken glen, whose sunless shrubs must weep,
> The tender azure of the unruffled deep,
> The orange tints that gild the greenest bough,
> The torrents that from cliff to valley leap,
> The vine on high, the willow branch below,
> Mix'd in one mighty scene, with varied beauty glow.

But this very quality of dazzling beauty makes the presence of an invading French army seem intolerable. Why should the Spanish people in particular, with their proud historic record, give up so much to foreigners? The same part of Canto 1 therefore includes a stanza which, in the spring of 1812, had up-to-the-moment political relevance:

> Awake, ye sons of Spain! awake! advance!
> Lo! Chivalry, your ancient goddess, cries;
> But wields not, as of old, her thirsty lance,
> Nor shakes her crimson plumage in the skies;
> Now on the smoke of blazing bolts she flies,
> And speaks in thunder through yon engine's roar
> In every peal she calls — 'Awake! arise!'
> Say, is her voice more feeble than of yore,
> When her war-song was heard on Andalusia's shore?

Byron's contemporaries responded no less eagerly to his thrilling declaration in favour of the cause of another country, Greece. The plight of Greece was much less familiar to the British people than that of Spain; there was in fact no reason why Britain should feel obliged to share it — war in Europe was burden enough. But the young were looking for an ideal. Such was Byron's clarity in summarizing the condition of a nation subject to Turkish overlords, that Greece suddenly ceased to seem remote.

He began once more by sharing with his readers his sense of the physical splendour of the Greek mainland and islands. Then he went on to contrast Greece's former glory as the classical home of freedom with her present fallen condition:

> Fair Greece! sad relic of departed worth!
> Immortal, though no more; though fallen, great!
> Who now shall lead thy scatter'd children forth,
> And long accustom'd bondage uncreate?
> Not such thy sons who whilome did await,
> The hopeless warriors of a willing doom,
> In bleak Thermopylae's sepulchral strait —
> Oh! who that gallant spirit shall resume,
> Leap from Eurotas' banks, and call thee from the tomb?

Destined to be quoted over and over again when he died a martyr for Greek independence twelve years later, this stanza and others like it communicated to his first readers the full force of Byron's passionate concern that Greece should one day be free.

But it was the confessional side of the poem which stamped

Childe Harold's Pilgrimage as daringly avant-garde in its morality. The Childe was subject to moods of remorse when he remembered the days he had misspent and the girls he had seduced:

> Sweet was the scene, yet soon he thought to flee,
> More restless than the swallow in the skies:
> Though here awhile he learn'd to moralize,
> For Meditation fix'd at times on him;
> And conscious Reason whisper'd to despise
> His early youth, misspent in maddest whim;
> But as he gazed on truth his aching eyes grew dim.
>
> To horse! to horse! he quits, for ever quits
> A scene of peace, though soothing to his soul:
> Again he rouses from his moping fits,
> But seeks not now the harlot and the bowl.
> Onward he flies, nor fix'd as yet the goal
> Where he shall rest him on his pilgrimage;
> And o'er him many changing scenes must roll
> Ere toil his thirst for travel can assuage,
> Or he shall calm his breast, or learn experience sage.

The revelation of this past shocked many people who wanted to admire the Childe and the poet. Samuel Rogers noted that 'two old maids in Buckinghamshire used to cry over the passage about Harold's "Laughing dames" that "long had fed his youthful appetite" '. They did not weep alone. And for every person who shed tears, a hundred others were made curious and felt both amused and disturbed at the completely unexpected disclosures.

The emphasis was not on sexual action, which Byron alluded to without much detail, but on the feelings of guilt haunting the restless Childe Harold. Walter Scott's own immensely popular verse tales, *The Lay of the Last Minstrel, Marmion,* and their successors, lacked any such *frisson* or suggestion of personal mystery. Scott was the least subjective, the most proper of poets. His works had enjoyed a great vogue because they were filled with exciting scenes of action, and because they offered the prospect of temporary escape from present actuality into a distant past and into an unknown geographical region, which might be the Scottish Borders, the Highlands, or, as in his latest poem, Spain. But his heroes had not sinned like Childe Harold, and they had none of his air of doom, world-weariness, and brittle disillusionment. Parents might deplore the change, but it quickly became clear that Byron, and not Scott, now commanded the interest of their sons and daughters.

Byron 'awoke to find himself famous' on 11 March 1812. Less than a fortnight previously, his prospects must have seemed very different. He had chosen to make his maiden speech in the House of Lords on the second reading of the Frame-work Bill, which the Government had introduced with a view to making frame-breaking punishable by death. Byron opposed the principles of the bill. There was nothing lacking in the eloquence with which he presented his case: rather, he had been only too eloquent. Most M.P.s and peers were extremely anxious about the threat to law and order posed by the machine-breakers, and they did not discriminate between an attempt to understand the causes of the machine-breakers' campaign and out-and-out support for them. Although Byron had consulted Lord Holland, a prominent figure among the moderate Whigs in the Lords, before he spoke, he had not altered the main argument of his speech; and in the judgment of the House, it was a radical rather than a Whig case which he put forward.

Newstead, Byron's ancestral home, was close to the Nottinghamshire textile factories where the rioting and frame-breaking said to have been ordered by 'General' Ned Ludd had begun the year before. Informing the Lords that every day brought reports of fresh acts of violence near Nottingham, and that on the day he left the county to come to London there was word of forty frames having been broken 'as usual, without resistance and without detection', Byron, without condoning this behaviour, had tried to find an explanation for it. The riots must be seen as a reaction to economic distress:

> ... nothing but absolute want could have driven a large, and once honest and industrious, body of the people, into the commission of excesses so hazardous to themselves, their families, and the community ... The rejected workmen, in the blindness of their ignorance, instead of rejoicing at these improvements in arts so beneficial to mankind, conceived themselves to be sacrificed to improvements in mechanism. In the foolishness of their hearts they imagined that the maintenance and well-doing of the industrious poor were objects of greater consequence than the enrichment of a few individuals by any improvement, in the implements of trade, which threw the workmen out of employment, and rendered the labourer unworthy of his hire.

Byron's sympathetic attitude to the frame-breakers certainly provoked disagreement from both Whigs and Tories. When he went on to blame

> the bitter policy, the destructive warfare of the last eighteen years, which

> has destroyed their comfort, your comfort, all men's comfort. . . that
> policy, which, originating with 'great statesmen now no more', has
> survived the dead to become a curse on the living, unto the third and
> fourth generation

it was too much for the Lord Chancellor, who, according to Byron, remained 'very much out of humour'.

Sir Frances Burdett congratulated Byron on 'the best speech by a Lord since "the Lord knows when" ', but Burdett was the leader of the notorious radical element in the Lords, not of the responsible Whig opposition. Byron himself made light of any error of judgment he might have shown, commenting to a friend,

> I spoke very violent sentences with a sort of modest impudence, abused
> every thing & everybody. . . As to my delivery, loud & fluent enough,
> perhaps a little theatrical.

'Perhaps a little theatrical.' In fact, despite the courage he had shown in pointing to causes of social unrest among the poor, he had probably spoiled his chances of a parliamentary career. 'Sound' views were valued far more highly than either intelligence or rhetorical skill. This was a matter of some significance to Byron. It had been his strongest ambition as a schoolboy to excel in oratory. He had won various prizes for recitation; and on his final Harrow Speech Day in 1805 had declaimed a passage from *King Lear* with such intensity that he was overcome with emotion and had to leave the room. From the time that he had taken his seat in the Lords in 1809 he had assumed that, sooner or later, he would become actively involved in parliamentary affairs. Since his return from overseas in the summer of 1811 he had been seeking the right opportunity to contribute to a major debate. Now it had come, and the dull dogs around him had taken offence. So much for his wish to be looked up to as an orator in the mould of Demosthenes or Cicero.

The same classical schooling and histrionic talent which lent individuality to his speech on 27 February went to create the resounding success of *Childe Harold's Pilgrimage*. Here no note of dissent was sounded. It was a poem of sustained rhetorical power; narrative and descriptive passages were finely balanced so as to complement each other. Those who shared Byron's knowledge of the Greek and Latin classics and his liberal outlook on European affairs were particularly impressed, no one more so than Lord Holland, who was quite ready to forgive the poet for making heavy weather of the Frame-work Bill.

Henry, third Lord Holland, was a clever, easy-going man, fifteen years older than Byron. In 1797 he had married Elizabeth Vassall, two days after her first husband, Sir Godfrey Webster, had divorced her, naming Holland as co-respondent. Lady Holland was ambitious, a natural high society hostess with a sharp tongue and a gossipy interest in the affairs of everyone she knew. At Holland House, set in the country in Kensington, she and her husband were famed for their generous hospitality and patronage of up-and-coming Whig politicians. As often as not, guests who came for dinner were invited to stay the night to avoid going back to town in the dark: it depended partly on whether Lady Holland found them witty and amusing. Talented opponents of the Government, whether or not they were in Parliament, had a friend in Lord Holland. They were assured at least of being admitted to what had the reputation of being the most brilliant and unconventional social circle in the country. Having been so long in opposition, the Whigs wanted to outshine the Tories socially, just as the Regent felt compelled to enjoy life more than George III.

Byron was frequently invited to Holland House, where he was treated with great kindness, as well as being displayed proudly by Lady Holland to her other guests — not for nothing was she known as the first 'lion-hunter' in the land. One introduction led to another, and soon he was being plied with invitations from two other hostesses of a distinction equal to Lady Holland's. Lady Melbourne, mother of the Whig statesman William Lamb — later as Lord Melbourne to become Prime Minister, and married to the totally unpredictable Caroline Lamb — was over sixty, but still attractive, and exceptionally intelligent. She and Byron at once took to each other; she was to be his confidante in a number of his most publicized love affairs during the next three or four years. To some extent, perhaps, he saw Lady Melbourne as an ideal mother-figure — his own mother, with whom he had not got on, having died in 1811 — but the relationship had its own piquancy: Byron would later comment, 'I have often thought, that, with a little more youth, Lady M. might have turned my head.' It was at Melbourne House that he first met Lady Sarah Jersey, a younger beauty, and a leading patroness of the fasionable balls at Almack's.

There was no question of romance between the poet and Lady

Jersey. But, like everyone else, he soon acknowledged her power and influence in society, writing that she was 'the veriest tyrant that ever governed Fashion's fools, and compelled them to shake their caps and bells as she willed it'. At Almack's, round the corner from White's, the sexes met; and even the dandies wanted to be seen to go there. Seven high-born ladies, with Lady Jersey in command, had the exclusive right to grant vouchers of admission to the subscription balls in Almack's Assembly Rooms on Wednesday evenings. No one was admitted without their approval, and after eleven o'clock there was no hope of getting in. (Lady Jersey once turned away the Duke of Wellington at seven minutes past eleven.)

Almack's was in certain respects decidedly old-fashioned, even dull. The only refreshments available in these rather cold, sparsely furnished rooms were bread and butter, stale cake, lemonade and tea. For a long time, too, the only dances permitted were of a decorous formality which kept partners at a distance from each other. Yet for girls new to fashionable society it was of the greatest importance to be on the list issued by Lady Jersey and her despotic colleagues. In the words of Henry Luttrell, a familiar and well-liked figure both at Almack's and in the homes of many who sought entry there:

> All on that magic LIST depends;
> Fame, fortune, fashion, lovers, friends:
> 'Tis that which gratifies or vexes
> All ranks, all ages, and both sexes.
> If once to Almack's you belong,
> Like monarchs, you can do no wrong;
> But banished thence on Wednesday night,
> By Jove, you can do nothing right.

Mothers knew that Almack's was the Mecca of London society, and that because it was under matriarchal control it was safe for their daughters.

But strict morality among the aristocracy ended with Almack's. The Holland House set prided themselves on their 'tolerance'. They assumed that numerous affairs, among both unmarried and married, were the normal pattern of life; and as far as peers of the realm were concerned, they were probably right. 'The Regency', someone has written in another connection, 'is where the eighteenth century dies.' But the tradition of eighteenth-century licence among the nobility did not look in the least like dying, so intense was its final phase. No doubt war had, as usual, relaxed moral attitudes. At any rate, many of the *ton* of both sexes and various ages were out to make hay while the sun shone.

Lady Caroline Lamb was three years older than Byron, and married, but that did not deter her. She read *Childe Harold's Pilgrimage* when it came out, and at once sent him a fan letter:

> I have read your Book & . . . think it beautiful. You deserve to be and you shall be happy. Do not throw away such Talents as you possess in gloom & regrets for the past & above all live here in your own Country which will be proud of you — & which requires your exertion.

This is typical of many letters Byron would receive from women over the next twelve years, making the point that he deserved to be made happier than evidently he was. But 'Caro', as he would soon be calling her, was uniquely impulsive, with a gift for self-dramatization which surpassed his own. When they met, a few weeks later, she wrote in her journal, 'mad — bad — and dangerous to know'. Her feelings were summed up in equally ominous words: 'That beautiful pale face is my fate.'

So indeed it proved, although at first her appearance did not interest Byron. He was to remember without gallantry, 'The lady had scarcely any personal attractions to recommend her. Her figure, though genteel, was too thin to be good. . .' However, her eager, darting personality and readiness to flout social convention more than compensated for this initial disappointment. Soon, the couple were meeting frequently, at the theatre, at balls, at private parties. According to Samuel Rogers, one of Byron's new literary friends and a diarist with an eye for gossip, 'She absolutely besieged him . . . she assured him that, if he was in any want of money, "all her jewels were at his service".' But if Lady Caroline Lamb was obsessed by Lord Byron, he also for his part became for some months her devoted lover.

He even spoke about eloping with her, and meant it. When she talked with other men he was seriously put out. Although he had cuckolded William Lamb, he felt jealous of him. Above all, he resented the fact that his clubbed right foot prevented him from dancing. Caroline liked dancing, especially on the spur of the moment, at parties in the gilded homes of her friends. And now there was a craze for a new and, as Byron thought, dangerously intimate dance, the waltz. When one of the controlling group at Almack's, the wife of the Russian Ambassador, Countess Lieven, had first whirled round the floor with 'Cupid' Palmerston, people had been shocked. But then Lady Jersey herself, not to be outdone, had taught herself and others how to waltz: after that, the dance had the approval of all Almack's. It was in vain that Byron brought out an anonymous satire which expressed his bitter feelings on the subject. . .

> Endearing Waltz! — to thy more melting tune
> Bow Irish Jig, and ancient Rigadoon.
> Scotch reels, avaunt! and Country-dance forego
> Your future claims to each fantastic toe!
> Waltz — Waltz alone — both legs and arms demands,
> Liberal of feet, and lavish of her hands;
> Hands which may freely range in public sight
> Where ne'er before — but — pray 'put out the light':
> Methinks the glare of yonder chandelier
> Shines much too far — or I am much too near;
> And true, though strange — Waltz whispers this remark,
> 'My slippery steps are safest in the dark!'

His 'volcanic little Caro' was shrewd enough to play on this nerve of sexual insecurity without giving him serious cause for being jealous. 'He liked', she said, 'to read with me & stay with me out of the crowd.' More often than not, she humoured Byron.

But it was not in her nature to keep out of the crowd, especially when she had captured so brilliant a literary lion as her lover. She would come to his rooms in her favourite disguise as a page boy (which incidentally may have appealed to the bisexual poet), write him notes at all hours of the day and expect answers by return, and make a particular point of being seen with him in his carriage late at night. Their affair had become the talk of the town, and this at a time when Byron was in constant demand socially. Caroline's exhibitionist behaviour acutely embarrassed him. He began to wish himself free of the entanglement. There were other bright eyes, after all.

Childe Harold's Pilgrimage was on every hostess's table. There were sometimes so many carriages bringing notes of invitation to his house in St James's Street that the traffic was held up. 'The subject of conversation, of curiosity, of enthusiasm almost, one might say, of the moment,' the Duchess of Devonshire wrote to her son in America, 'is not Spain or Portugal, Warriors or Patriots, but Lord Byron! . . . courted, visited, flattered, and praised wherever he appears.' She was using 'enthusiasm' in its eighteenth-century sense of fanatical devotion or uncontrollable ecstasy.

At a ball given by a Miss Johnson in late June 1812, the Regent himself was present, and asked to meet the poet. Byron was genuinely impressed by his knowledge of literature: his praise clearly meant more than that of less well-read persons. They talked about a number of contemporary writers, and especially about Walter Scott. Remembering that the Prince was anything but popular with the moderate Whigs whom he was held to have betrayed, Byron had to be careful not to make too much of the occasion to Lord Holland. All he wrote was,

> The other night at a Ball I was presented by order to our gracious Regent, who honoured me with some conversation & professed a predilection for Poesy.

Nevertheless, it pleased him that the Regent liked his work. He took the chance to write a very courteous letter to Scott, about whom he had foolishly been rude many years before in one of his early poetic satires. Scott replied no less generously, describing Byron's current fame as richly deserved. As a result of this exchange – and indirectly therefore of the Regent's admiration for both – a warm friendship sprang up between the two. In 1815, they were to have long conversations at the premises of John Murray, their publisher, in Albemarle Street; and Byron would later send Scott a magnificent silver urn containing the ashes of Greek heroes from the Long Walls of Athens. He thought of Scott as in a class of his own, both as man and writer.

Certainly Byron did not lack congenial and gifted male companions now. Perhaps it was the Celtic blood in him which made him respond to fellow-Celts: at any rate, two of those whose friendship he valued most highly were Irishmen, Richard Sheridan and Thomas Moore. Sheridan he had admired since his schooldays. Indeed, if there was any single Harrovian whose example was taken by Byron as a model, it was this legendary figure, wit, playwright – Byron never wavered in his opinion that *The School for Scandal* was the outstanding comedy of modern times – and parliamentary orator worthy of being compared with the great Fox. By now, 'Sherry' had been reduced by drink and political disappointment to a shadow of his former self; but Byron thought more of him drunk than of most people sober. 'In society', he wrote, 'I have met him frequently: he was superb.' Moore was a complete contrast, a tiny, cheerful poet and song-writer whose talents for writing mildly erotic verse and the words of lyrics set to Irish melodies had raised him from a humble background as the son of a Dublin grocer. He was frequently asked into the homes of the great, being an engaging talker as well as a fine singer of his own songs. Like Scott, Moore had been mocked by Byron in *English Bards and Scotch Reviewers*. He sent the now famous poet a half-hearted challenge to fight a duel; Byron declined, recognizing that such an event would be even sillier than their original quarrel with each other; a correspondence between them began, at first stiff with their sense of the Regency code of honour: then suddenly they left all that behind them, and became firm friends.

At the height of his passion for Lady Caroline Lamb, Byron was aware that Moore and his devoted wife Bessy (who seldom ventured into high society with her husband, but who shared his secrets) were 'distressed' at his conduct. This merely amused him at the time; but later it more than once crossed his mind that if he were to follow Moore's advice by marrying a girl less giddy and headstrong than Caroline he would be spared at least one kind of trouble. When the long-suffering William Lamb took his erring wife off for a holiday in Ireland, it was with relief that Byron wrote to Moore:

> On Monday, after sitting up all night, I saw Bellingham [Spencer Perceval's assassin in the House of Commons] launched into eternity, and at three the same day I saw xxxxx launched into the country.

In seeking to escape from her attentions Byron came to rely, odd though it may seem, upon the advice of Caroline's mother-in-law, Lady Melbourne. Presumably reasoning that her son was now old enough to look after himself, she dispensed worldly wisdom with good humour to Byron and at the same time kept a kindly eye on Caroline's welfare. When she felt, for instance, that Byron was too abrupt in seeking to make a final break with Caroline, she warned him that her daughter-in-law's hysteria might lead to suicide.

Like Moore, Lady Melbourne spoke to Byron of the advantages of marriage. Byron, however, was still sowing wild oats. In the winter of 1812-13 he was captivated, as a number of other men had been before him, by the physical charm of Lady Oxford, now forty and the mother of a brood of children whose uncertain paternity led to their being called 'The Harleian Miscellany' after a collection of rare tracts in her husband's library. Byron spent some weeks in the country with Lady Oxford, whose company he found altogether less taxing than Caroline's. Caroline meanwhile began to take her 'revenge' by burning his effigy and along with it copies of the letters he had sent her — she kept all the originals. She dressed some of her neighbours' children in white and had them recite verses as she carried out this ritual. Presumably they had little idea of what it meant. (Her other, literary, revenge came later, in 1816, when she published *Glenarvon,* a novel about fashionable life, in which more than one of the letters she had received from Byron was reproduced in a thinly disguised context.) She also wrote to Lady Oxford, bitterly accusing her of stealing her lover. Lady Oxford herself paid little attention to this — it may have pleased her vanity that she had been preferred to a younger woman — but Byron was put out that she had been subjected to such a 'German tirade'.

There was talk of Byron following the Oxfords when they went abroad in the sping of 1813. But the affair had run its course, and Lady Oxford and Byron were content to drift apart. Their brief and, Byron always insisted, delightful liaison was followed by something much more serious. In the summer Byron began to spend a lot of time in company with his married half-sister Augusta Leigh. Five years older than himself — at this stage he displayed a need to be loved by an older woman — Augusta was pretty, uncritical, and amusing. Colonel Leigh tended to be an absentee husband, devoted to race-going. There were three young daughters. Augusta, or 'Guss' as he called her, shared with Byron certain childhood memories, and she was now his only close surviving relative. He was later to say that he felt at ease with her as with no other woman, for she had the Byron pride and sense of fun.

Byron kept this new relationship secret. Even the Holland House circle would have drawn the line at the idea of incest. Yet it is doubtful if anyone would have felt as deep a sense of shock as Byron did himself. In his boyhood in Aberdeen he had been subject to gloomy Calvinist influences — something the sunny-natured Augusta had entirely escaped — and now he felt obsessed by sexual guilt. How much he knew of the long history of such illicit consanguineous affairs among the Byrons is not recorded. What is certain is that he felt Augusta and he were *fated* to love each other.

Both his brooding sense of guilt and his fatalism colour the verse 'Turkish tales' which he had now begun to write and publish as a way of capitalizing on the success of *Childe Harold*. These poems, drawing on his special knowledge of Turkish life and history, were if anything more popular than *Childe Harold's Pilgrimage*, partly because the note of doom which sounds through their action is stronger than before. Conrad, in *The Corsair* (10,000 copies of which were sold on the day of publication in 1814), is a characteristic 'hero', torn between conflicting emotions, heroic yet antisocially motivated:

> 'Twas vain to paint to what his feelings grew —
> It even were doubtful if their victim knew.
> There is a war, a chaos of the mind,
> When all its elements convulsed — combined —
> Lie dark and jarring with perturbed force,
> And gnashing with impenitent Remorse —
> That juggling fiend, who never spake before,
> But cries 'I warned thee!' when the deed is o'er.

Conrad's alienation at once mirrored and helped to create the mood of the alienated young, who felt their world to be somehow out of joint. Byron wrote *The Corsair* and poems like it as a kind of instant therapy, to work off the 'lava' of his troubled emotions.

The near-disclosures and half-confessions of his fictional heroes, which so strongly appealed to the reading public, came after very different but no less cryptic hints in Byron's letters to his closest friends. On 22 August 1813 he wrote wryly to Moore:

> I am at this moment in a far more serious, and entirely new, scrape than any of the last twelve months, — and that is saying a good deal. It is unlucky we can neither live with nor without these women.

Moore must have wondered if anything could possibly be more serious than the passionate feud between Byron and Lady Caroline Lamb! This letter was written two days after one to Lady Melbourne which opened with the comment, 'When I don't write to you or see you for some time you may be very certain I am about no good.' It was to Lady Melbourne that Byron came closest to being explicit in the next few months about what had taken place between Augusta and himself during the summer of this year.

Deeply alarmed by something which went beyond both her own experience and the taboos of society, Lady Melbourne again thought it wise to remind Byron of the one kind of romantic attachment he had still to experience. He might marry. There was no lack of attractive young women, or indeed of well-educated ones. Her own niece, for example, Annabella Milbanke, just turned twenty-one, had been strictly brought up in the bracing atmosphere of Seaham in County Durham; she was fully capable of discussing intellectual subjects with anyone, and she was very pretty. Byron might not of course come up to the high standards Annabella would look for in a husband, but he had already met her and exchanged letters with her. Why not keep in touch with her, at least? She, Lady Melbourne, could act as intermediary if need be. After all, she had had some practice in his affair with Caroline!

In the meantime, however, diversion was important both as a means of turning Byron's thoughts away from Augusta and of letting him see that, however harshly he might judge himself, others were ready to accept him. Therefore Lady Melbourne made no attempt to discourage him when he wrote to her admitting that he felt strongly tempted to make love to Lady Wedderburn Webster, the beautiful and romantically inclined young wife of a man he knew well and thought rather selfish and loud-mouthed.

Frances Wedderburn Webster, in fact, much to Byron's surprise, was eager to run away with him. On the other hand, she was not willing to indulge in casual adultery like Lady Oxford. Torn between her desires and her moral scruples, she smuggled love-letters to the poet in her husband's billiard-room, presumably while he was demonstrating his skill at the game. 'Is not all this a comedy?', wrote Byron to Lady Melbourne, while Frances continued to wrestle with her conscience; and he went on:

> ... it has enlivened my ethical studies on the human mind beyond 50 volumes — how admirably we accommodate our reasons to our wishes!

In the end, 'Platonics' prevailed and he 'spared' Frances — he seems to have been too fond of her to do otherwise. But, as he noted wistfully to Lady Melbourne, the young lady's charms were very real. There might indeed be merit, he began to think, in forming an association of which society might approve with a girl who, as Lady Wedderburn Webster did, combined the beauty and the innocence of twenty-one.

This was a frame of mind into which Byron drifted gradually. It would be wrong to suggest that he formed any very firm plan as a result of the Wedderburn Webster escapade to seek the hand in marriage of someone newly come of age, or for that matter of anyone at all. But since he had himself lost the personal innocence natural to youth, he must look to a woman younger than himself to supply that quality.

[5]

Home Thoughts from Abroad: Byron Rejected

Byron was always to look back on the year before he married as a time of delightful freedom, the high point of his social life in London. Nostalgically, he wrote to Moore from Italy in 1822: 'Do you recollect, in the year of revelry 1814, the pleasantest parties and balls all over London?' The war had taken a decisive turn in Britain's favour by 1814. Napoleon abdicated in the spring, and this gave rise — if a little prematurely — to victory celebrations in Britain. It was in June of this 'Year of the Sovereigns' that the Regent received as the nation's guests the Tsar of Russia, Blücher and other victorious foreigners. They were welcomed with every kind of festivity from elaborate firework displays to summer balls, and the rest of society made merry at the same time.

The news about Napoleon shocked Byron, who, like many another, had come to think of him as invincible. His attitude to the Corsican was one of mingled contempt and admiration. He had no time for tyranny, and he judged that latterly Napoleon had been nothing better than a tyrant. But on the other hand he recalled clearly, as few of his countrymen now seemed willing to do, that before being corrupted by love of power Napoleon had been France's and Europe's liberator. In his journal for 9 April 1814 he wrote,

> I mark this day!
> Napoleon Buonaparte has abdicated the throne of the world. 'Excellent well' . . . I won't give him up even now; though all his admirers have, 'like the Thanes, fallen from him'.

In the months which followed, it pained him to notice how willing people were, both in Britain and on the Continent, to see the

Bourbon monarchy restored in France. Before long, he reflected, reactionary statesmen would force all Europe to accept old-style monarchical régimes. Something must be done to prevent them from having their way.

Dining out on summer evenings in 1814, Byron was frequently appalled as he listened to violently anti-French, and in his view politically antediluvian, talk. The French Revolution might as well never have taken place. How ironical it would be if the mighty uprising of the French people in 1789 were to result in the imposition throughout Europe of forms of government more repressive than any known before. But then of course, it occurred to him, policies were dictated by the few. 'Society', in England at least — those who even now were flattering him, who gave parties in their town and country houses, who governed the nation — consisted of only a tiny fraction of the British people. Beyond the couple of square miles where they entertained and had their being, there lay an unknown land and an unknown populace. How tiny, how unrepresentative, was 'The World'!

For the time being, none the less, Byron was part of 'The World' and its quest for pleasure. His valet Fletcher was a countryman with no sense of the sartorial niceties which appealed to dandies like Brummell. But Byron turned this to advantage by deliberately wearing loose cloaks and by throwing away stiff cravats, which he loathed. Soon he had set a new style in dress, including a fashion for open-necked shirts. The dandies simply accepted that he was different. As he wrote much later,

> I liked the Dandies; they were always very civil to *me*, though in general they disliked literary people.

He added, with characteristic honesty,

> The truth is, that, though I gave up the business early, I had a tinge of Dandyism in my minority, and probably retained enough of it, to conciliate the great ones, at four and twenty. I had gamed, and drank, and taken my degrees in most dissipations; and having no pedantry, and not being overbearing, we ran quietly together. I knew them all more or less, and they made me a Member of Watier's (a superb Club at that time), being, I take it, the only literary man (except *two others*, both men of the world, M. and S.) in it.

As this passage reveals, it was important to Byron, both in 1814 and subsequently, that he should be seen to be something quite different from a mere 'literary man'. He was a man of the world or nothing. The style of life he led proclaimed this, from the nonchalant ease with which he spoke in the Lords to the screen decorated with portraits of famous boxers which stood in his superb Albany rooms in Piccadilly. Action was much more valuable in his own eyes than writing, which he thought of as a recreation and certainly not as a 'career'.

There may have been 'a tinge of Dandyism' in this attitude, or at any rate of affectation, but Byron's mind was far too energetic to be at home for long in the Watier's Club world. He might jest to John Murray that he wrote *Lara*, the verse tale which came after *The Corsair*, 'while undressing after coming home from balls and masquerades in the year of revelry 1814' — the carelessness of some parts of the poem certainly indicates that *Lara* was written in haste — but even writing in haste and very casually, Byron remained inventive:

> There was in him a vital scorn of all:
> As if the worst had fallen which could befall,
> He stood a stranger in this breathing world,
> An erring Spirit from another hurled;
> A thing of dark imaginings, that shaped
> By choice the perils he by chance escaped;
> But 'scaped in vain, for in their memory yet
> His mind would half exult and half regret:
> With more capacity for love than Earth
> Bestows on most of mortal mould and birth.
> His early dreams of good outstripped the truth,
> And troubled Manhood followed baffled Youth.

If this came dangerously close to self-parody, it was still well beyond the reach of any dandy. In portraying Lara, Byron described conflicts within himself.

These internal conflicts continued to make him very restless. At times he thought of going abroad again, perhaps to Italy or preferably to the Near East, where he could leave behind him all the unhappy and broken relationships of the recent past, and make a fresh start. But he still loved Augusta intensely. Going abroad would solve nothing. It would simply make them both miserable. Instead, his thoughts turned again to finding himself a wife.

For a while he toyed with the idea of courting Frances Wedderburn Webster's younger sister. She looked like Frances, yet at the same time intriguingly different. But he judged her rather silly, and who in any case would want James Wedderburn Webster as a brother-in-law? Then Augusta took a hand in the matter by proposing that he should instead woo Lady Charlotte Leveson Gower, who was also young, extemely pretty, and — unlike the girl he had in mind — modest as well. Byron was ready enough to comply with any idea of Augusta's. He had seen and admired the 'shy antelope', Lady Charlotte. But because she was known to be shy, he thought she might confide initially in Augusta rather than in himself: he suggested that Augusta should befriend her and find out how things stood. Meanwhile, he himself was corresponding again, he told his half-sister, with Annabella Milbanke. He had even been invited to visit Annabella and her parents at Seaham in the north.

Privately, Augusta thought Annabella too serious-minded to be Byron's type. She applied herself vigorously to her own commission. One of the things she most liked about Lady Charlotte was that she had a ready sense of humour. . . But then it turned out that Lady Charlotte, who was of course polite about Byron and ready to be persuaded of his merits, was already 'promised' by her parents to another family, by one of those annoying arrangements that were still being made. Nothing could be done about it, and indeed by the end of the year Lady Charlotte was married. The lucky man turned out to be wealthy and high-born, the only son of the Duke of Norfolk. Small wonder that Lady Charlotte's letters to Augusta had seemed somewhat skittish and enigmatic.

Whether Byron felt piqued or not in learning that the 'antelope' was unavailable is not entirely clear. But he certainly acted with speed when Augusta told him of the 'compact elsewhere' which ruled out the Leveson Gowers, explaining to Lady Melbourne afterwards:

> I then said to X[Augusta], after consoling her on the subject, that I would try the next myself, as she did not seem to be in luck.

'The next' was Annabella. On 9 September he sent off a letter of proposal to Seaham; then immediately began to have doubts. After all, he might still go to the Continent and join the indulgent and lovely Lady Oxford, who had asked him the year before, 'Have we not passed out last month like the gods of Lucretius?' (In his journal Byron added after this question the words, 'And so we had'.) While waiting for a reply from the north, he wrote to his old travelling companion J. C. Hobhouse,

100

> . . . if a circumstance (which may happen but is . . . unlikely to
> happen. . .) does not occur — I have thoughts of going direct and directly
> to Italy — if so, will you come with me?

It can be deduced from this that his pride was going to be hurt if
Annabella's answer was 'No'. Acceptance, on the other hand, would
remove the peronal freedom he valued very dearly.

He was with Augusta when eventually Annabella's reply came.
She wrote delightedly, 'I will *trust* to you for all I should look up to
— all I can love.' Every moment of her life would be devoted to
making her husband happy. The prospect of marriage suddenly
terrified Byron. What had begun as a light-hearted diversion was now
serious, and he must go through with it. Deadly pale, he handed
Annabella's letter over the dinner-table to Augusta, saying as he did
so 'it never rains but it pours'.

He was of course now invited to come to Seaham as soon as he
could; Annabella's parents were looking forward to meeting their
future son-in-law. He knew that he must brace himself for a quiet
and probably boring time in the home of Sir Ralph and Lady
Milbanke. But he delayed for as long as he decently could, spending
time on the way at Newstead, until Augusta positively ordered him
to continue his journey. His feelings were utterly confused. Annabella's good looks, her cool intelligence and her 'prim and pretty'
letters attracted him strongly. But he would have to give up so much.
To begin with — and to end with — there was Augusta. Then there
was his ancestral home. For years he had been trying to sell Newstead (which was worth at least £100,000 in the currency of the
time), in order to pay off substantial debts. A buyer had been found
in 1812, but he had repented the bargain and withdrawn with a
promise to pay the contracted deposit of £25,000. This sum had
taken until now to come through, and the house *must* be sold soon
anyway or he and his bride would be dogged by financial worries.
Sentimentally, Byron carved his and Augusta's initials in an oak tree
in the 'Devil's wood' on Newstead estate; the least he and his
half-sister could do was to mark their attachment to each other and
to the place he would no longer be able to think of as his own.

Annabella, too, was out of her emotional depth. An only child,
she had grown up to expect whatever she asked her parents to
provide. She was sensible, strait-laced, and extremely interested in
all things mathematical; she was able, for example, to hold her own

in discussions with Charles Babbage, the man who invented the first computer. Byron felt proud, amused, and a little frightened at this talent. In letters to Lady Melbourne he referred to Annabella as his 'Princess of Parallelograms'.

At Seaham he found as he expected that Annabella's father was distinctly tedious; he told all his stories many times over. However, Byron put himself out to be agreeable, and quickly fell into the routine of the household. Thus he spent lengthy periods in the library with his fiancée, which suited him very well, and went for walks with her on the cliff-tops where, if he missed the sight of the Mediterranean which would have greeted him if he had gone to Italy, he at least drew in lungfuls of good sea air. At the end of his fortnight's visit he still felt deeply uneasy about marrying so correctly educated and inexperienced a young woman, but then he recalled the tempestuous nonsense of Lady Caroline Lamb, and realized how much he had to be thankful for.

The wedding was arranged for the beginning of January 1815. Annabella had hoped to be married in church, but Byron insisted that he should apply to the Archbishop of Canterbury for a special licence, 'because we can be married at any hour in any place without fuss or publicity'. Sensing the strength of his opposition to her wishes, Annabella could only agree that the ceremony should take place at Seaham, where, as he put it, 'mama will lend us a cushion each to kneel upon'.

As the day approached, Annabella waited eagerly for Byron to arrive with his friend Hobhouse. But again Byron dawdled in the Midlands, making himself wretched by spending Christmas at Newstead. 'Never was lover less in haste', wrote Hobhouse in his diary. Eventually, the pair reached Seaham, unannounced, on the evening of 30 December. The weekend was spent in making preparations for Byron's and Annabella's journey to Halnaby Hall, forty miles away in Yorkshire, which Sir Ralph was lending them for the honeymoon. On Monday 2 January 1815 the marriage was solemnized, as quietly as Byron had stipulated, in the drawing-room at Seaham. In addition to two clergymen and Annabella's parents, the only persons there to witness it were her former governess, Mrs Clermont, and Hobhouse. 'Hobby' slipped a set of Byron's poems bound in yellow morocco into the carriage as a gift for Lady Byron when it was about to set off across the wintry countryside to Halnaby Hall. 'If I am not happy,' she told him, 'it will be my own fault.'

There was a Gothic side to the honeymoon, what with the bleak cold, a Yorkshire moor, and strange remarks from the bridegroom such as 'it *must* come to a separation' (Byron remembered that his father and mother had been unable to live together). But, as he later insisted, the honeymoon was 'never down at zero'. The three weeks which he and Annabella passed at Halnaby Hall were certainly not idle. She saw to it that he worked in the library on *Hebrew Melodies*, a collection of words for traditional tunes of the Jewish people which he was currently producing; she herself acted as his amanuensis.

All was not well, however. When Lady Caroline Lamb learned that Byron was to marry Annabella she wrote to John Murray, 'She is very learned and very good, and the top of her face is handsome.' Then she added that Byron would 'never be able to pull with a woman who went to church punctually, understood statistics and had a bad figure'. The slur on Annabella's appearance was unfair. Nevertheless, Byron's cast-off mistress had put her finger on an underlying cause of incompatibility between the poet and his bride. Byron's easy-going morality belonged to the raffish tradition of the eighteenth-century aristocrat. He had written to Lady Melbourne when he became engaged,

> I suppose a married man never gets anybody else, does he? I only ask for information.

Lady Melbourne understood and enjoyed such naughtiness; but her niece, who, significantly, disapproved of the correspondence between the two, was of the serious-minded nineteenth century in her outlook — a different world altogether. Annabella took things literally. She lacked the trick, possessed by many women, of humouring Byron when he was moody. Instead, she sought to discuss every real or imaginary problem rationally, and her probing intelligence sometimes only added to his irritability. 'I can make Augusta laugh *at any thing*', he complained.

Tension grew when Byron announced in March that he would have to go to London to settle his financial affairs, and Annabella stated that she was going to come with him. They had been living at Seaham since the end of January. Byron was not tired of Annabella, but he felt in need of a spell on his own; bachelor habits were reasserting themselves. After losing his temper and making it up, he agreed that his wife should accompany him. On the way south, he said, they must visit Augusta. It was time that Annabella met her.

The visit to Augusta's home at Six Mile Bottom was a disastrous mistake — the mistake Byron's fatalism had been provoking him to make every since Annabella agreed to marry him. Augusta herself was very kind, giving a warm welcome to her sister-in-law, but Byron behaved incomprehensibly towards Annabella. For instance, he would send her off to bed at night with the comment, 'We don't need *you*, my charmer'; then the next day he hinted that Augusta and he had been lovers. Neither woman could cope with him in this, his blackest frame of mind. Had she not been deeply in love with him, it is likely that Annabella would have gone straight back to her parents. As it was, she suffered silently, relying on Augusta's natural cheerfulness to keep her going. Her spirits lifted if at any time Byron relaxed and smiled in her direction, but more often he frowned.

Things were a little better once they had left Cambridgeshire and Augusta, and moved into the house in Piccadilly which Hobhouse had leased on their behalf from the Duchess of Devonshire. Here at last, Annabella thought a little desperately, she could coax her husband into settling down. And indeed, friends and observers at the opera and other social functions noted the apparent happiness of the young couple. Byron was solicitude itself towards his wife, or so it seemed. He was forever hanging over the back of Annabella's chair, inquiring if she was comfortable, carrying her shawl or rug.

In this, he was acting like any other man who has learned that he is about to become a father. But he was still subject to fits of gloom. These made him drink heavily and take up with his old companions of the gambling clubs and the Drury Lane 'green room' — he had a short-lived affair at this time with Susan Boyce, an actress. The main reason was acute and recurring worry over money. The £25,000 which he had recently received as a result of the abortive attempt to sell Newstead had been used up at once, much of it going to pay off old debts. Yet his foolish lawyer, Hanson, was no further forward in the necessary business of trying to sell off the family properties. He would even have to sell his *books* to keep the duns from his door.

As Annabella's pregnancy advanced, Byron's drinking increased. A few hours before she went into labour she thought he was trying to torment her by dashing soda bottle tops against the walls and roof of the room beneath her. It seems much more likely that he was simply seeking to allay his masculine anxiety; as Hobhouse could have told her, it was a favourite habit of Byron's to break the heads off soda bottles with a poker, rather than open them in the usual way. Annabella's baby was born on 10 December, a girl. She believed later that her husband would have preferred a boy. Certainly, his odd behaviour continued after the birth: leaning over the cradle one day he exclaimed, 'Oh, what an instrument of torture I have acquired in you!' Outside the family, however, and usually also at home, he gave every indication of being both proud and happy at his daughter's arrival. She was christened Augusta Ada. Byron seems to have chosen both names, the first after his half-sister and the second because it was simple and biblical. He was content that the little girl should be known as 'Ada'.

It might have been expected that Ada's birth would bring a new degree of harmony into her parent's lives. Instead, and for reasons that are not wholly clear, Annabella decided within a month that her husband was mentally deranged and that she and her baby would have to leave him. She read an article in the *Medical Journal* describing the disease of hydrocephalus, and convinced herself that Byron showed the symptoms of this distressing illness. Furtively, she instructed her doctor to observe him and confirm what she suspected. And on 15 January 1816 she and Ada drove away from the Piccadilly house, bound for the north and her parents' protection. She was never to see her husband again.

The accumulated insults of the early months of marriage had provoked Annabella, who objected also to Byron's recent liaison with Susan Boyce. But the curious thing is that she should have kept everything to herself until this point and then acted so uncompromisingly. Post-natal depression may have played a part. She seems to have feared, most unreasonably, for the safety of the baby, and her suspicions about her husband's hydrocephalus were also without foundation. Once away from Byron, she applied her logical mind to the question of how to establish evidence in support of her action, seeking medical support for her theory that he was deranged. But a second doctor told her gravely that he could find 'nothing like a settled lunacy' in Lord Byron. There was nothing for it but a series of harrowing, complicated discussions with her father and mother and their legal advisers, in which she went over the disquieting facts, until now hidden from everyone, of her year of wedded life. Sir

Ralph soon wrote to Byron, making plain that Annabella would not be coming back, and indeed blaming his son-in-law for turning her out.

Byron, meanwhile, was wounded to the quick, and also bewildered. If Annabella had failed to understand him, he had seriously underestimated the strength of her will. She was, he belatedly realized, the kind of person who instead of flaring up and expressing anger at the time of a quarrell remembered and brooded upon every slight, every word uttered in haste. But why should she walk out on him now? No woman had ever walked out on him before — let alone a wife. It was she who had acted inconsistently and irrationally. He showed Hobhouse the first two letters, full of affectionate phrases and diminutives, which she had written to him after going away. What could be done with a woman like that?

Once having got the bit between her teeth, however, Annabella was implacable. It was hopeless for Byron to write to her promising to reform and imploring her to return, and when he sent her a poem, 'Fare Thee Well', the tenderness of which would have melted many a heart, she made no reply at all. Just as some fifteen months earlier she had resolved that nobody should deter her from marrying the man of her choice, now she made up her mind that nothing on earth — not even the love she still felt for him in one part of her being — would persuade her to go back to him.

Tongues had begun to wag as soon as she had left London, and soon all kinds of rumours were rife. Byron had threatened his wife and child; he was in debt and would soon be declared a bankrupt; there were other women; there was his own *sister*. There were two main sources for the stories about Byron and Augusta, which, when eventually they reach Byron at third or fourth hand, worried him far more — out of fear for Augusta's future peace of mind — than anything else. Annabella had begun to recount everything she could remember from his conversations with and about Augusta to her lawers. Either from a natural propensity to gossip, or from calculated policy, her lawyers were less discreet than they ought to have been. (They probably acted deliberately, realizing that the more sympathy could be created in the public mind for their client, the better her chance of success at law might be.) Secondly, Lady Caroline Lamb was indiscretion itself. She requested an interview with Annabella, promising to help her, and supplied Byron's estranged wife with corroborative 'evidence' relating not only to his half-sister, but also, at an earlier period of his life, to adolescent boys. Then she saw to it that some of this information leaked out. Annabella had become so obsessed by the need to construct a case which would justify her own conduct that she does not seem to have stopped to think that 'Caro' still loved Byron and was delighted to keep her apart from him.

While the Milbankes were bent on securing a legal separation, they wished at all costs to avoid court publicity. In March and early April 1816 there took place a to-ing and fro-ing of lawyers and other family representatives with a view to getting Byron to agree to a deed of separation. By this time Byron knew that there was no hope of a reconciliation. In the end, he could only allow the document to be completed. He signed it himself on 21 April, and three days later he left England for good.

He had made up his mind some time earlier to quit the country, at least for some months, and travel in Europe. His debts made it convenient for him to do so and so escape hungry creditors, while the opening up of Europe as a result of the allied victory at Waterloo meant that he was only doing what others had set out to do in large numbers during the past eight months. But what finally drove him abroad was the scandal. The last three weeks had brought more unpleasant incidents than even he could take. He had not minded being 'cut' in certain circles in society until the evening of 8 April when Lady Jersey, loyal as ever, had invited him to Almack's. As he entered, a chilly silence had come over the company; then people had scattered to right and left, isolating him. A week later, the Press had begun to hound him. He had made the mistake — in retrospect he supposed it must have been a mistake — of asking Murray to print fifty copies of 'Fare Thee Well' and of a quite different sort of poem, a satirical 'Sketch' of Mrs Clermont, Annabella's former governess who had stayed on in town after his wife's departure — to spy on him, as he believed. Mrs Clermont had largely been responsible, or so he thought, for poisoning Annabella's attitude towards him, and in 'A Sketch' he had written without restraint. . .

> Born in the garret, in the kitchen bred,
> Promoted thence to deck her mistress' head. . .
> With eye unmoved, and forehead unabashed,
> She dines from off the plate she lately washed.

Quick with the tale, and ready with the lie,
The genial confidante and general spy —
Who could, ye gods! her next employment guess —
An only infant's earliest governess!

Somehow, perhaps through the agency of Annabella's lawyer Henry Brougham, the Sunday *Champion* had got hold of one of the fifty copies and published both poems, along with a long self-righteous commentary, on 14 April . . . no doubt the editor wanted to boost circulation. The *Sun*, the *Courier*, the *Times* and other journals had followed suit. Lord Byron, they trumpeted, was a cruel monster. And scarcely a soul had spoken up for him. What fickleness and hypocrisy, if one day 'society' and 'public opinion' were united in praising someone, indeed in fawning upon him, and the next they ignorantly and completely rejected him! To stay in England would be unthinkable after this.

John Murray, who had refused to let the separation scandal affect his relationship with Byron, had stated that he would be very glad to publish a further Canto of *Childe Harold's Pilgrimage*. After all, half the country seemed to be on their travels now; every Tom, Dick and Harry had turned scribbler. Something from Byron's pen about the field of Waterloo, or the condition of France after the long war would be worth more than all the *Tours* and *Visits* pouring from the press. Murray had shrewdly guessed that the sensation in which Byron had been involved, so far from lessening his appeal as a poet, might actually increase it. Now more than ever the public would be eager to read his work in the hope of solving the mystery of his personality and tragic marriage.

Byron was in no mood to humour the British public, yet he agreed readily enough to Murray's proposal. Writing, he liked to think, distracted him from his other worries. He had made this point the year before in his journal,

> To withdraw *myself* from *myself* (oh that cursed selfishness!) hath ever been my sole, my entire, my sincere motive in scribbling at all; and publishing is also the continuance of the same object, by the action it affords to the mind, which else recoils upon itself.

Now, in a time of adversity, he had a chance to test out the truth of his theory.

Travelling with a young Italian physician named Polidori (who had a publisher's contract for a prose journal of their *Tour*), he headed first for Belgium. Lockhart Gordon, an old friend and Scottish army officer, escorted Byron and Polidori over the scene of Wellington's most famous victory, answering questions about how many men had been deployed in the battle, the scale and number of the losses which had taken place, and the story that some of the British officers had rushed to the battleground from the Duchess of Blenheim's ball. Byron lost no time in beginning his new Canto. After explaining as succinctly as he could his motive for resuming the poem

> 'Tis to create, and in creating live
> A being more intense, that we endow
> With form our fancy, gaining as we give
> The life we image

he produced what was to become a celebrated description of the ball the night before the battle and of how it was interrupted by a call to arms. His imagination vividly reconstructed a happy, carefree scene. . .

> The lamps shone o'er fair women and brave men;
> A thousand hearts beat happily; and when
> Music arose with its voluptous swell,
> Soft eyes looked love to eyes which spake again.

But while this passage would be quoted and anthologized time and time again — it is a major influence behind the 'Georgette Heyer tradition' of portraying Regency society — Byron was doing something more than paying tribute to the gallantry of Wellington's officers. He hinted at a subversive code of values, one which would be summed up a hundred and fifty years later in the catch-phrase 'make love not war'. And he asked directly what had been achieved by the defeat of Napoleon.

In 1814, at the height of his fame in London, Byron had been made apprehensive by the thoughtless jingoism of his fellow-Britons. Now he dared to criticize publicly the Congress of Vienna, as a result of which Europe had been parcelled up among the allies who had triumphed over the Imperial French Army at Waterloo. How far he was driven to do so by the acute personal unhappiness he felt at this time can only be guessed; he was in a reckless, devil-may-care frame of mind. What is certain is that nobody else had asked such a searching question about the victory of the allies as he put in four short words, 'is Earth more free?':

109

Fit retribution! Gaul may champ the bit
And foam in fetters; — but is Earth more free?
Did nations combat to make *One* submit?
Or league to teach all Kings true Sovereignty?
What! shall reviving Thraldom again be
The patched-up Idol of enlightened days?

Later in the Canto he suggested that only those battles fought by the few against the many to defend life and freedom were worthwhile. He named Marathon as an example. Waterloo, by contrast, had taken place to satisfy the ambition of governments addicted to power politics.

From Brussells, Byron and Polidori made for the Rhine and Cologne. They travelled south fairly quickly, and in the mid-summer of 1816 reached Switzerland. Byron at once took to Lausanne, with its backdrop of snowy peaks, and was even more strongly attracted by Geneva, where he rented a large villa. Not only was the setting of Geneva unlike that of any city he had seen before in combining views of a lake and of mountains; it held associations which were precious to him. Jean-Jacques Rousseau, whose novel *Julie* he had long admired for its intensity of feeling and ability to evoke the natural scene, had lived here. For a while at least, he thought, he could find some kind of release from mental suffering in the neighbourhood of the Villa Diodati.

One unlooked-for complication arose very soon. Before leaving England Byron had had a brief affair with Claire Clairmont, an eighteen-year-old girl who importuned him to make love to her until finally, with no thought of possible consequences, he agreed. She had written to him in April when his world seemed to be falling apart, 'I shall ever remember the gentleness of your manners and the wild originality of your countenance.' He, though, had been glad to escape from a liaison which mattered little to him. Now he discovered that she had made her way to Switzerland, and was even now trying to meet him again. This was bad enough, but to make things more awkward, it turned out that Claire was travelling along with Percy Shelley and his second wife Mary. Shelley was a poet and a fellow aristocrat, and Byron was keen to make his acquaintance. How on earth could he spend some time with Shelley without being thrown together with Claire?

In the event, he took up once more for a few weeks with Claire. As he put it in a letter to Augusta,

> I was not in love nor have any love left for any, but I could not exactly play the Stoic with a woman who had scrambled eight hundred miles to unphilosophize me.

Claire offered, too, to copy out the new Canto of *Childe Harold's Pilgrimage*, to which Byron had been rapidly adding under the inspiring influence of Switzerland and the Alps. Meanwhile, Shelley and he became firm friends. They sailed together on the Lake of Geneva, exploring the haunts of the chief characters in Rousseau's *Julie* and sitting up half the night to discuss poetry and politics. Byron listened a little wistfully to Shelley's enthusiastic talk about Wordsworth and the transcendental glories of nature. He himself was too much of an eighteenth-century realist and sceptic to believe for long in nature-worship. As he saw it, nature offered a delightful escape from 'the crushing crowd'. He had loved rugged landscapes since his boyhood in Scotland, so that the country in which he now found himself was very congenial. 'High mountains are to me a *feeling*', he wrote — but he stopped short of Shelley's (and Wordsworth's) mysticism. So eloquent was Shelley, however, that it was tempting for the time being to share his faith and swallow 'the Wordsworth physic'.

It was a genuine meeting of minds. Shelley at once recognized in Byron the most gifted writer he had come across anywhere. He worried a good deal over Byron's bouts of cynicism and despondency, when he would come out with superstitious, bitter remarks, the talk of a man lacking faith. But what struck him most forcibly was the fact that, fundamentally, Byron was not a gloomy or misanthropic figure like Childe Harold or Manfred — the suicidally inclined hero of the 'Witch Drama of the Alps' written during this autumn — but rather a brilliantly witty man and spontaneous humorist. In the preface to *Julian and Maddalo*, a poem of his own which commemorates his friendship with Byron, Shelley summed up his main impression of the other poet's behaviour:

> I say that Maddalo is proud, because I can find no other word to express the concentered and impatient feelings which consume him; but it is on his own hopes and affections only that he seems to trample, for in social life no human being can be more gentle, patient, and unassuming than Maddalo. He is cheerful, frank, and witty. His more serious conversation is a sort of intoxication; men are held by it as by a spell. He has travelled much; and there is an inexpressible charm in his relation of his adventures in different countries.

111

He wanted to see Byron devote himself to some long poem which would be worthy of his talents.

When Canto III of *Childe Harold* came out in November, the average reader could not have guessed that the author's character was as Shelley understood it to be. The Childe counted for less in this Canto, Byron himself for more. He even referred directly to his estranged wife and daughter, describing Ada as

> The child of Love! though born in bitterness,
> And nurtured in Convulsion!

The Canto was in this way more revealing than anything he had published before, with the emphasis in the autobiographical passages placed squarely upon what Byron saw as his undeserved suffering. But if Canto III withheld from the public any sign of the cheerfulness which delighted Shelley, it certainly bore witness to Byron's pride:

> I have not loved the World, nor the World me. . .
>   I stood
> Among them, but not of them — in a shroud
> Of thoughts which were not their thoughts.

His readers judged the poet to be superbly eloquent in this new part of his serial poem. Some critics were quick to realize that Canto III contained poetry of a different order from its predecessors. His recent experiences had matured Byron. It was clear that he cared greatly about political freedom in Europe. As if to drive the point home, Murray brought out, within a month of *Childe Harold* III, *The Prisoner of Chillon*. In this work of sustained imaginative insight, Byron described the feelings of Bonnivard, a sixteenth-century political prisoner in the Swiss Castle of Chillon; he excelled especially in showing how bewildering is the experience of being set free after a long period of isolation in the dark. The main poem was preceded by a sonnet, the first lines of which soon became very famous as an invocation to the principle of liberty for which Bonnivard — and Byron — stood:

> Eternal spirit of the chainless mind!
> Brightest in dungeons, Liberty!

Byron was now, or would very shortly become (the translators were hard at work), a leading poet not only in Britain but throughout western Europe. In the eyes of the young who distrusted the Vienna settlement and all it represented, he was *the* leading poet. There was to be another, no less successful Canto of *Childe Harold's Pilgrimage* before the poem was complete. But Byron himself wrote to Moore about Canto III,

> I am glad you like it; it is a fine indistinct piece of poetical desolation, and my favourite. I was half mad during the time of its composition, between metaphysics, mountains, lakes, love unextinguishable, thoughts unutterable, and the nightmare of my own delinquencies. I should, many a good day, have blown my brains out, but for the recollection that it would have given pleasure to my mother-in-law.

It was a typically truthful summing-up.

Byron had now crossed the Alps into Italy. He at once fell in love with the country. Everything made him feel at ease: the warm sunshine, the splendour of Italian towns and cities (especially the decaying grandeur of Venice), and the fiercely amorous Venetian women. Of the latter, there were many. He began by forming 'one of the happiest — unlawful couples on this side of the Alps' with Marianna Segati, the wife of his first landlord in Venice. Marianna's reign lasted for many months. She was followed by an equally direct and passionate girl, Margarita Cogni, the *fornarina* or baker's wife, whose charms he described as

> . . . firstly, her person — very dark, tall, the Venetian face, very fine black eyes — and certain other qualities which need not be mentioned. She was two and twenty years old, and, never having had children, had not spoilt her figure, nor anything else — which is, I assure you, a great desideration in a hot climate where they grow relaxed and doughy, and flumpity a short time after breeding.

La fornarina had a tolerant, unpossessive attitude towards the English milord, and his list of conquests among the women of Italy grew. This period of dissipation made up, in his own eyes, for the hypocritical conduct he had been subjected to by Annabella, Caroline and other high-born English females.

Byron's father had ended his days as a roué in exile from his native land. From one point of view, therefore, Byron was merely reverting to type in leading a dissolute life at La Mira in Venice. He had rented a large and dilapidated house there, and through its various rooms there trod his strange menagerie of pet birds and animals and a long succession of indulgent, frequently quarrelsome Italian women.

But this exiled aristocrat had been thinking, and to some purpose. His mind ran on contrasts between Italy, the land he had virtually adopted, and England. Very soon he was experimenting with forms of verse which would allow him to comment sardonically on some of the main points of difference. A psychological, as well as a physical, release had taken place in Byron's life since coming to Italy. On 10 March 1817 he had written to Tom Moore complaining that Francis Jeffrey in the *Edinburgh Review* had formed the wrong idea of his personality from *Childe Harold* Canto III:

> I wish you would also add, what you know, that I was not and, indeed, am not even *now*, the misanthropical and gloomy gentleman he takes me for, but a facetious companion, well to do with those with whom I am intimate, and as loquacious and laughing as if I were a much cleverer fellow.

Now for the first time he felt able to write poetry expressing his sense of life's comedy and England's absurdity.

His conversation and letters had been full of amusing things all along, so that this new development can be seen as a sudden breakthrough allowing Byron to write verse as freely and cheerfully as he communicated with his friends. Interestingly, the first poem in the new style and *ottava rima* stanza, *Beppo*, exploits an idea mentioned in a letter to Moore from Milan in December 1816; it is as if the poet felt inspired to turn the story into verse when he knew it had been well received in prose. (The most recent British comic poem of outstanding quality before *Beppo* was *Tam o' Shanter*. Burns, like Byron, followed this course of 'testing out' his narrative in a letter before forming the idea of writing a poem.)

Byron had met in Milan a 'very excellent, good-natured Irishman', Colonel Fitzgerald. He was fascinated by one anecdote told about him:

> Six-and-twenty years ago, Col. Fitzgerald, then an ensign, being in Italy, fell in love with the Marchesa Castiglione, and she with him. The lady must be, at least, twenty years his senior. The war broke out; he returned to England, to serve — not his country, for that's Ireland — but England, which is a different thing; and *she* — heaven knows what she did. In the year 1814, the first annunciation of the definitive treaty of peace (and tyranny) was developed to the astonished Milanese by the arrival of Col. Fitzgerald, who, flinging himself full length at the feet of Madame Castiglione, murmured forth, in half-forgotten Irish Italian, eternal vows of indelible constancy. The lady screamed, and exclaimed, 'Who are you?' The Colonel cried, 'What! don't you know me? I am so and so', etc., etc., etc.; till, at length, the Marchesa, mounting from reminiscence to reminiscence, through the lovers of the intermediate twenty-five years, arrived at last at the recollection of her *povero* sub-lieutenant. She then said, 'Was there ever much virtue?' (that was her very word) and, being now a

widow, gave him apartments in her palace, reinstated him in all the rights of wrong, and held him up to the admiring world as a miracle of incontinent fidelity, and the unshaken Abdiel of absence.

Some months later, Byron heard a similar story concerning a far-travelled Italian from Pietro Segati, the husband of his current mistress Marianna. On this basis he constructed his imaginary tale of Beppo, who, after a very long absence in Turkey, returns to Venice, bearded, tanned mahogany and at first not recognized even by Laura his wife, who has long since given him up for dead and taken a 'vice-husband, chiefly to protect her'. After staring possessively at Laura, Beppo declares to her *cavalier servente*, who is a count, 'That Lady is *my wife*', whereupon

> She said, — but what could she say? Why not a word;
>   But the Count courteously invited in
> The Stranger, much appeased by what he heard:
>   'Such things, perhaps, we'd best discuss within,'
> Said he; 'don't let us make ourselves absurd
>   In public, by a scene, nor raise a din;
> For then the chief and only satisfaction
> Will be much quizzing on the whole transaction'.
>
> They entered, and for Coffee called — it came,
>   A beverage for Turks and Christians both,
> Although the way they make it's not the same.
>   Now Laura, much recovered, or less loth
> To speak, cries 'Beppo! what's your pagan name?
>   Bless me! your beard is of amazing growth!
> And how came you to keep away so long?
> And you not sensible 'twas very wrong?'

Once having launched into her wifely interrogation, Laura has some difficulty in stopping. However, after a brief account of Beppo's doings while absent for so long abroad, the poem itself ends — according to Byron, because he has reached the bottom of a page. Beppo has regained his home and spouse, evidently without any serious altercation. 'I've heard', Byron writes, 'the Count and he were always friends.'

This anti-climax is deliberately designed to shock 'moral' English readers. Byron, describing himself as

> but a nameless sort of person
> (A broken Dandy lately on my travels)

takes delight everywhere in *Beppo* in drawing attention to the un-Englishness of Italy. His casually spun digressions continually touch on differences between northern and Mediterranean customs. The behaviour of Italian women during the carnival appears outrageous? At least, the poet hints, they openly share a relaxed moral code, instead of taking refuge in hypocrisy. In contrast to

Our cloudy climate, and our chilly women

there is warmth in Italy. Could it conceivably be England — the question is implied rather than asked directly — which is less than admirable? English society ('twenty score of well-bred persons called "*The World*" ') gives itself so many strange airs and graces. Why, even the Turkish women among whom Beppo spent part of his exile from Italy were not subjected to such intellectual fashions as oppress their counterparts in England:

No Chemistry for them unfolds her gases,
No Metaphysics are let loose in lectures,
No Circulating Library amasses
Religious novels, moral tales, and strictures
Upon the living manners, as they pass us;
No Exhibition glares with annual pictures;
They stare not on the stars from out their attics,
Nor deal (thank God for that) in Mathematics.

Not even the final line of this passage, with its obvious reference to Lady Byron, is allowed to disturb the festive and comic mood of *Beppo*. Throughout the poem Byron's tone is light and good-humoured. At one point he remarks, almost apologetically,

I fear I have a little turn for Satire.
And yet methinks the older that one grows
Inclines us more to laugh than scold, though Laughter
Leaves us so doubly serious shortly after.

Beppo is comic entertainment edged with satire, and not a satirical production first and foremost like *English Bards and Scotch Reviewers* or his other early poems in the manner of Pope.

But precisely because the tale he has to tell is genuinely amusing, Byron's throwaway allusions in *Beppo* to 'The World' of Regency London have force. Someone at his ease telling a funny story can direct criticism where he will and be listened to. Having found this out and mastered *ottava rima* at the same time, Byron was not going to forget the secret. Soon he felt himself inclined to indulge further his 'little turn for satire' in a longer comic tale cast in the same verse form.

116

Don Juan, begun in July 1818 and left unfinished at an early point in Canto XVII at the time of Byron's death six years later, has been described as 'the most readable long poem in English'. Writing it gave Byron a great deal of fun, which must surely help to explain why it is so enjoyable to read. He had chosen a congenial theme, and rejoiced in the central irony whereby his hero, Juan, travelling the length and breadth of Europe, is more often seduced by pretty women than he is himself the seducer. And he came to enjoy greatly the opportunities which the comic epic form gave him to tease and bait his English readers. A love-hate relationship grew up between Byron and an English public who had never before read anything so daring as *Don Juan*. Those who had swooned over *Childe Harold's Pilgrimage* were now treated to a brilliant serial display of subversive humour. 'How terribly shocking!', exclaimed '*The World*', and read on.

As in *Beppo*, the digressions in *Don Juan* count for as much as the narrative (im)proper. Byron's *persona* is once again that of 'a nothing sort of person, a Dandy lately on my travels'; he offers disquisitions on every topic under the sun from moral education to cooking. This is often done with an air of mock innocence. But running through the early Cantos is a fairly constant *leitmotif* of satire on the ways of the 'tight little island' which had made Byron suffer so much. His aim, he said, was to be 'a little quietly facetious upon everything'. Then in Canto X he brings Juan to England, and immediately the satire takes on a new intensity. 'I've no great cause to love that spot on earth', writes Byron in stanza 66. From this point he begins to level his social criticism quite deliberately at the West End dwellers who had made so much of him, and then proved so heartless, during his first 'years of fame'.

Juan is on a diplomatic mission for Catherine the Great of Russia, whose lover he has recently become. He arrives in London splendidly dressed and bringing with him magnificent diamonds, the tokens of Catherine's personal favour. Byron was almost certainly recalling that year of 1814, when the Tsar and other privileged visitors from Moscow were to be seen in the streets of the capital. Just as James Joyce was to remember in astonishing detail from his Continental exile nearly a hundred years later the sights and nuances of Dublin life in 1904, so Byron kept vividly in mind the appearance of London in 'the Year of the Sovereigns'.

> From a distance, Juan sees only
> A mighty mass of brick and smoke and shipping.

He is attacked on Shooter's Hill by highwaymen, which allows Byron both to comment on the quality of the nation's welcome and to show that he has studied Pierce Egan and picked up the language of the streets:

> Poor Tom was once a kiddy upon town,
>   A thorough varmint and a real swell,
> Full flash, all fancy, until fairly diddled,
> His pockets first and then his body riddled.

Juan moves on 'through coaches, drays, choked turnpikes, and a whirl of wheels' into town. Every physical detail which Byron takes to be characteristic of life in the capital is evoked; and, throughout, there is a note of irony, for he is bent on stripping away illusions.

> Over the stones still rattling up Pall Mall
> Through crowds and carriages, but waxing thinner
> As thundered knockers broke the long-sealed spell
> Of doors 'gainst duns, and to an early dinner
> Admitted a small party as night fell,
> Don Juan, our young diplomatic sinner,
> Pursued his path and drove past some hotels,
> St. James's Palace and St. James's hells.

For a variety of reasons, among them his possession of wealth, Juan is welcomed by

> the great world — which being interpreted
> Meaneth the West or worst end of a city
> And about twice two thousand people bred
> By no means to be very wise or witty.

The number of people who make up 'The World' has gone up since *Beppo*. But this is only because Byron wishes to make their collective inanity the more apparent. He stresses time and again in the Cantos which follow the coldness of spirit which prevails in such a self-absorbed society. Lady Adeline Amundeville, a smug hostess who is ready to fall for Juan as the poem tantalizingly breaks off, is typical. She has some passion and much hypocrisy, and Byron compares her to frozen champagne. (Dickens was to model Lady Dedlock, his frozen anti-heroine in *Bleak House*, upon Adeline.) This is a world without a soul.

Byron, in other words, was getting his own back on those who had closed their ranks against him. No facet of their way of life was

spared, from the obsession with cash to the eager perusal of the
Morning Post,

> As thus: 'On Thursday there was a grand dinner.
> Present: Lords A. B. C.' Earls, dukes, by name
> Announced with no less pomp than victory's winner.

To balance the picture, he also described the excitement of high life,
and especially the pleasure of evening entertainment in the region of
St James's:

> Then dress, then dinner, then awakes the world!
> Then glare the lamps, then whirl the wheels, then roar
> Through street and square fast flashing chariots, hurled
> Like harnessed meteors.

But the insistent theme is 'All is vanity here'. Nothing lasts in such a
society, which has at its heart hypocrisy and coldness of spirit.

Bulwer Lytton, Dickens, Thackeray and many others were to
satirize the Regency in the next few decades. The model and
prototype of all such satire is a passage in Canto XI of *Don Juan* in
which Byron produces a superbly ironical variation on the 'Ubi
sunt?' catalogue of questions famous in classical literary tradition:

> 'Where is the world?' cries Young[1] at eighty. 'Where
>   The World in which a man was born?' Alas!
> Where is the world of eight years past? 'Twas there —
>   I look for it — 'tis gone, a globe of glass,
> Cracked, shivered, vanished, scarcely gazed on, ere
>   A silent change dissolves the glittering mass.
> Statesmen, chiefs, orators, queens, patriots, kings,
> And dandies, all are gone on the wind's wings.
>
> Where is Napoleon the Grand? God knows.
>   Where little Castlereagh?[2] The devil can tell.
> Where Grattan, Curran, Sheridan,[3] all those
>   Who bound the bar or senate in their spell?
> Where is the unhappy Queen with all her woes?
>   And where the daughter, whom the isles loved well?[4]
> Where are those martyred saints the five per cents?[5]
> And where, oh where the devil are the rents?

---

[1] The poet Edward Young (1683-1765) published *Resignation* when he was eighty
years old.
[2] Castlereagh committed suicide in 1822.
[3] Parliamentary orators who had won sympathy for Ireland.
[4] Princess Charlotte died in 1817.
[5] five per cents: British bonds. Byron wrote to a friend on 18 January 1823 that he
wanted 'to get out of the tremulous funds of these oscillating times'.

Where's Brummell? Dished. Where's Long Pole Wellesley?[1] Diddled.
    Where's Whitbread?[2] Romilly?[3] Where's George the Third?
Where is his will?[4] That's not so soon unriddled.
    And where is 'Fum' the Fourth, our 'royal bird'?[5]
Gone down it seems to Scotland to be fiddled
    Unto by Sawney's violin, we have heard.[6]
'Caw me, caw thee.' For six months hath been hatching
This scene of royal itch and loyal scratching.

Where is Lord This? And where my Lady That?
    The Honourable Mistresses and Misses?
Some laid aside like an old opera hat,
    Married, unmarried, and remarried (this is
An evolution oft performed of late).
    Where are the Dublin shouts and London hisses?
Where are the Grenvilles?[7] Turned as usual. Where
My friends the Whigs? Exactly where they were.

Where are the Lady Carolines and Franceses?[8]
    Divorced or doing thereanent. Ye annals
So brilliant, where the list of routs and dances is,
    Thou *Morning Post*, sole record of the panels
Broken in carriages and all the phantasies
    Of fashion, say what streams now fill those channels?
Some die, some fly, some languish on the Continent,
Because the times have hardly left them one tenant.

Some who once set their caps at cautious dukes[9]
    Have taken up at length with younger brothers.
Some heiresses have bit at sharpers' hooks;
    Some maids have been made wives, some merely mothers;
Others have lost their fresh and fairy looks.
    In short, the list of alteration bothers.
There's little strange in this, but something strange is
The unusual quickness of these common changes.

[1] William Pole Tylney Long Wellesley was a notoriously spendthrift dandy.
[2] Samuel Whitbread, a prominent Whig, had committed suicide in 1815.
[3] Sir Samuel Romilly, another leading Whig, had taken his own life in 1818.
[4] George III had made a will in 1810 but because he failed to sign it, it was not accepted as official; a will he had made forty years before had to suffice, although many of its provisions related to people now dead.
[5] Byron's friend Tom Moore wrote a satire entitled *Fum and Hum, The Two Birds of Royalty*, referring to George IV at Brighton as 'the Chinese Bird of Royalty'; 'Hum' was a common nickname for the King.
[6] George IV visited Scotland in 1822. 'Sawney' (Sandy) is a derisive term for a Scotsman.
[7] William Wyndham, Baron Grenville (1759-1834) was a social reformer early in his career but later became a repressive Tory. His brother Thomas was out of Parliament after 1818.
[8] Lady Caroline Lamb and Lady Frances Wedderburn Webster.
[9] Byron had heard gossip to the effect that Lady Frances Wedderburn Webster had been flirting with the Duke of Wellington.

Talk not of seventy years as age. In seven
   I have seen more changes, down from monarchs to
The humblest individual under heaven,
   Than might suffice a moderate century through.
I knew that nought was lasting, but now even
   Change grows too changeable without being new.
Naught's permanent among the human race,
Except the Whigs *not* getting into place.

When he left England in 1816, not even the most loyal admirer of Byron's poetry could have guessed that he would write a long poem given over to humour, let alone one having as its climax this re-creation of the vanished Regency 'World' which had first idolized and then rejected him. In those stanzas written in the autumn of 1822 the Regency passed into history, summed up by one uniquely qualified to pass judgment upon it.

[6]

Poetry, Painting and Nature

Ah, THEN, if mine had been the Painter's hand,
To express what then I saw; and add the gleam,
The light that never was, on sea or land,
The consecration, and the Poet's dream. . .
(Wordsworth, 'Elegiac Stanzas suggested by a Picture of Peele
Castle, in a Storm')

In the history of British poetry and painting the Regency stands supreme, just as the Elizabethan period does in drama. Other ages have their individual glories, but no other time offers such a range of achievement. All the major poets since labelled 'Romantic' were at work; and in addition to Blake, Coleridge, Wordsworth, Byron, Keats and Shelley, the Northamptonshire labourer John Clare, recently described by G. M. Ridenour as 'the greatest nature poet, in the strict sense, in the language', was beginning to express his unique vision. In painting, Lawrence and Raeburn enjoyed considerable and well-deserved fame for their portraits, while Turner and Constable made daring innovations in the representation of landscape. It is natural to ask what accounts for all this brilliance. Is there any underlying unity or indication of a common inspiration behind the richly varied output of Regency poetry and visual art?

No single factor in isolation inspired all these differently gifted individuals, but it is clear at least that the shock of recent political events had stimulated poets and painters to perceive the world about them in an original way. A poet-artist like Blake, who had grown up with the French Revolution, seen it topple into violence, and brooded over the reactionary politics of Pitt and his successors, responded in a complex way to the age in which he lived. The lyrical note in his work was very strong, because he hoped for and envisaged a new order of freedom — both personal, social and political. At the same time his awareness of the difference between what might be and what actually was led him to make frequent use of irony as he strove to render human experience in words and pictures. Blake's progress from revolutionary political hope to disillusionment and temporary despair, and from there to renewed optimism about the possibilities facing man, was directly paralleled by Shelley, who resembled him further in expressing himself through a series of constantly changing general myths. Turner showed a kindred sense of being engaged in a lifelong quest for a pristine joy and beauty which might somehow have continued to exist despite the presence of powerful forces of destruction. These three 'visionaries', whose works frequently proved too original to be appreciated on their first appearance, communicated through the language of pure symbol and colour what was conveyed in other terms by their contemporaries, namely the heady excitement and challenge of living in an age of revolution.[1]

Throughout Western Europe in the early nineteenth century, artists had been affected by public events and by expectations of change on an altogether greater scale than hitherto. There had come into being a 'spirit of the age' — to use a phrase made popular by Hazlitt in the 1820s — in the sense of a widely shared commitment to the primary values, and especially to the idea of freedom, which lay behind so much of the political activity of the time. The impulse to create which was part of this new complex of feeling and thought (in time to be known as Romanticism) crossed national frontiers, just as Napoleon had done, and before him the words 'Liberty, Equality, Fraternity'. Thus it was not the special prerogative of the British to pursue, in Wordsworth's words, 'the gleam, the light that never was', nor to meet the destructive energy of war by dwelling tenderly on love's beauty and mutability. Delight in the splendours of the natural world was by no means confined to British poets and painters. Elsewhere in Europe, others were discovering a new depth or an old

---

[1] Blake's poems and paintings were admired by a few people at this time, but scarcely known to the general public; he was better known as a book-illustrator. His work in the Regency ranges from his completion of the last of his long 'Prophetic Books', *Jerusalem*, to the execution of a series of woodcut illustrations to Virgil's Eclogues (now in the Tate Gallery).

innocence in their experience of nature, coupled with a sharp recognition of the transitoriness of such beauty. Beethoven is the outstanding example, running the whole gamut of feeling as he does from serene pastoralism in his Sixth Symphony to the defiant statement of joy which crowns his Ninth Symphony. An equally clear instance of radical Romanticism can be seen in the lyrical poetry of Leopardi, a tragically unhappy Italian who found in the dazzling yellow broom plant growing close to a deadly volcano a lesson in the art of living. Like Beethoven, Leopardi displays emotions of joy and sadness as intense as anything in Blake or Turner.

But if Romantic art was being produced all over Europe, it nevertheless took distinctive forms in Regency Britain. Britain was the first nation to experience the combined effects of the Industrial and Agricultural Revolutions. Her poets and painters, sensing a threat to natural beauty and to the continuity of country life, responded by creating images of well-loved landscapes. Native cultural traditions helped: Wordsworth and his fellow poets who wrote of the simple yet profound pleasures to be derived from the English countryside in a mood of 'Learn to love that well which thou must leave ere long' were sometimes following in the steps of such predecessors as Spenser and Milton; continuity made new experiment possible. Similarly, there was a long history of landscape painting in England before the art gained into particular new intensity, and a visitor to the 1808 exhibition of 'the Associated Artists in Watercolours' noticed

> the overwhelming proportion of landscapes, a proportion almost as unreasonable as that of the portraits at Somerset House. In pacing round the rooms the spectator experiences sensations somewhat similar to those of an outside passenger on a mail-coach making a picturesque and picturizing journey to the North. Mountains and cataracts, rivers, lakes, and woods, deep romantic glens and sublime sweeps of country, engage his eye in endless and every-varying succession.

For both poets and painters, to return thus to Nature was to take up afresh a well-tried theme. What was new was the conviction that there resided in fields and rivers and woods a power almost divine, a vital principle. Or one might put it another way and say that this was a very old idea, which had been forgotten by rationally minded men and women in the classical eighteenth century, and whose rediscovery was felt as liberating. Coleridge went to great lengths to expound the 'theory' of living Nature in his very involved autobiographical treatise *Biographia Literaria*, published in 1817. (Byron commented naughtily,

Coleridge, too, has lately taken wing,
But like a hawk encumbered with his hood, —
Explaining metaphysics to the nation —
I wish he would explain his Explanation.)

Essentially, the idea Coleridge put forward was of a transaction taking place between the mind of the individual looking at the external scene and a spark of life inherent in the landscape and waiting to be revived by this agency. According to Coleridge the source of the creative transaction lay in the human being, within the faculty which he called 'Imagination'. There was no question of an artist who described or painted Nature being merely a copyist of what he saw (as had often been assumed in the past), as his Imagination helped to create the 'world' before him. He was something much more important than simply a copyist, being instead a maker; as such, his status was second to nobody's.

This doctrine had been worked out by Coleridge many years before the Regency opened, in conversations with Wordsworth, and he took his main examples in illustration of what he now shared with the public from Wordsworth's poetry. Not everyone paid attention either to the argument or to Wordsworth's poems as a result of opening *Biographia Literaria*; but the claims which Coleridge made about the importance of the arts were to have far-reaching effects. Poets and other 'makers' would increasingly be thought of as specially endowed persons, who had not only mastered the particular skills or 'technique' of their art but who served society by being its seers or prophets. It was no longer intellectually respectable, at any rate where Coleridge's writings were known, for those who cared little about poetry and painting to talk patronizingly of mere technical accomplishment as their contribution to civilization. No less significantly, many artists in the future would be encouraged by one side of what Coleridge wrote in *Biographia Literaria* to think themselves above any obligation to society and would thus allow themselves to become 'alienated' from their fellow men whenever they suffered neglect or misunderstanding.

Wordsworth and Coleridge both enjoyed a considerable vogue in the later Regency, after a period of comparative obscurity. Their poetry appealed strongly to a generation which had been harassed by war and unable to travel abroad. Beyond this, their best poems were marked by the temper of the 1790s, when they had come of age as men and as writers. The Regency revived that radical, independent mood. It was a delight to the young in 1816 to read 'Kubla Khan' and 'Christabel', both now published for the first time although Coleridge had written them almost twenty years earlier . . .

> The moon shines dim in the open air,
> And not a moonbeam enters here.
> But they without its light can see
> The chamber carved so curiously
> Carved with figures strange and sweet,
> All made out of the carver's brain.

In the decade when these words were written, Wordsworth and Coleridge had been fired by the democratic and republican sentiments of the new France, despising British governments and conventional ethics as outmoded and reactionary. Indeed, along with his brother-in-law and fellow poet Robert Southey, Coleridge had gone so far as to draw up a plan for emigrating to North America, where he hoped to establish a commune on the banks of the Susquehanna River, but the scheme came to nothing. The failure of other hopes was disillusioning: in particular, all three poets were horrified by the growing imperial ambitions of France. Their opinions altered, and there were no half-measures about the change. As irony would have it, now that their early poems were finding an admiring public in the Regency, they had become, to a man, passionate Tories and supporters of Church and State.

They were often referred to as 'the Lake poets', as if they shared the same address and set of poetic principles. But in fact, while all three lived for many years in the Lake District until Coleridge moved to London on hearing from a common friend that Wordsworth had said he was 'an absolute nuisance', they were very different from each other, and subscribed to no common literary doctrine during the Regency. Southey was Poet Laureate, having been glad to accept that office when Walter Scott turned it down in 1813. He was the very epitome of Establishment attitudes, and rushed to celebrate every incident which was to the credit of John Bull. (Conventional as he was, however, Southey wrote a lively *Life of Lord Nelson*, and amused his children by making up for them the story of *Goldielocks and the Three Bears*.) Coleridge with his labyrinthine mind had settled for a role as a kind of freelance intellectual adviser to the nation, someone who could be consulted on a whole range of subjects from German philosophy to the English Constitution. He frequently wrote on political questions in the *Courier*, and was recognized as the best talker or at any rate the most brilliant monologuist in London.[1] As such, he was much in demand at dinner-parties, although hostesses sometimes discovered to their chagrin that his addiction to opium made him a decidedly erratic performer. His unpredictable degree of self-possession — or lack of it — also tended to interfere with the success of lecture-courses which he was asked to give to London audiences on Shakespearean subjects. When he was on form, there was nobody to touch him, except perhaps his former friend the critic Hazlitt (politics had come between them), who made the most of the opportunities for lecturing which were created by popular interest in the arts.

Wordsworth, being a canny northerner, had attained a more respectable authority by other means. His political wild oats had long since been forgotten — except, once again, by Hazlitt, who remained a radical and was therefore in bitter disagreement with Wordsworth — and the public knew nothing of his early tempestuous love affair in France with a girl called Annette Vallon. Little did they dream that this grave-faced man (someone in the Lake District once commented, 'You could tell fra the man's faace his potry would niver have no laugh in it') had once lain in the arms of a foreign beauty, fathered her child, then deserted her. There seemed to be no more exemplary Tory and pillar of family morality in the land. Now happily settled at Rydal Mount, high on the hills between Grasmere and Ambleside, with his wife Mary and sister Dorothy, he had been rewarded for his loyalty with a Government sinecure as Distributor

---

[1] In a letter to his brother and sister-in-law in America, Keats described a meeting with Coleridge one day in 1819: 'I walked with him at his alderman-after-dinner pace for near two miles I suppose. In those two miles he broached a thousand things — let me see if I can give you a list — Nightingales, Poetry — on Poetical Sensation — Metaphysics — Different genera and species of Dreams — Nightmare — a dream accompanied by a sense of touch — single and double touch — A dream related — First and second consciousness — the difference between will and volition — so many metaphysicians from a want of smoking the second consciousness — Monsters — the Krakens — Mermaids — Southey believes in them — Southey's belief too much diluted — A Ghost story — Good morning — I heard his voice as he came towards me — I heard it as he moved away — I had heard it all the interval — if it may be called so. He was civil enough to ask me to call on him at Highgate. Goodnight!'

of Stamps for Westmoreland (the Distributor's main responsibility, the stamping of legal documents, was discharged by a clerk). Browning was to write a generation later of Wordsworth's action in accepting this office as a betrayal of liberty, in a poem entitled 'The Lost Leader':

> Just for a handful of silver he left us,
>   Just for a riband to stick in his coat —
> Found the one gift of which fortune bereft us,
>   Lost all the others she lets us devote . . .
> We that had loved him so, followed him, honoured him,
>   Lived in his mild and magnificent eye,
> Learned his great language, caught his clear accents,
>   Made him our pattern to live and to die!
> Shakespeare was of us, Milton was for us,
>   Burns, Shelley, were with us, — they watch from their graves!
> He alone breaks from the van and the freemen,
>   He alone sinks to the rear and the slaves!

But Wordsworth was not troubled by any sense of political remorse, and he had the Duke of Wellington's capacity for simply disregarding the existence of those people whose views he did not wish to hear. The Distributorship enabled him to live the life of a frugal country gentleman, on visiting terms with Lord Lonsdale and Sir George Beaumont; he could walk, and write, whenever he wanted, without any longer worrying unduly about money. When he had made one of his rare visits to the capital he expected to be accepted on his own terms, as the country's leading poet and sage. Haydon the painter, who fully recognized his genius and treated him with the deference he required, has a story of a party he gave in Wordsworth's honour, to which he invited Wordsworth's old friend Charles Lamb, Keats, Ritchie the explorer, 'who was going to penetrate by Fezzan to Timbuctoo', and others. On the morning of the day of his 'immortal dinner',

> . . . a gentleman, a perfect stranger, had called on me. He said he knew my friends, had an enthusiasm for Wordsworth, and begged I would do him the happiness of an introduction. He told me he was a comptroller of stamps, and often had correspondence with the poet. I thought it a liberty; but still, as he seemed a gentleman, I told him he might come.

The party was held in Haydon's painting-room, 'with Jerusalem [his unfinished historical painting, "Christ's Triumphal entry into Jerusalem"] towering up behind us as a background'. Lamb became 'exceedingly merry' as the evening wore on . . .

128

When we retired to tea we found the comptroller. In introducing him to Wordsworth I forgot to say who he was. After a time the comptroller looked down, looked up and said to Wordsworth, 'Don't you think, sir, Milton was a great genius?' Keats looked at me, Wordsworth looked at the comptroller. Lamb who was dozing by the fire turned round and said, 'Pray, sir, did you say Milton was a great genius?' 'No, sir; I asked Mr Wordsworth if he were not.' 'Oh,' said Lamb, 'then you are a silly fellow.' 'Charles! my dear Charles!' said Wordsworth; but Lamb, perfectly innocent of the confusion he had created, was off again by the fire.

After an awful pause the comptroller said, 'Don't you think Newton a great genius?' I could not stand it any longer. Keats put his head into my books. Ritchie squeezed in a laugh. Wordsworth seemed asking himself, 'Who is this?' Lamb got up, and taking a candle, said, 'Sir, will you allow me to look at your phrenological development?'[1] He turned his back on the poor man, and at every question of the comptroller he chanted:

> Diddle diddle dumpling, my son John
> Went to bed with his breeches on.

The man in office, finding Wordsworth did not know who he was, said in a spasmodic and half-chuckling anticipation of assured victory, 'I have had the honour of some correspondence with you, Mr Wordsworth.' 'With me, sir?' said Wordsworth, 'not that I remember.' 'Don't you, sir? I am a comptroller of stamps.' There was a dead silence; — the comptroller evidently thinking that was enough. While we were waiting for Wordsworth's reply, Lamb sung out

> Hey diddle diddle,
> The cat and the fiddle.

'My dear Charles!' said Wordsworth, —

> Diddle diddle dumpling, my son John,

chanted Lamb, and then rising, exclaimed, 'Do let me have another look at that gentleman's organs.' Keats and I hurried Lamb into the painting-room, shut the door and gave way to inextinguishable laughter.

'It was delightful to see the good humour of Wordsworth', he added, 'in giving in to all our frolics.' 'Giving in' or humouring is the key idea, however, for Wordsworth himself did not readily lose his dignity. Although he had seen years before that poets have to 'create the taste' by which they are appreciated, he was not ready to compromise in his view either of his own claims to poetic fame or those of others. Byron he frankly hated as a playboy aristocrat who had no business writing poetry, let alone becoming a popular favourite. He still admired Coleridge's intellect, but was increasingly tempted to despise his old friend's lack of staying power and grit.

---

[1] 'Phrenology', the study of the shape of the skull as a means of indicating personality, was a pseudo-scientific craze of the time.

Scott was a 'sound' man, who seemed to be abandoning poetry for other things. Only Southey was still to be relied on. Nobody else seemed to have written much of note. There were too many frivolous poetasters who allowed themselves to be deflected by the passing fancies of their readers. His true peers, he reflected, were the great poets of the past.

It was entirely natural for Wordsworth to think such thoughts, however arrogant he might seem to be. He was above all a dedicated poet, who had been patiently seeking to realize certain well-defined aims ever since he and Coleridge had published *Lyrical Ballads* in 1798. He hoped to complete nothing less than a modern epic poem, dealing with 'Man, Nature, and Human Life', a sort of latter-day equivalent to *Paradise Lost. The Excursion* (1814), on which Francis Jeffrey commented unkindly, 'This will never do', and his unpublished long poem on the Growth of a Poet's Mind, later to be known as *The Prelude*, were conceived as small parts of this grand whole. As he saw it, all he needed was more time, with freedom from distractions. He had schooled his family into sharing this view: Mary had created for him a stable and loving home, and Dorothy's eyes were 'watchful in minutest observation of Nature' on his behalf.

Coleridge, whose own marriage had broken down, did not think it good for a poet to be 'living wholly among *Devotees* — having every the minutest Thing, almost his very eating and drinking, done for him by his Sister, or Wife', but it is a tribute to Wordsworth's wife and sister, as well as to his own skills, that he alone of the 'Lake poets' continued throughout the Regency to write poetry which is still enjoyed today. The lyrical gift usually belongs to the young, and just as scientists very often produce their best work in their twenties and early thirties, poets tend to 'burn themselves out' before they reach the age of forty. Wordsworth was forty in 1810. It is true that he seldon now had the intense mystical experiences, the 'dizzy raptures', of an earlier period — in poem after poem, indeed, he lamented the loss of that special power. But his faith in the restorative strength of contact with Nature remained, and in place of his former perceptions he could offer a wider understanding of how people are sustained by the beauty of the external world. These qualities are present, for example, in a poem written in 1817 and published three years later, 'Composed Upon an Evening of Extraordinary Splendour and Beauty'. Standing high on a Lakeland hillside, the poet gazes at distant ridges of the surrounding hills which are lit up by the setting sun so as to form 'a kind of Jacob's Ladder, leading to Heaven'. The air is so clear that he can make out the shepherds at their work and the glistening antlers of stags. He is convinced that such a magnificent prospect has a special meaning for people who are suffering or unhappy:

> And, if there be whom broken ties
> Afflict, or injuries assail,
> Yon hazy ridges, to their eyes
> Present a glorious scale,
> Climbing suffused with sunny air,
> To stop — no record hath told where! . . .
> — Wings at my shoulders seem to play;
> But, rooted here, I stand and gaze
> On those bright steps that heavenward raise
> Their practicable way.
> Come forth, ye drooping old men, look abroad,
> And see to what fair countries ye are bound!

This leads him to recall that when he was much younger, colours as brilliant as those now before him streamed before his eye 'where'er it wandered'. He admits that their disappearance filled him at one time with regret. Now by contrast he values the peace and calm which have followed youth's turbulence, and feels very grateful for his glimpse on this occasion of 'the light full early lost . . . fruitlessly deplored' and, for the moment, 'by miracle restored'. As a result he can rejoice in 'a second birth'.

The extempore poem might be expected to end on this triumphant note, but even as Wordsworth is meditating on the glorious spectacle, he notices a change in the sky:

> — Tis past, the visionary splendour fades,
> And night approaches with her shades.

These last lines underline the transitoriness of what he has been describing. Wordsworth has rendered the whole experience, including chill moments at its end, and not merely its high point. This kind of stubborn truthfulness adds something important to what he has to say about Nature's capacity to transform and renew. As he stated in *The Prelude*, he wished to be considered 'as a teacher, or nothing'. Poetry, in his eyes, must deal in everyday reality no less than in 'extraordinary beauty'.

Someone who came under Wordsworth's influence and readily

accepted his claim to be considered *the* foremost poet of the day, at any rate in the description of Nature, was Haydon's friend John Keats. Keats was only fifteen when the Regency opened. His entire literary career was crammed into the few years after Waterloo, and by the time of the Coronation in 1820 he knew himself to be dying of consumption. Unlike Wordsworth, he was town bred. Seizing on this, *Blackwood's Magazine* sneered at him in a review whose cruelty was exceeded only by its pettiness, that he was 'a Cockney poet'. In fact, Keats possessed to an exceptional degree that strong love of all rural things which is common among so many city-dwellers. He travelled widely in the south of England, in addition to visiting both the Lake District and the Western Highlands, and his opportunities to gain first-hand experience of Nature were much more extensive than the words 'Cockney poet' implied. But then the *Blackwood's* attack was part of a Tory journalistic campaign against Leigh Hunt, Hazlitt and other London Whigs and radicals to whose 'set' Keats seemed to belong. In truth, its ferocity was due not so much to the fact that as a 'townie' he had presumed to write about Nature, as to what was held to be his impertinence in writing poetry at all when he lacked the passport of a gentlemanly education. Keats had broken the social rules. After all, the *Blackwood's* line of argument ran, whatever one might think of Wordsworth, he not only lived in the heart of the countryside about which he wrote; he had a liberal education and had studied at one time in Cambridge like Lord Byron himself. Keats, as far as one could make out, was merely the upstart son of a vulgar fellow who had kept livery-stables. He had 'walked the London hospitals' for a few years, but only in the lowliest capacity possible, as a surgeon's assistant. There was no question of his having any professional standing or other claim to notice. Instead, he was that most objectionable of creatures, an underbred and under-educated man who did not know his place. As such, he deserved to be taught a lesson.

The 'lesson' which Keats tried to teach himself as a result of being mercilessly traduced by snobbish reviewers was high-minded enough for anyone. 'Praise or blame', he wrote, had only a momentary effect on any artist who genuinely loved beauty; he himself had 'loved the principle of Beauty in all things'. But although he held to this ideal, and suffered in silence, thoughtless criticism troubled him, for he was instinctively generous and free from the sort of small-minded-ness which confuses social irrelevancies with other things. He knew himself to be a different *kind* of poet from Wordsworth

> Of the cloud, the cataract, the lake,
> Who on Helvellyn's summit, wide awake,
> Catches his freshness from Archangel's wing

but the difference was a matter of temperament and poetic outlook rather than of social rank. Wordsworth's gift was for bringing Nature into relationship with himself and investing everything he wrote about with powerful subjective feeling. 'The wordsworthian or egotistical sublime', Keats wrote to his friend Richard Woodhouse in October 1818, 'is a thing per se and stands alone.' The type of poetical character to which he felt drawn himself was altogether more mercurial in its workings:

> ... it is not itself — it has no self — it is everything and nothing — It has no character — it enjoys light and shade; it lives in gusto, be it foul or fair, high or low, rich or poor, mean or elevated — It has as much delight in conceiving an Iago as an Imogen.

He went on to comment that his sort of poet was not shocked by immorality like 'a virtuous philosopher' — or, he might have added, like Wordsworth. Instead, he was a chameleon, whose secret consisted in becoming closely identified with any person or surroundings he might choose. Elsewhere, he gave to this talent for self-effacement or suppression of prejudice practised for the sake of artistic gain the name 'Negative Capability':

> ... that is to say when a man is capable of being in uncertainties, mysteries, doubts, without any irritable reaching after fact and reason.

Coleridge's speculative approach to a topic showed that he possessed Negative Capability, Wordsworth's dogmatism that he did not. Shakespeare, as the finest *dramatic* writer in the language, had it in abundance (Keats's hope, when illness struck him down, had been 'to write a few fine plays'): by setting aside everything connected with his own personality he had become free to get right inside his characters.

Keats's letters remain, with Byron's, the most vivid of the Regency. As a correspondent, he applied his own poetic principle and took on the colours of those to whom he wrote, whether they were relations like his brother George in America and 'baby' sister Fanny, literary friends like Benjamin Bailey and J. H. Reynolds, or very special young women, such as Fanny Brawne, whose sultry beauty and enigmatic behaviour delighted and tormented him in almost equal measure throughout the spring and summer of 1819 when he was living in Wentworth Place, Hampstead, and writing his famous Odes.[1] 'If a Sparrow come before my window', he explained to Bailey in 1817, 'I take part in its existence and pick about the Gravel.' Places he visited and people he met found their way into his letters, caught forever in some seemingly throwaway sentence or paragraph. Thus for example he travelled from the Isle of Wight to Winchester in August 1819 and wrote to Fanny Brawne of the difference between the two:

> The little coffin of a room at Shanklin is changed for a large room, where I can promenade at my pleasure — looks out onto a beautiful — blank side of a house. It is strange I should like it better than the view of the sea from our windows at Shanklin. I began to hate the very posts there — the voice of the Old Lady over the way was getting a great Plague. The Fisherman's face never altered more than our black teapot. . .

This made him reflect that he was 'getting a great dislike of the picturesque', but then he remembered how different was Fanny's outlook. She liked conventionally attractive views, and often asked him to describe incidents which she could pass on to her friends in London. Without needing any further pretext, he added:

> One of the pleasantest things I have seen lately was at Cowes. The Regent in his Yatch (I think they call it) was anchored opposite — a beautiful vessel — and all the Yatchs and boats on the coast were passing and repassing it; and circulating and tacking about it in every direction — I never beheld anything so silent, light, and graceful.

Bardic solemnity was not for Keats, serious though he could be when he wanted. 'Let us have the old Poets, and Robin Hood', he commented in one letter to Reynolds, and in another to his publisher John Taylor, 'If Poetry comes not as naturally as the Leaves to a tree it had better not come at all.' He believed firmly that poets should avoid all posturing, and frequently used his friend Hazlitt's

---

[1] Now 'Keats House' with the original internal dividing walls removed, Wentworth Place had been built in 1815 as a pair of semi-detached houses. Keats lived in one of these from 1818 until 1820 with his friend Charles Brown, and Fanny Brawne and her widowed mother rented the adjoining house from Brown from the summer of 1818 — the garden was shared. Wentworth Place clearly helped to make possible both Keats's love-affair with Fanny Brawne and his composition of the Odes; a phrase such as 'cooled a long age in the deep delved earth' takes on fresh meaning for the visitor to Keats's wine-cellar, situated several feet below the level of the garden where he heard the song of the nightingale which inspired his poem.

term 'Gusto' to describe the quality of concentrated vitality which he prized most highly in every art. He had been helped by the journalist-poet Leigh Hunt, both during and after Hunt's imprisonment in Horsemonger Gaol, and by Haydon, who dreamed of an age of heroic and Grecian achievement in English poetry and painting; but so phenomenally rapid was Keats's growth as a poet that he soon outstripped those who had influenced his early work. While he had learned much of value from both men, neither Leigh Hunt's tendency to dwell on the merely pretty in Nature, nor Haydon's obsession with large-scale ambitions, prevented his art from developing. His confident divergence from Wordsworth's potentially overpowering example has already been mentioned. Even more striking was the decisive way in which he rejected Byron as a model. The deficiency in Byron's work, as he thought, was a lack of true depth. He wrote to his brother and sister-in-law in February 1819,

> A Man's life of any worth is a continual allegory, and very few eyes can see the Mystery of his life — a life like the scriptures, figurative — which such people can no more make out than they can the hebrew Bible. Lord Byron cuts such a figure — but he is not figurative — Shakespeare led a life of Allegory: his works are the comments on it.

When a few months later the same correspondents likened his ability to Byron's, he explicitly repudiated the comparison:

> You speak of Lord Byron and me — There is this great difference between us. He describes what he sees — I describe what I imagine. Mine is the hardest task. You see the immense difference.

The letter in which this statement occurs does not indicate which poem or poems he had in mind, but it seems a reasonable deduction that when he wrote 'he describes what he sees — I describe what I imagine' he was thinking of his disadvantage in trying to write of Greece when he had travelled only in the realms of imagination with Lemprière's *Classical Dictionary* and Chapman's translation of Homer: Byron had actually been there. It makes sense to look for a specific connection between what Keats may have judged to be his most important treatment of a Greek theme and Byron's work. Such a link can be found, and it not only confirms what Keats claims in this letter, but supplies part of the original Regency context for one of his best-known poems. In the 'Ode on a Grecian Urn', he had to rely on his imagination — whatever inspiration he may have received from looking at classical urns and vases — for his rendering of the 'feel' of life in Tempe or Arcady. Not so Byron in *Childe Harold's Pilgrimage*. But to what end had Byron used his enviable privilege of travel in Greece? Merely to be rude about Lord Elgin (whose action in bringing Greek sculpture and urns to England Keats by contrast believed to be in the best interests of art), and to underline a bleak philosophy: 'remember to die'.[1] At the opening of Canto II of *Childe Harold* Byron warned an imaginary passer-by not to molest an urn he had in view near the Temple of Olympian Zeus in Athens, and summed up the wisdom of the urn in a saying of Socrates:

> All that can be known on earth is: nothing can be known.

The ending of the 'Ode on a Grecian Urn' replies to this pessimistic saying with an assertion of Keats's aesthetic faith by his Urn:

> When old age shall this generation waste,
> Thou shalt remain, in midst of other woe
> Than ours, a friend to man, to whom thou say'st,
> 'Beauty is truth, truth beauty — that is all
>   Ye know on earth, and all ye need to know'.

Keats's disagreement with what he takes to be Byron's false philosophy is here summed up in the words 'Beauty is truth, truth beauty', which directly oppose the claim 'Nothing can be known'; it is a disagreement sharpened by the two poets' completely different views about the value and propriety of taking the Elgin Marbles to Britain. There could scarcely be a clearer proof of Keats's poetic originality than the skill with which on the one hand he disengages himself from the opinions of Byron, a noted authority on Greek subjects, and on the other creates for his readers an ideal Greece and an ideal world of unchanging art. Yet it is all done with the minimum of self-advertisement. As he put it in a letter,

> . . . we hate poetry that has a palpable design upon us . . . Poetry should

[1] The Earl of Elgin (1766-1841) collected the Marbles from the frieze and pediment of the Parthenon in Athens between 1799 and 1803, and ordered them to be shipped to England, 'to protect them from the Turks': the ship conveying them was wrecked, but they reached London safely. Lord Elgin was heavily criticized, notably by Byron, who considered his action theft from Greece. After many years of bitter argument about the morality of what Lord Elgin had done, and about the quality of the sculpture now offered to the British people, in 1816 the Marbles were bought and placed in the British Museum. Keats and Haydon, who had campaigned vigorously in defence of the genuineness of the Marbles as classical work of the best period, were delighted; but many people thought the cost to the nation was too high, especially at a time of social distress and economic crisis (see Plate 18).

be great and unobtrusive, a thing which enters into one's soul, and does not startle or amaze it with itself, but with its subject.

In this decade of 'Nature poetry', the natural world was known to different poets in a variety of ways, and to none more painfully, or intimately, than to John Clare, an agricultural labourer who lived in the village of Helpston, 'on the brink', as he put it, 'of the Lincolnshire fens', between Peterborough and Stamford. Clare was two years older than Keats, and belonged to no literary 'set'. He had known nothing but poverty since birth, and had grown up a

> . . . ragged boy,
> Prest ere a child with man's employ.

The formal schooling he received amounted to very little, but he loved words, and his sensitivity to the sights and sounds of the open would have been exceptional anywhere. All through the Regency he was labouring, observing, writing. It was in this period that he found his 'voice' as a poet, and a number of the themes which were to lend distinction to his first book, published in 1820, *Poems Descriptive of Rural Life and Scenery. By John Clare, a Northamptonshire Peasant*. Prominent among these was a countryman's bitter regret at the destruction and changes which were associated with enclosure. Clare wrote of the subject as someone who had lived in Helpston all his life and who had recently seen alteration forced upon its centuries-old pattern of fields. (The Act of Parliament for the enclosure of Helpston and five neighbouring villages on the Fitzwilliam Estate was passed in 1809. But the middle of 1813 new roads had been planned, and the actual enclosing, which involved ditch-digging, road-building, and redistribution of land, took place in the next three years.) What distressed him most was the chopping down of a favourite line of willows close to the village at a place called Round Oak Waters. He believed that enclosure had been carried out merely to increase the wealth of the landowner and a handful of tenant-farmers, and several times singled out this particular deed as an example of their selfishness:

> Dire nakedness o'er all prevails;
> Yon fallows bare and brown
> Are all beset with posts and rails
> And turned upside down. . .
> Oh, then what trees my banks did crown!
> What willows flourished here!
> Hard as the axe that cut them down

> The senseless wretches were.
> But sweating slaves I do not blame,
>   Those slaves by wealth decreed;
> No, I should hurt their harmless name
>   To brand then with the deed;
> Although their aching hands did wield
>   The axe that gave the blow,
> Yet 'twas not them that owned the field
>   Nor plann'd its overthrow.

A modern economic historian might dismiss Clare's objections to enclosures as sentimental and short-sighted. But while it is true that Clare was too upset to admit how, in the long run, everyone stood to benefit from agricultural improvement, or else simply failed to understand the possibility, this in itself is important evidence of how someone of his background reacted to 'the improvements'. There were numerous poetasters at work who had nothing to add to Goldsmith's classic lament for 'Sweet Auburn' and the unimproved countryside in *The Deserted Village*. Clare was quite free from the spurious emotions of these writers, who merely exploited a cause without being personally involved. In common with nearly everyone else who had any interest in poetry, Clare had read Goldsmith, but his understanding of Helpston and its environs as his own 'place' ensured that his response to enclosure was all his own. His attachments were particular and localized. He knew every bird's nest and every species of flower in his parish — as, at this time, very many other working folk did in theirs. Each had for him associations of some kind, however trivial these might have seemed to outsiders, and when he wrote about the scenes around him he sometimes used dialect words, as naturally as Burns had done in Ayrshire, for there was no other way to give everything its proper identity.

'I found the poems in the fields', was how he explained his art. There shines through all of Clare's work an unaffected love of Nature which contrasts favourably with some of Wordsworth's more portentous statements and intuitions. He is endlessly curious, and notices little things. Often he chooses to describe creatures about which poets had not previously written — insects, for instance. In 'Summer Evening' he surprises his reader with a glimpse of frogs, as exact as it is unexpected:

> From the hay-cock's moisten'd heaps,
> Startled frogs take vaunting leaps,

> And along the shaven mead,
> Jumping travellers, they proceed:
> Quick the dewy grass divides,
> Moistening sweet their speckled sides. . .

The same poem shows that he feels about birds as he does about trees — they are to be cherished, not treated with contempt. Cruel boys in the village have amused themselves by killing fledgling sparrows. Clare grows angry as he remembers them:

> Come, poor birds! from foes severe
> Fearless come, you're welcome here;
> My heart yearns at fate like yours,
> A sparrow's life as sweet as ours.
> Hardy clowns! grudge not the wheat
> Which hunger forces birds to eat:
> Your blinded eyes, worst foes to you,
> Can't see the good which sparrows do.
> Did not poor birds with watching rounds
> Pick up the insects from your grounds,
> Did they not tend your rising grain,
> You then might sow to reap in vain.

His vision is of all living things as interrelated; and this is no idle armchair ecologist's dream, but a way of looking, born of his detailed knowledge of how humans depend for their crops on the co-operation of the whole creation, and confirmed by what he has heard in church. Thinking about how man needs sparrows to help in the production of food leads him to pray,

> O God! let me what's good pursue,
> Let me the same to others do
> As I'd have others do to me,
> And learn at least humanity.

Even if these lines appear a little trite, like some of the improving texts which children were being made to learn by heart and sew on samplers at the time when he was writing, his was no false piety. *Poems Descriptive of Rural Life and Scenery* proves again and again that, just as his eye was trained like the wood engraver Thomas Bewick's to note 'every shivering bent and blade', so his heart responded to many forms of suffering.

In a poem entitled simply 'Enclosure', recording both what had happened to Helpston and his sense of lost innocence on growing up, Clare described the characteristic appearance of the old open landscape as he had known it in his boyhood before it was fenced 'in little parcels little minds to please'. The dominant impressions are of Fenland flatness and of what Clare calls the 'circling sky':

> A mighty flat, undwarfed by bush and tree,
> Spread its faint shadow of immensity,
> And lost itself, which seemed to eke its bounds,
> In the blue mist the horizon's edge surrounds.

So long as the sky was the only boundary he felt entirely free; that feeling disappeared later on, especially as a result of the enclosures. It is highly probable that John Constable had as a boy experienced a similar emotion in the valley of the River Stour in Suffolk, and that in a number of his best-known paintings, beginning with 'Dedham Vale: Morning' (1811), in which the sky is no less his subject than what lies below it, he was seeking to recapture the sense of limitless freedom he enjoyed then. Constable's Suffolk was almost as low-lying as Clare's Northamptonshire. That these otherwise very different regions of England should have produced two artists so completely dedicated, in their individual styles, to capturing the beauty of the clouds on the one hand and of their place of birth on the other is of considerable interest. Chance obviously played a major part; but in this instance there seems to have been an artistic kinship of the plain and sky, which can be contrasted with the common interest in mountainous scenery of, say, Wordsworth and Scott. Clare's 'Description of a Thunderstorm' is only one of a group of his poems which share their subject and inspiration with such skyscapes by Constable as 'Cloud Study with Verses from Bloomfield' (1819), now in the Tate Gallery.

Yet there the similarity virtually ends. Constable was the son of a prosperous watermill owner, and he instinctively understood the viewpoint of those who introduced changes in agricultural methods in the Stour valley — even although he was happy to leave the responsibility for carrying on his father's business to his young brother Abram. Enclosure held no terrors for him. His love for East Bergholt, Flatford Mill and the surrounding district was obsessive, drawing him back from London year after year for most of his life on a painter's pilgrimage, but he was never restricted to this single corner of the country by 'sad necessity'. Instead, he was able to travel to various parts of England, including the Lake District — where in 1806-7 he produced a number of his most advanced early drawings — and to take lessons from some of the leading painters of the time. In comparison with Clare's, his life was very comfortable.

When in 1816 he at last married Maria Bicknell, the granddaughter of the Rector of East Bergholt, despite the elderly patriarch's refusal to give his consent, his painting at once received an access of light and colour. In 'Osmington Bay', painted during his honeymoon in Dorset, sunshine and skudding clouds reveal his new happiness. Now for the first time he felt confident enough to begin work on a series of large paintings of Suffolk scenes which he hoped would incorporate all that he had learned about draughtsmanship and composition, ways of adding to the interest of landscape by introducing one or two human figures, and above all the play of light from the sky upon trees, land and water. 'Scene on a navigable river', better known today as 'Flatford Mill', was painted in 1817 and exhibited that year at the Royal Academy. It shows a view Constable had known all his life, from the southern end of the footbridge at Flatford looking along the towpath to Flatford Lock and the mill buildings beyond.

'Scene of a navigable river' is now so firmly established among the masterpieces of English landscape painting — with 'The Hay Wain' (1821) and 'The Leaping Horse' (1825) that it is hard to understand why Constable had to wait till 1829 before being elected a member of the Royal Academy. Only very gradually did the Academy — and indeed the general public — learn to recognize in his art a more comprehensive approach to the representation of the everyday country scene than anything previously known in England. Interestingly, Constable's reputation abroad grew more quickly than among the arbiters of artistic fashion in London; he may have been at a disadvantage in his native land through not joining in the intrigues and social round favoured by some of the Academicians. At any rate, it was only very slowly that professional success came to this most thorough and committed of landscape artists. In this light it does not seem surprising that in a course of lectures at the Royal Institution in 1836 he should have stressed the need to understand his kind of painting 'not only as a poetic inspiration, but as a pursuit, legitimate, scientific, and mechanical', and one which required on the part of painters 'long and patient study, under the direction of much good sense'. Nor that he should have commented, with his own struggles in mind, 'the field of Waterloo is a field of mercy to ours'.

J. M. W. Turner enjoyed to the full the recognition which, for so long, was denied to Constable. Admittedly, Sir George Beaumont could see nothing but 'pea-green insipidity' in 'Crossing the Brook' (1815), and Beaumont had influence; but nevertheless Turner had unquestionably 'arrived'. He had been elected to full membership of the Royal Academy as early as 1802, when he was only twenty-seven, and from 1807 was Professor of Perspective. (The fact that he disliked lecturing and was said to speak with a 'vulgar pronunciation' does not seem to have counted against him, for he retained his position until 1837. Latterly, he was not expected to lecture at all; and he wrote this wry quatrain on 'Professors':

> Professors (justice so decreed)
> Unpaid must constant Lectures read;
> On earth it often doth befall
> They're paid and never read at all.)

Yet there was about his work none of the stiffness or complacency which might have been expected to overtake someone who had conquered the citadel of high art in England so young. Still less was he an Academy gossip and self-appointed authority on everyone else's work, like his contemporary the diarist Farington. Instead, he was probably the most versatile and prolific artist in the country, an earthy, secretive creature whose whole life centred on his painting and drawing.

Turner's versatility, his readiness to produce every kind of painting, including the historical canvasses so well liked by the age, is the key to his luck in comparison with Constable, toiling away so faithfully in the Stour valley. The Professor of Perspective may have been uncouth — he was short and fat, dressed untidily, and lived in some squalour with a musician's widow who bore him three children — but he got about the country and discharged with prompt efficiency the commissions which came his way. In some ways he resembles no one in the period so much as John Nash: he put all his technical skills to work, took into account the wishes of clients and patrons, and allowed nothing to discourage him. Not only was he filled with the same restless energy as the Regent's architect, he was as totally professional in his outlook. There was a ruthlessly practical side to his nature, which allowed him, for example, to satisfy popular demand by painting subjects of topical interest like 'Richmond Hill, on the Prince Regent's Birthday' in 1819. Whereas Constable in all probability would have painted the scene when it lacked the additional interest of a royal holiday crowd, Turner

142

cheerfully exploited this association both in the painting itself and in the lines from Thomson which accompanied it at the Academy exhibition:

> Which way, Amanda, shall we bend our course?
> The choice perplexes. Wherefore should we chuse?
> All is the same with thee. Shall we wind
> Along the streams? or walk the smiling mead?
> Or court the forest-glades? or wander wild
> Among the waving harvests? or ascend,
> While radiant Summer opens all its pride,
> Thy Hill, delightful Shene?

No prisoner of public taste, he nevertheless respected the actual preferences of Regency society.

Having proved that he could paint and draw in a variety of styles which were acceptable to patrons, Turner had more scope than most painters to experiment in his work. As yet he kept within fairly strict limits in the methods he used; his most daring departures from convention belong to a later period. But already the way was being prepared, and the liberties he took intrigued those who had been following his career. A significant turning-point was reached with the large historical painting, 'Snow Storm: Hannibal and his Army Crossing the Alps', exhibited in 1812. Here for the first time he created a vortex at the centre of his composition, expressing in its whirling movement the anger of mountains and sky directed at the helpless Carthaginians shown in the dark foreground of the picture. Turner had made a sketch in a thunderstorm while staying with his patron Walter Fawkes at Farnley Hall in Yorkshire two years before, and according to Fawkes's son, this gave the painter the idea for 'Snow Storm':

> One stormy day at Farnley, Turner called to me loudly from the doorway, 'Hawkey — Hawkey! — come here — come here! Look at this thunderstorm! Isn't it grand? — isn't it wonderful? — isn't it sublime?'
> All this time he was making notes of its form and colour on the back of a letter. I proposed some better drawing-block, but he said it did very well. He was absorbed — he was entranced. There was the storm rolling and sweeping and shafting out its lightning over the Yorkshire hills. Presently the storm passed, and he finished. 'There', said he, 'Hawkey; in two years you will see this again, and call it Hannibal Crossing the Alps.'

There seems no reason to doubt that Turner was inspired in this way by the thunderstorm he had seen in Yorkshire, far-fetched though 'Hawkey's' last sentence may be. At any rate he had captured effects of sunshine, storm and shadow in a design without any known pictorial precedent. Turner insisted that the painting should be hung low so that people should have the sense of being drawn into it. Interestingly, most of those who commented on 'Snow Storm' in 1812 were very enthusiastic. The critic of *The Examiner* described it as 'a performance that classes Mr Turner in the highest rank of landscape painters', noting especially the terrible magnificence in the shining of the sun . . . and in the widely circular sweep of snow, whirling high in the air'; the 'mysterious effect' of the painting was praised no less highly in *The Repository of Arts*; and a writer in the *St James Chronicle* also admired Turner's 'peculiar felicity' in painting the sun:

> . . . the warm tinting from the great source of light struggling through the blackness of the storm, gives a fine relief to the subject, which is still further improved by the introduction of a corner of cloudless sky on the left.

This last critic, however, was unhappy about Turner's decision to show Hannibal's soldiers 'crouching' as they tried to protect themselves from the elements instead of behaving 'in a manner more becoming hardy warriors'. He had failed to grasp the point, which Turner made explicit in an accompanying quotation from 'The Fallacies of Hope' (a poem of his own), that, whatever his dreams of empire, man is puny in relation to the power of Nature:

> . . . the fierce archer of the downward year
> Stains Italy's blanch'd barrier with storms.

There is still disagreement among art historians about whether Turner identified Hannibal with Napoleon (who, coincidentally, was to be held up on the retreat from Moscow later in 1812), or, in contrast, saw a connection between the decline of Carthage through easy living and the possible fate of self-indulgent Regency Britain. But in terms of his overall artistic development, neither of these intriguing allegorical interpretations counts for as much as his new skill in displaying vertiginous forces at work in the external world, forces beside which imperial ambitions in human beings are seen to be totally insignificant. Like Byron, Turner had made the discovery that the struggle between England and France, which, like the ancient enmity of Rome and Carthage, had gone on for a very long time, was ultimately a less stirring theme than 'wonderworks of God

11 A dandy (1817), etching by George Cruikshank. *Victoria and Albert Museum, Crown Copyright*

12 Byron (1813) by Richard Westall. *National Portrait Gallery*

13 William Wordsworth (1818), chalk drawing by B. R. Haydon. *National Portrait Gallery*

14 Mary Shelley (1841) by
Richard Rothwell. *National
Portrait Gallery*

15 Sir Walter Scott (1824) by
Edwin Landseer. *National
Portrait Gallery*

16 'Boatbuilding near Flatford Mill' by John Constable. *Victoria and Albert Museum, Crown Copyright*

17 'Tom and Jerry at the Exhibition of Pictures at the Royal Academy' (1821), engraving by Isaac and George Cruikshank. *Victoria and Albert Museum, Crown Copyright*

18 'The Elgin Marbles! or John Bull buying Stones at the time his numerous Family want Bread!!' (10 June 1816) by George Cruikshank. *British Museum*

London. Publish'd May 1,1812, at R.Ackermann's Repository of Arts 101 Strand

Etch'd by Rowlandson.

DOCTOR SYNTAX TUMBLING INTO THE WATER.

19 'Doctor Syntax Tumbling into the Water' from *The Tour of Doctor Syntax, in search of the picturesque. A Poem* (1812), with etchings by Thomas Rowlandson, published by Rudolph Ackermann.

20 The opening of Waterloo Bridge by the Prince Regent on 18 June 1817, as depicted on a plate belonging to the Saxon Service (Meissen), presented to Wellington by King Frederick Augustus IV of Saxony. *Apsley House*

and Nature's hand'. In the years ahead he would experiment end-lessly with the aim of conveying through his art the movement and dazzling colour of Nature's spectacular 'wonderworks'.

What, finally, of the criticism that the preoccupation of poets and painters with the countryside in this period was merely a sophisti-cated kind of escapism? Were Wordsworth, Keats, Constable, Turner and the rest running away from harsh social and environmental realities, having failed to come to terms with the Industrial Revolu-tion? It can certainly be argued that one important element in the creation of a number of works of art during the Regency was a wish to escape from painful experience, whether caused by the oppres-siveness of living in large cities or by other factors. Especially relevant here are the Odes of Keats, who had known a great deal of misery brought about by illness and deaths in his family, and who sometimes found London like a prison as a result: then he longed to be free like the nightingale and leave the world unseen

> And with thee fade away into the forest dim:
> Fade far away, dissolve, and quite forget
>   What thou among the leaves hast never known,
> The weariness, the fever, and the fret
>   Here, where men sit and hear each other groan;
> Where palsy shakes a few, sad, last grey hairs,
>   Where youth grows pale, and spectre-thin, and dies.

But the ode created by Keats in this mood amounts to something much more than a memorial to a wish to escape: it is instead a celebration of a kind of beauty which, to his delight, he has found to be no less a part of his life than acute suffering. As such, it is typical of British Romantic art, which is more concerned with the renewal of hope than with dwelling on unpleasant things. So intense is the perception of beauty in Nature by the poets and painters of the Regency that their art, so far from being judged 'escapist' or 'nega-tive', is to be valued in terms the very opposite of these. Threatened by what seemed to be the wanton destruction of the countryside by social forces beyond their control, these artists had responded by producing works of such splendour that no one who explores Regency poetry and painting can doubt that they express in its purest form the spirit of freedom which ran through the age.

[7]

Fiction for All

Whilst it would be unwise to attempt to reconstruct a picture of any society from the evidence of its fictional creations alone, these nevertheless have a unique value, because they express a people's myths, in the sense both of their values and their dreams. Provided one takes care to distinguish between what is literally true and what belongs to the realms of imagination, fiction can be used to illuminate history, and the aspirations and beliefs of an entire social group may be gleaned from their favourite novels.

This idea has particular force when applied to the Regency, as the decade was one of unprecedented activity on the part of novelists, evidence in itself of a widespread desire for the special kind of satisfaction offered by fiction. Had there not existed a powerful demand, there would have been no Waverley novels to follow *Waverley*, published as 'an experiment upon the public taste' in 1814. As it was, Scott produced by 1820 no fewer than ten novels, each of them a bestseller, which won for him a fame greater than that known by any earlier novelist anywhere in the world.

There was not a little envy of Scott's sales and popularity. Coleridge as a poet and literary critic had known lean times, and wrote with some asperity of the reasons which had made hundreds of thousands of readers turn to what he judged to be undemanding fiction:

> The absence of the higher beauties and excellencies of style, character, and plot has done more for Sir Walter Scott's European, yea, plusquam-European popularity, than ever the abundance of them effected for any previous writer. His age is an age of *anxiety* from the crown to the hovel, from the cradle to the coffin; all is an anxious straining to maintain life, or *appearances — to rise*, as the only condition of not falling.

'An age of *anxiety* from the crown to the hovel.' So far from seeing the period as one of leisure or deep civilization — as it has appeared to some social historians of our own time — Coleridge here diagnoses a frantic concern with status to be its leading characteristic. Already, there has come into being that complex of pressures summed up in the ugly twentieth-century phrase, 'the rat-race'. More people are reading books than in the eighteenth century, according to Coleridge. Indeed, he says 'every man is now a reader'; but the clear implication is that they read with less discrimination than before, simply in order to get away from it all. . .

> Interest? A few girls may crave purity, and weep over *Clarissa Harlowe,*[1] and the old novelists! For the public at large, every man (for every man is now a reader) has too much of it in his own needs and embarrassments. He reads, as he smokes, takes snuff, swings a chair, goes to a concert, or to a pantomime, to be *amused*, and forget himself.

Several major issues arise out of this passage, in which Coleridge sounds like a disillusioned educational élitist of today. Instead of bringing enlightenment, he maintains, the new fiction has merely catered to the escapist temper of the times, and this is a symptom of a lowering of cultural standards and of a lessening of intellectual seriousness. The terms in which he expresses this criticism of Scott and his readers are revealing. Coleridge shares with nearly all his educated contemporaries the habit of taking the reasonably well-to-do part of the population (that part which he describes here as 'anxious') for the whole, at any rate in discussing such subjects as literature. When he refers to 'the public at large', he almost certainly has in mind not every section of British society, but the middle and upper classes alone. Any other interpretation seems out of the question, because at the time when he wrote, large numbers of men and women could neither read nor sign their names, let alone tackle three-volume novels — which in any case were far too dear for them to buy and unavailable in any other way as there were virtually no free public libraries.

*   *   *

Scott, like Byron, grew up lame in one foot. If one accepts the theory of artistic creation put forward by Edmund Wilson in *The Wound and the Bow*, he wrote prolifically as a way of compensating

---

[1] A novel in seven volumes (1747-8) by Samuel Richardson.

for this physical defect, in order to make good a flawed world. This may explain why the best of his works, produced in the Regency, have appeared to many readers to be, in Hazlitt's phrase, 'like a new edition of human nature' — he was generous in creating likeable characters and happy endings because he longed to recover wholeness. When taunted about his lameness as a schoolboy, he fought furiously, again like Byron; later, perhaps significantly, he was silent on the subject. He did acknowledge, however, that he had always been a dreamer, and said that in giving himself up to story-telling, which came as naturally to him as breathing, he had 'worn a wishing-cap'. There are various hints in the *Journal* which he began to keep in the last few years of his life that he was aware of a connection between certain painful emotional experiences which he had undergone when much younger and the 'wishing-cap' world of his prose fiction.

But while it is necessary to go back to Scott's youth in order to understand the deeper springs of his artistic inspiration, there is no mystery about what it was that drove him to try his hand as a novelist in 1813-14. He had recently bought and begun to 'improve' (by building, planting trees, and purchasing further land in the neighbourhood) a small estate round a tumbledown farmhouse at Cartleyhole in the Tweed valley, between the ancient abbey town of Melrose and the new textile-making town of Galashiels; and he needed money. Scott was nearly always short of cash. While integrity mattered to him above everything, he was very much a man of his age, living on credit and paying off today's debts with the undertaking to make good his bond in six months' time. Few Regency gamblers took larger risks in the matter of issuing promissory notes to pay, and in speculating on land. He had a steady income from two legal appointments — he had been Sheriff of Selkirkshire since 1799 and Clerk of the Court of Session in Edinburgh since 1806 — and had in addition made substantial sums from his already numerous books, especially from the series of verse tales which had begun with *The Lay of the Last Minstrel* in 1805. But he could seldom refuse a plea for help, whether from stranger, acquaintance, or relative; he and his wife were openhanded in entertaining their friends in their house in Castle Street in the fashionable Georgian New Town of Edinburgh; their teenage family required to be clothed and educated in style; and Scott wanted

Abbotsford, as he had decided to name the house which replaced Cartleyhole, to be much more than a country cottage.

Although he had been born an Edinburgh lawyer's son, Scott thought of himself as a Borderer, because most of his forbears on both sides of his family had lived in the Scottish Border country, and because he himself had been sent as a small boy to his grandfather's farm at Sandyknowe in Roxburghshire, beside the old stone keep of Smailholm, which had once belonged to the Scotts, and which commands views of both the Eildon and the Cheviot Hills. He was a kinsman of the Scotts of Buccleuch (already the Dukes of Buccleuch were among the most prosperous landowners in Britain), and he had a great desire to re-establish and then pass on to his descendants a Scott estate which would not disgrace his branch of the family.

Therefore, while part of Abbotsford was furnished in the latest country-house style, and Mrs Scott enjoyed playing hostess in an elegant drawing-room and dining-room, it also boasted many antique features, both in its imitation-Gothic architecture, which marks the start of the Gothic architectural revival in domestic Scottish building, and in the truckloads of historical relics with which Scott proceeded to fill it. One very large room became the armoury, and was soon full of swords, spears, clubs, guns and suits of armour of many times and many lands. Scott had a collector's passion, and thought nothing of asking his London friends, such as the actor Daniel Terry, to bid in shops and showrooms on his behalf for weapons or other objects with particular associations which interested him. The same kind of activity went on all the time north of the Border, his printer John Ballantyne earning his thanks on one typical occasion for declining to buy someone's collection of books for the well-stocked library at Abbotsford unless the sword which Charles I had presented to the Marquis of Montrose for his services to the Royalist cause was included in the sale. Scott's capacity for literary work matched in scale his appetite for land, family status and what he referred to, quoting Burns, as 'old nicknackets', or he must surely have run into financial disaster at Abbotsford before Waterloo was fought and won.[1]

---

[1] Characteristically, he showed an eye for the main chance after Waterloo by visiting the battlefield, publishing a record of what he saw in *Paul's Letters to his Kinsfolk*, and bringing home armour of Napoleon's Imperial Army, including some very large ornamental helmets.

In deciding to meet Byron's strong challenge to his supremacy as a popular poet by writing a novel, Scott was backing his own judgment against advice once given him by a friend. Years before, he had begun under the title 'Waverley' a prose tale in which he intended to draw on his knowledge of eighteenth-century Scottish history, and especially of the '45 Rebellion; his idea was to combine with a narrative of adventure the appeal of Highland scenery, which he had already described in a way that the public liked in his poem *The Lady of the Lake*. After completing the first half-dozen chapters, which described the upbringing in England of the hero of the projected story, Edward Waverley, he had shown the work to his former university classmate William Erskine, only to be told that he would do better to stick to verse. Scott had carelessly stuffed the manuscript into a drawer of an old desk, and for a long time could not lay his hands on it, though it crossed his mind more than once that perhaps it would be worth while to go ahead and finish it.

While hunting for fishing-tackle one day in 1813 for one of the many house-guests he welcomed to Abbotsford, he had come across these early chapters, and necessity now suggested that he complete the novel lying in this embryonic state. Once he was well into the story and had his hero on Scottish ground undergoing various trials of loyalty as he found himself falling first for one girl (Rose Bradwardine) and then for another (Flora MacIvor), siding first with the Hanoverian army, then with the forces supporting Charles Edward Stuart, it did not take Scott long to write. The copy for volumes two and three of the three-volume novel — which ended with Edward Waverley bidding a reluctant farewell to Jacobite sympathies and reasserting his commitment to the first girl he loved and to King George II — was produced in three weeks of sustained composition when legal work slackened in June 1814. By 7 July, thanks to the author's close collaboration with James Ballantyne (the brother of John), who supervised the work of the printers and kept them hard at it, *Waverley: Or 'Tis Sixty Years Since* was on sale in the bookshops of Edinburgh.

Scott had followed the example of many other novelists of the period in bringing out *Waverley* anonymously. Not only was it hardly the thing to be known in polite society as someone whose name appeared on the title-page of a mere prose romance; he had shrewdly realized that if the work failed to sell or was heavily

150

criticized, his reputation as a poet would suffer. He need not have feared, as things turned out, for after a week or two sales of *Waverley* in Scotland were excellent, which in turn helped to create interest in the south. When reviews began to appear, they were full of praise. Not since the appearance of Burns's *Poems, Chiefly in the Scottish Dialect* twenty-eight years before had any literary work by a Scottish writer caused such excitement. Everyone wanted to know who could have written such a stirring and well-informed historical tale, which delighted both by the range of attractive characters it contained, from Flora MacIvor and her warlike brother Fergus to Rose Bradwardine and her kindly, irascible father, and by portraying convincingly something previously untouched in fiction, Highland Perthshire and the way of life north of 'the Highland Line' in the middle of the last century. There were some wild guesses about the authorship of *Waverley,* but a number of readers who knew the cast of Scott's mind from his poems, historical writings or conversation — Scotland, after all, is a small country — were quick to make the right deduction. The *British Critic* commented in August,

> A very short time has elapsed, since this publication made its appearance in Edinburgh, and though it came into the world in the modest garb of anonymous obscurity, the northern literati are unanimous, as we understand, in ascribing part of it at least to the pen of W. Scott. As that gentleman has too much good sense to play the coquet with the world, we understand that he perseveres in a formal denial of the charge; though from all we can learn, the *not guilty* which he pleads to the indictment, proceeds almost as faintly from his mouth, as from the tongue of a notorious offender at the bar of the Old Bailey.

This was an accurate summary of Scott's position. He had made up his mind on two points straightaway: not to admit publicly to having written the novel, and to follow up his success, which was no less notable in England than in Scotland, as soon as possible. In that part of his complex nature which belonged to the Court of Session and to everything concerning landed estates, he was slightly shocked by his latest venture into the literary market-place. It seemed better by far to preserve anonymity, even though he had been found out by intelligent sleuths. A gentleman might publish poems under his own name, but to do this with novels would be to risk losing social standing among solid Edinburgh burghers and country lairds who had been brought up to think of fiction as little better than sensational nonsense. At the same time, it would obviously be folly not to cash in on the popularity which he appeared to have attained through *Waverley* . . . otherwise how was he to continue enjoying a gentlemanly standard of living? He therefore set to work and in six weeks at Christmas-time 1814 wrote *Guy Mannering*, a novel set mainly in the Borders in the later eighteenth century, dealing once again with the vicissitudes in love of an impressionable young hero, and, this time, with the struggle to rebuild the fortunes of an ancient Scottish family. He was rewarded for his boldness in taking this course in February 1815, when *Guy Mannering* proved to be an instant success.

Coleridge's charge that Scott missed the 'higher beauties' of fiction through being too anxious to pitch his work at a level which would appeal to a public longing above all to be amused and taken out of themselves admittedly contains a good deal of truth. Scott himself wrote of *Waverley*,

> The tale was put together with so little care that I cannot boast of having sketched any distinct plan of the work. The whole adventures of Waverley, in his movements up and down the country with the Highland cateran Bean Lean, are managed without much skill. It suited best, however, the road I wanted to travel, and permitted me to introduce some descriptions of scenery and manners, to which the reality gave an interest which the powers of the Author might have otherwise failed to attain for them.

Waverley and *Guy Mannering* both lack the kind of scrupulously worked out plot associated with, say, Jane Austen or Henry James, or with Samuel Richardson, whose novels Coleridge seems to have taken as a standard of excellence. It is quite easy to detect loose ends in *Waverley* at the point where Scott resumed writing in 1813, and again in the book's over-hasty last few chapters; while *Guy Mannering* suddenly ceases to be concerned with the supernatural predictions of Guy Mannering, who is an astrologer, because Scott realized in the course of writing that to make too much depend on astrology in a novel about recent times was a mistake in that it strained credulity.

The evidence of his haste and carelessness is certainly there, but so also is a masculine originality of a quality not seen in British fiction since Fielding published *Tom Jones*. On balance, there can be no doubt that Scott's 'hab nab at a venture' or improvisational style of composition suited him far better than a more strictly controlled approach to writing would have done. This does not mean that he was right to leave whole chapters of his books unrevised, or to spin out the story of *The Heart of Midlothian* (1818) simply because he wanted to fill a third volume; but it was by following intuition rather than the plan with which he always tried to begin that he was able to develop many of his finest characters, and to make them speak in unforced Lowland Scots — a feature which the Regency reading public took in its stride or at any rate accepted as appropriate in 'Scotch Novels'.

Guy Mannering bears all this out, for Scott was on his home territory in describing Border society, and certain characters whose original place in his scheme of the novel was clearly minor, simply took hold of his imagination and broke free from the plan.[1] Thus Dandie Dinmont, a hill farmer from the remote valley of Liddesdale with a great love of field sports and of his large family, became a companion for the hero and a source of good humour throughout the novel; and the rather dry and academic astrology of Colonel Mannering was balanced by prophecies memorably uttered in dialect by Meg Merrilees, whose character was based on that of gypsies Scott had met and heard much of around the village of Yetholm, which lies close to Cheviot itself at the northern extremity of the Pennine Way.

One argument in support of Coleridge's view that people became addicted to the Waverley novels in the Regency out of a wish to leave behind anxiety over their 'needs and embarrassments' is that all but one of the series — and *St Ronan's Well* was not published until 1824 — concerned the past rather than the present. It suited a war-weary nation to be entertained with imaginary deeds of love and heroism from a remote time: many readers, of different generations, had had a surfeit of the nineteenth century in their own lives.

Yet it would be misleading to conclude that the relationship between Scott and his public was merely that of someone peddling escapism to willing dupes. Scott's passionate interest in the past came about in part because he saw in human continuity and change a way of understanding the present. He had been trained at Edinburgh University in the discipline of historical sociology, and was intellectually indebted to Adam Fergusson, whose *Essay on Civil Society* (1767) is an early attempt to show how different societies evolve in

---

[1] When asked to explain how he had created the character of Jeanie Deans in *The Heart of Midlothian*, Scott replied, 'the lassie kept tugging at my heart-strings'.

response to changing political systems and external pressures. It was as a serious student of social change that Scott wrote in the Advertisement to *The Antiquary* (1816):

> The present work completes a series of fictitious narratives, intended to illustrate the manners of Scotland at three different periods. *Waverley* embraced the age of our fathers, *Guy Mannering* that of our own youth, and the *Antiquary* refers to the last ten years of the eighteenth century.

He added, in justification of what had come instinctively while he was writing,

> I have, in the two last narratives especially, sought my principal personages in the class of society who are the last to feel the influence of that general polish which assimilates to each other the manners of different nations.

This was not a spurious attempt on Scott's part to inject into his fiction what has since become known as 'working-class interest'. In creating a character like Edie Ochiltree, the 'bluecoat' or licensed beggar who in *The Antiquary* rescues from certain death by drowning a number of his social superiors, he remained true to his firsthand observation of country life among poor people in the previous century. The point was simply that in his experience the Edie Ochiltrees of the world spoke with a degree of individuality and a freedom from inhibition which gave them more interest as subjects for fiction than persons conforming to the demands of middle-class society usually displayed.

Scott aimed to treat impartially in his novels individuals from different nations and many walks of life, and made a point wherever possible of stressing by implication the interdependence of various groups, highborn and lowborn, Highland and Lowland, English and non-English, in nineteenth-century Britain. The Irish authoress Maria Edgeworth had in his opinion done a great deal through the success in mainland Britain of her novel *Castle Rackrent* (1800), which was set in Ireland and peopled by Irish characters, to 'consolidate the Union'. Scott as a good Tory wanted his own fiction to serve a similar purpose by increasing the familiarity of English readers with Scotland, and as a result reducing the distrust of his native land which was a legacy from the time of the '45 and that of Lord North's corrupt Scottish influence on the government of Great Britain in the 1770s. He did not often spell out the social philosophy behind his work, but he scarcely needed to, because his belief in the need for social unity and in the natural dignity of the common man was conveyed so clearly through the action and characterization of novel after novel.

While his readers were happy to absorb much history they had not known before in reading *Waverley* and its successors, some were sceptical of his claim that he had tried to examine systematically 'different stages of society'. J. W. Croker, for instance, reviewing *The Antiquary* in the *Quarterly Review*, thought this sounded like an explanation dreamed up after the books had been written in order to make them appear to have a greater degree of historical connectedness and authenticity than in fact they possessed:

> We admit that, provided the author succeeds in amusing us, it is, in ordinary cases, of little consequence on what theory he may choose to proceed, or to say that he proceeds; but when he affects, as in the present instance, to write a work in some degree historical of men, and professedly historical of manners, it becomes our duty, as contemporaries, as well as reviewers, to withhold our testimony from what we consider a misrepresentation. We believe that the manners of Guy Mannering are as much the existing manners of the day, as those of the Antiquary; and we are satisfied that the able and ingenious author, after having written these three very amusing romances, has indulged himself in a fanciful classification of them, and, waiving his higher claims, prefers the humbler one of writing on a *system*, which he never thought of, and in which, if he had designed it, we should have no hesitation in saying that he has, by his own confession, failed.

Clearly, Croker was willing to forgive Scott his presumption in claiming to have a consistent historical method, 'provided the author succeeds in amusing us'. The test was always the same, whatever a reader's attitude towards Scott's treatment of the past, and the author of *Waverley* seldom failed to pass it. Hazlitt's dislike of Scott's Toryism provoked him to write on one occasion,

> His is a mind brooding over antiquity — scorning 'the present ignorant time'. He is 'laudator temporis acti' — 'a prophesier of things past'. The old world is to him a crowded map; the new one a dull, hateful blank. He dotes on all well-authenticated superstitions; he shudders at the shadow of innovation.

But he nevertheless went on to admit that in his fiction Scott

> does not enter into the distinctions of hostile sects or parties, but treats of the strength or infirmity of the human mind, of the virtues or vices of the human breast, as they are to be found blended in the whole race of mankind.

It was, in Hazlitt's opinion, largely because people responded to his quality of 'candour', that Scott had become 'undoubtedly the most popular writer of the age — the "lord of the ascendant" for the time being'.

But what of the criticism that Scott 'shuddered at innovation'? Hazlitt has put his finger on a paradoxical truth about the Regency itself and at the same time identified an aspect of Scott's outlook which demands to be considered if he is to be understood either as man or as artist. It may appear contradictory to state that old-fashioned politics and old-fashioned morality actually helped to sell Scott's novels during the very decade when, as we have already seen, Byron's very different and essentially subversive code had become fashionable. However, there were two moral camps in the Regency, and the more powerful, at any rate among middle-class readers, was very far from welcoming any departure from traditional values. The Evangelical revival was well under way, and tracts were being distributed throughout the land to the poor and the not-so-poor by ladies with an earnest glint in their eyes; Dr Bowdler was already at work selecting from classic authors of an earlier day those passages which could be read without a blush in the classroom,[1] while Hannah More campaigned tirelessly for stricter moral standards; three-volume novels with such titles as *Self Control* and *Discipline* were in demand. In short, the 'fathers and mothers of the Victorians' were already on the scene.

To such leaders of moral counter-revolution — for so many men and women saw themselves — the 'Scotch novels' appeared deeply reassuring. Without exception, these were stories which celebrated the virtues of political stability and ethical conservatism. There was nothing anarchic or dangerously lax in the conduct of Scott's well-bred heroes and heroines. Chivalrous courtships abounded; but not even the most restrained description of physical love was to be found, least of all in what is possibly his greatest masterpiece, *The Heart of Midlothian,* although the whole action of this novel springs from an illicit love-affair.

The explanation lies partly in Scott's having submitted to the prevailing convention of reticence in fiction — few novelists dared flout the prudish standards of the 'blue stockings' — and partly in

[1] Bowdler's *Family Shakespeare* was published in 1818.

something which had happened to him twenty years before he published *Waverley*. He had loved and lost to a wealthy rival a girl who meant so much to him through 'three years of dreaming and two years of wakening' that although, as he put it himself, his heart had been 'handsomely pieced' by marriage to someone else, 'the crack would remain to my dying day'. This robbed him of the confidence a novelist needs to write frankly of love between man and woman, and made him in the words of a recent biographer, 'distrustful of violent emotion, unreined passion, excess'. As the same period in the 1790s had seen the French Revolution plunge finally into political chaos, it is hardly surprising that, through a process of psychological reaction, Scott had developed into someone whose gift it was to re-create imaginatively old, far-off things and battles long ago: the present was altogether too disturbing. . .

> Nothing is perhaps more dangerous [he once wrote] to the future happiness of men of deep thought . . . than the entertaining an early, long, and unfortunate attachment. It frequently sinks so deep into the mind, that it becomes their dream by night and their vision by day — mixes itself with every source of interest and enjoyment; and, when blighted and withered by final disappointment, it seems as if the springs of the spirit had dried up along with it.

Nothing of this early period of emotional storm and stress was known to the general public, who assumed correctly that Scott must be a cheerful, well-adjusted person. How else, they reasoned, could he fill his novels with such amusing characters as Dugald Dalgetty, the far-travelled mercenary in *A Legend of Montrose* who is always quoting the Latin he learned 'at the Marischal College in Aberdeen', or that man of few words, the Laird of Dumbiedykes in *The Heart of Midlothian*, who thinks to win the hand of Jeanie Deans by opening his money-hoard ('A' gowd, Jeanie') and letting her gaze on it with the rapture he feels himself? Scott's readers took him to be serene, good-humoured, and above life's ordinary struggles, a kind of universal favourite uncle. Few of them guessed that in his twenties he had been swept off course by an unrequited passion of such strength that the thought of it could make him break down and weep thirty years later, or realized that he was even now being driven to live dangerously in a time of soaring land prices by a relentless inner compulsion which would not allow him to be satisfied with less than a country laird's social standing: in this sense, he was indeed 'The Great Unknown'.

157

The success of *Waverley* provoked this wry comment in a letter sent by an English parson's spinster daughter to her niece Anna on 28 September 1814:

> Walter Scott has no business to write novels, especially good ones. — It is not fair. — He has Fame and Profit enough as a Poet, and should not be taking the bread out of other people's mouths. — I did not like him, & do not mean to like Waverley if I can help it — but fear I must.

She added, with playful spite, 'I have made up my mind to like no Novels really, but Miss Edgeworth's, Yours & my own.' Jane Austen, who had already published *Sense and Sensibility* (1811), *Pride and Prejudice* (1813), and, just four months before, *Mansfield Park*, here recognized that Scott was destined to become a bestselling novelist in a way that she was not. But while none of her books would sell within her lifetime more than two or three thousand copies, in contrast to, say, *Rob Roy*, which sold ten thousand copies within a fortnight in 1817, she nevertheless enjoyed a growing reputation among discerning readers as a writer of 'clever' fiction. The first two novels had both gone into a second edition in 1813, *Pride and Prejudice* within a few months of being published, and to someone with as small a private income as Jane Austen returns of £100 or £200 were riches indeed. She was now on the point of changing her publisher to the fashionable John Murray (of whom she said characteristically 'he is a rogue of course but a civil one'). Work on her next book, *Emma*, which she had told someone was going to be about 'a heroine whom no one but myself will much like', was giving her considerable satisfaction that autumn. On the suggestion of his Librarian, *Emma* would be dedicated in 1815 to the Prince Regent, who had been quick to detect exceptional literary talent in her works, a complete set of which she was told he kept not just in Carlton House but in each of his residences.

Annabella Milbanke described *Pride and Prejudice* as 'a very superior work ... the *most probable* fiction I have ever read', adding, in words which reveal that many people liked to be made to weep by novels, 'It is not a crying book, but the interest is very strong.' Scott, who gave *Emma* an excellent review in the *Quarterly*, wrote in his Journal after reading *Pride and Prejudice* for a third time, that Jane Austen had a talent for describing

> the involvements and feelings and characters of ordinary life, which is to me the most wonderful I ever met with. The Big Bow-wow strain I can do

> myself like any now going; but the exquisite touch, which renders ordinary commonplace things and characters interesting, from the truth of the description and the sentiment, is denied to me.

As well as being an accurate and objective summing-up of the nature of Jane Austen's achievement in *Pride and Prejudice* and her other books, this points to the great difference between her kind of fiction, depending for its success on the exact observation of '3 or 4 Families in a Country Village', and the 'Big Bow-Wow strain' of Scott's own picaresque historical romances.

Yet while Jane Austen was in many ways a different kind of novelist from Scott, there were fascinating resemblances between them. They had in common, to begin with, the habit of bringing out their novels anonymously. All that appeared on the title-page of *Sense and Sensibility* were the words 'by a lady'. In subsequent books, the formula was changed to 'by the author of . . .'; Jane Austen did not wish to be known as a professional writer, despite her pride in her craft. It could no doubt be claimed that her case was really very unlike that of Scott, as she was not already known for other publications before taking up fiction, and as a result therefore the number of her admirers who learned her identity was small: nevertheless, the two shared the practice of not owning up to their authorship except to their families and closest friends.

Jane Austen resembled Scott, too, in communicating through her stories a firm and essentially conservative set of social and moral values. She rejected the cult of 'sensibility' or unrestrained feeling as something likely to lead to all kinds of trouble, including, in *Sense and Sensibility,* a young girl's seduction. Her first novel, and *Waverley*, use different means to underline the same warning, that it is not healthy for the young to live exclusively in a world of romance and daydreams. Jane Austen, like Scott, had been brought up in a Christian household, and believed that as a writer she had a responsibility to instruct, through the indirect channels of fiction, as well as to entertain. ('I am by no means convinced', she wrote in 1814, 'that we ought not all to be Evangelicals.') Finally, she made a similar choice to Scott in deciding not to write often or at length in her novels about stirring events in her own times. Instead of aiming to catch the public interest by bringing in well-known personalities, or by setting her stories in the West End of London, she wrote of what she knew best, middle-class localities scarcely disturbed by rumours of war against Napoleon or of popular riots; and, by concentrating on family affairs in a provincial setting, quietly excluded the more spectacular sides of modern experience.

The similarity between Jane Austen and Scott in what they opted *not* to handle becomes very clear when their approach to fiction is contrasted with that of the greatest British novelist of the Victorian period. Dickens treated in such novels as *Bleak House* (1853) and *Hard Times* (1854) topical social issues concerning the poor, and frequently wrote with the zeal of someone who wanted to see a re-distribution of wealth and opportunity. So far from excluding present-day conflicts and tensions in society, he made the exploration of them central to his mature art. But whereas Dickens belonged by upbringing to London, experienced extreme poverty in his childhood, and inherited a vigorous tradition of popular journalistic writing from Pierce Egan and others, both Jane Austen and Scott came from a partly rural and wholly middle-class background, in which quite different norms and taboos operated, and where fictional expectations certainly did not include committed writing about 'low life'.

If Jane Austen was understandably more interested in examining with controlled wit and irony the foibles of 'country gentlefolk' than anything else, this did not prevent her from making innovations in the art of the novel nor from analysing in some detail in her later work the assumptions of specifically contemporary Regency social types. She died at the age of forty-two in 1817; and her brother Henry had the task of seeing through the press the following year both *Northanger Abbey*, the first version of which dates from as long before as 1797-8, and her last completed work, *Persuasion,* which had been written in the last two years of her life. Like almost everything else which she wrote, these two works have a degree of polish and a quality of internal order in the construction of their narratives wholly lacking in Scott's novels. Together they illustrate the remarkable continuity in her fiction from an early point in her career to its close, while *Persuasion* shows how the Regency world helped her to perfect her gift for satire and exact social observation.

Northanger Abbey is a brilliant 'send-up' of the Gothic novel, a form which had held its popularity throughout Jane Austen's writing career. The most successful of all Gothic tales, *The Mysteries of Udolpho* (1794), has such a strong fascination for Catherine

Morland, the novel's adolescent heroine, that she ceases for the time being to be able to distinguish between the imaginary and the real, and when invited by friends to visit their home, Northanger Abbey, becomes convinced that it must be a place of dreadful secrets, like the Castle of Udolpho, and believes that her host, General Tilney, is an unspeakable tyrant who has murdered his wife. All this is shown to be false, and when Henry Tilney, the General's son, with whom she has fallen in love, gently reproves her for becoming a prey to such delusions, Catherine is humiliated. One of the lessons she has learned is that the terrors of Udolpho need not be feared in England, 'at least in the midland counties'; and Henry's willingness to overlook her nonsense proves to her that she has 'nothing but to forgive herself and be happier than ever'.

Yet Jane Austen has created a finely ironical situation, for while everything is to work out for Catherine and Henry in the end, General Tilney does indeed behave at one stage in a cruel and arbitrary way, by abruptly announcing that Catherine is to leave Northanger Abbey. He turns out to be a complete materialist, in whose eyes a girl without an assured large dowry is not good enough to marry into his family:

> She was guilty only of being less rich than he had supposed her to be. Under a mistaken persuasion of her possessions and claims, he had courted her acquaintance in Bath, solicited her company in Northanger, and designed her for his daughter in law. On discovering his error, to turn her from the house seemed the best, though to his feelings inadequate proof of his resentment towards herself, and his contempt of her family.

As it is only through good luck and his son's determined opposition to the General's dismissal of Catherine that the young couple become free to marry, the point is put beyond doubt that an obsession with position, or still worse, with wealth, is in Jane Austen's view the equivalent crime 'in England and among the English' to the outrageous cruelty practised by the Master of Udolpho in the novel she has been parodying. Society, she implies, has certain natural divisions, and it is only proper that people should know their place within their own social rank; but snobbery is a blight on the face of the land because it lessens the sum of human happiness.

Snobbery is held up to scorn once again in *Persuasion*, but in this novel, set in 1814, Jane Austen is not producing a literary parody and can therefore proceed more directly. 'Sir Walter Elliot, of Kellynch-hall, in Somersetshire', we learn from the first sentence of Chapter 1,

> was a man who, for his own amusement, never took up any book but the Baronetage; there he found occupation for an idle hour, and consolation in a distressed one; there his faculties were roused into admiration and respect, by contemplating the limited remnant of the earliest patents; there any unwelcome sensations, arising from domestic affairs, changed naturally into pity and contempt, as he turned over the almost endless creations of the past century − and there, if every other leaf were powerless, he could read his own history with an interest which never failed . . .

Pride in his own birth and good looks (there is more than a touch of the dandy about him) are what matter above everything else to Sir Walter. He is no slave of Mammon, like General Tilney, but a vain and absurd man whose family somehow has to come to terms with the nineteenth century: and out of all this Jane Austen creates sparkling social satire. What Coleridge was to complain of as 'a straining to maintain life − or appearances' has caused Sir Walter to incur heavy debts. Neither he nor his equally haughty eldest daughter can think of ways of economizing without compromising their dignity, but after a time they are persuaded to consider letting out Kellynch-hall and moving temporarily to Bath. The thought of how they will give themselves airs in Bath dismays Anne Elliot, the heroine of the story; but her preference for a smaller house in the country is ignored by her elders.

The new tenant is Admiral Croft, recently returned from the war; he and his wife, as well as several other much younger naval officers, are described by Jane Austen in consistently sympathetic language, as cheerful, patriotic and considerate individuals, perfectly capable of taking good care of anyone's property. The Admiral is 'quite the gentleman', in the words of Mr Shepherd, Sir Walter's lawyer, and later also applied to a curate named Wentworth; but his criteria are not acceptable to Sir Walter Elliot, who protests,

> You misled me by the term *gentleman*. I thought you were speaking of some man of property: Mr Wentworth was nobody, I remember; quite unconnected . . .

One of the issues of direct relevance to Regency society which *Persuasion* presents lies precisely here: is service to one's community or country to be allowed to count for as much in post-war Britain as inherited social position? Jane Austen's attitude is not in doubt at any point in the novel, which can be read as a sustained tribute to returning naval heroes — Wellington's army, interestingly, is not even mentioned in *Persuasion* — by an Englishwoman who had anxiously followed the course of the war at sea since before Nelson's victory at Trafalgar, and whose youngest brother, Charles, himself rose to the rank of Admiral.

Neither has she any illusions about the attitude of such survivors from the past as Sir Walter Elliot. Only their need for money makes them look on nautical men with anything but contempt. This is made plain through the story of Anne Elliot's love for Captain Wentworth, brother of the 'quite unconnected' curate. Many years before 1814, Anne had been engaged to Wentworth, at that time an impecunious but promising young officer, but had yielded to strong pressure from her father and his neighbour Lady Russell, who united in thinking her fiancé a nobody, and broken off the engagement. Now at last, through a series of happy accidents, Captain Wentworth and she meet again, discover that they still love each other, and plan to marry. This time,

> Sir Walter made no objection, and Elizabeth did nothing worse than look cold and unconcerned. Captain Wentworth, with five-and-twenty thousand pounds, and as high in his profession as merit and activity could place him, was no longer nobody. He was now esteemed quite worthy to address the daughter of a foolish, spendthrift baronet, who had not had principle or sense enough to maintain himself in the situation in which Providence had placed him, and who could give his daughter at present but a small part of the share of ten thousand pounds which must be hers hereafter.

There could be no clearer proof that, in the world of Jane Austen's novels, money talks loudest. In her own way, she makes the same criticism of her contemporaries as Byron, 'cash rules'. Yet there is an additional stricture, for it is no accident that both General Tilney and Sir Walter Elliot are *men*, who lack the steadying influence of a sensible woman. Although no militant liberationist, Jane Austen frequently draws attention both to such instances of male stupidity, and to the difficult position of girls in a society which was in important ways dominated and controlled by men.

No writer conveys more vividly the elegance and charm of the way of life enjoyed in Regency country houses. The instinctive sense of artistic proportion revealed in her descriptions of rooms, furnishings and dresses — an art seen at its height perhaps in *Mansfield Park*, where a particular house and its setting are especially important — is matched only by the fine aesthetic taste of the people who created these things in the late eighteenth and early nineteenth centuries. Today it is necessary to visit the Museum of Costume in Bath, a city which Jane Austen knew well but, like Anne Elliot, heartily disliked, in order fully to appreciate the beauty of the domestic interiors and well-designed clothes which form part of the background in all of her novels. For many people, Jane Austen's heroines in their flowing dresses, whether pictured in a conversation piece in their own neat drawing-rooms, or being escorted to the dining-table in the homes of their friends, are 'the essential Regency' as nothing else is save possibly the finest furniture which has been handed down from the period. To have been able to project in this way an image of the age as one of calm, leisured living, and equipoise — however much this leaves out of the historical reckoning — is an achievement almost without parallel in English literature. And it is obvious that, but for the cruel illness (Addison's disease) which put a premature end to her life, Jane Austen would have gone on to provide even more insights into Regency England, for in the uncompleted *Sanditon* she had begun to analyse with her customary flair a phenomenon she had not treated in depth before, the minor seaside spa town and its highly distinctive residents. As she knew well, such places were being 'developed' all along the south coast, at a quite alarming rate; living at Chawton, near Winchester, she had probably heard much about how these places of resort were changing people's lives in previously quiet corners of England. To judge from the fragment of *Sanditon* which is all that she had time to write between January and March 1817, Jane Austen was greatly amused by the talk of individuals who sought to make out that the particular resort where they lived was in every way superior to its rivals. Without condemning modern civic improvements, she mocks at excessive local patriotism and at an unqualified belief in progress, shown for example in the person of Mr Parker, a founding father of the spa at Sanditon, who, on noticing after a month's absence that the shoemaker's shop has on display blue shoes and nankeen boots, which he assumes to be the latest fashion, exclaims innocently, 'Civilization, civilization indeed!'

One of the attractions at Sanditon is the circulating library, run by a milliner, Mrs Whitby, who as well as lending out to subscribers fashionable novels, sells toiletries and rings and brooches. Mr Parker is disappointed when he looks at the library subscription book, which is a reliable indicator of who has come to Sanditon during his month away:

> The list of subscribers was but commonplace. The Lady Denham, Miss Brereton, Mr and Mrs Parker, Sir Edward Denham and Miss Denham, whose names might be said to lead off the season, were followed by nothing better than — Mrs Mathews — Miss Mathews, Miss E. Mathews, Miss H. Mathews. — Dr and Mrs Brown — Mr Richard Pratt. — Lieutenant Smith R.N., Captain Little, — Limehouse. Mrs Jane Fisher. Miss Fisher. Miss Scroggs. — Rev. Mr Hanking. Mr Beard — solicitor, Grays Inn. — Mrs Davis and Miss Merryweather. Mr Parker could not but feel that the list was not only without distinction, but less numerous than he had hoped. It was but July however, and August and September were the months . . .

This passage gives a good idea of the importance of circulating libraries in Regency spas as places where the upper and middle classes came together. As one might expect, however, from the way in which Mr Parker mentally classifies the subscribers into two groups, the larger lacking 'distinction', in the circulating library, as elsewhere, cash ruled! There were normally several categories of subscription, only one of which entitled the subscriber to borrow the latest novels, magazines and reviews. Jane Austen does not go into detail, but if the 'terms for subscribers' to the Sanditon library were devised in the usual way, it is possible to deduce that for a yearly subscription of one guinea or more Lady Denham had the run of the place, whereas Miss Scroggs, say, would probably have paid five shillings for the privilege of borrowing during the summer quarter any books in Mrs Whitby's stock with the exception of those which had newly arrived from the bookseller.

Given their association with light reading and a life of ease — the hero in *Frederick and Caroline* (1800) visits the library at Margate and asks, 'Where, in these enlightened days is there a bathing-place without such a necessary receptacle of literary knowledge?' — it is hardly surprising that circulating libraries were looked down on by some lovers of literature. Coleridge sneered at people who frequented them, most notably in *Biographia Literaria*:

> I dare not compliment their pass-time, or rather kill-time, with the name of reading. Call it rather a sort of beggarly day-dreaming, during which the mind of the dreamer furnishes for itself nothing but laziness, and a little mawkish sensibility . . . indulgence of sloth, and hatred of vacancy.

165

Leigh Hunt, on the other hand, thoroughly enjoyed losing himself in the sensational Gothic and equally undemanding romantic novels which were published in Leadenhall Street by the Minerva Press, and wrote in his *Autobiography*:

> I can read their three-volume enormities to this day without skipping a syllable; though I guess pretty nearly all that is going to happen from the mysterious gentleman who opens the work, in the dress of a particular century, down to the distribution of punishments and the drying of tears in the last chapter. I think the authors wonderfully clever people, especially those who write most, and I should like the most contemptuous of their critics to try their hand at anything half so engaging.

The general public, as distinct from consistently fastidious persons, was on the side taken by Leigh Hunt. Many addicts would have agreed with Charles Lamb that Minerva Press novels were 'scanty intellectual viands', but they bought or borrowed books all the same. The clearest proof of this lies in the number of titles brought out — on average, eighteen a year throughout the Regency — at William Lane's 'fiction manufactory'. Lane had grasped that fiction was a marketable product for which the well-to-do were ready to pay handsomely. By controlling both publication and distribution (his evening newspaper, *The Star*, proclaimed that he was ready to set anyone up in business in a circulating library filled with Minerva Press novels), he made a large fortune, and was able to drive about London in a splendid carriage attended by footmen with gold-headed canes and cockades. It was well said of him when he died, 'no man knows the world better, and none better how to manage and enjoy it'.

Various attempts have been made to account in psychological or sociological terms for the phenomenal popularity of Gothic novels at this time. Historians of the place of women in society argue that the many abductions and near-rapes which take place in these stories are proof of how inadequate were contemporary ideas about a woman's role; Gothic novels were avidly read by women, who, according to this form of analysis, must have been brain-washed into thinking of themselves merely as 'sex objects', whose existence was boring at best. Another theory is that there was a connection in the subconscious public mind between the perilous situations faced by the heroes and heroines of these stories and the sharp threats to security which society had faced and continued to face in a revolutionary era. Psychologically, according to this view, it was reassuring to read about imaginary situations which were at once more stressful than those in real life and yet which nevertheless had a happy ending. But however deep may have been the societal forces which summoned the Gothic novel into favour, there was nothing profound in the common run of Minerva Press Gothic fiction. That the main idea was to create from the beginning a mood of suspense, which was then maintained by a series of unexpected twists and turns in the plot, can be seen from the opening paragraph of *The Confessional of Valombre* (1812), one of fourteen Gothic or pseudo-historical tales by Louisa Sidney Stanhope:

> It was at the close of the festival of St Fabian, when the last sonorous tone of the organ had ceased, and the pale glimmer of the tape had expired, when nature had sealed the eyes of fanaticism, and even the vigil virgin had ceased to watch, that a stranger paused at the gate of the convent of Valombre. The stilly gloom of the hour, the hollow moaning of the blast, the darkened concave of the heavens, from which no star, no casual reflection of light was emitted, recalled to mind the object of his embassy. He started — he drew from beneath his cloak a dagger; and as he grasped the hilt, as carefully he replaced the folds of his habit, burying under their dark disguise the burden his left arm supported, a fiendlike smile distorted his visage; he cast a scowling glance around; his mind seemed pregnant with some weighty matter; he looked the slave of impulse — he felt the man of blood. 'Pity is transient', he muttered, 'down, down, damned weakness! memory, be thou the goading spur of action; revenge, be thou eternal.'

The atmosphere is shamelessly melodramatic, the diction filched from an earlier day than 1812, but this four-volume novel pleased admirers of the Gothic, and Louisa Stanhope was to oblige by publishing many others of the same kind in the next few years, until tempted by the success of Scott's mediaeval re-creation in *Ivanhoe* to devote no fewer than five volumes to *The Crusaders: An Historical Romance of the Twelfth Century* (1820), for which there was also a keen demand. Evidence of this kind goes to show that in the early nineteenth century fiction had come to serve as the main leisure interest of the largest part of the British reading public; William Lane's 'stable' contained many authors no less prolific than Louisa Stanhope.

In view of the number of writers who brought into the world Gothic novels without any claim to literary distinction, it seems only justice that one should have created a masterpiece. Strictly speaking, Mary Shelley's *Frankenstein: Or The Modern Prometheus* (1818) belongs to the genre of 'terror' rather than the Gothic, in that it lacks the historical element of such lucubrations as *The Confessional of Valombre*, but while there is no mediaeval monastery, the creation of suspense and use of fear as the psychological pivot of the novel shows the author's familiarity with the Gothic form. It was while Byron was their near neighbour at Geneva in the summer of 1816 that Shelley and Mary decided to experiment by writing 'ghost stories'. Byron and his physician companion Polidori took part in the enterprise with them; there was a volume of German ghost-stories lying about, and it seemed an amusing idea to while away the wet evenings by producing their own stories. Byron and Shelley failed to complete anything substantial, and Polidori's story of a 'skull-headed woman' quickly reached a point where, in Mary's view, he did not know what to do with the characters he had invented — although, interestingly, a very popular Victorian tale of terror, *The Vampyre*, was based on Polidori's work.

Only Mary took the challenge seriously, partly no doubt because Shelley kept insisting that she should write something. As she later recalled, for a long time, she 'could not think of a story', and would go off to bed in a glum mood while the men cheerfully told each other about their latest Gothic imaginings. Then one evening the wide-ranging talk of Byron and Shelley turned to scientific experiments allegedly made by Dr Erasmus Darwin, and to the report that he had

> preserved a piece of vermicelli in a glass case, till by some extraordinary means it began to move with voluntary motion.

It would not be in this way, the poets reasoned, that life might one day be artificially created by human beings. Instead,

> perhaps a corpse would be re-animated; galvanism had given a token of such things: perhaps the component parts of a creature might be manufactured, brought together, and endued with vital warmth.

Mary had an extremely powerful visual imagination, and that night she found that she could not sleep for thinking of 'a horrid thing... with yellow, watery, but speculative eyes' let loose upon the world by an over-ambitious man of science and returning to torment his creator. She succeeded in thoroughly frightening herself, but realized that her search for a subject and a story was at an end. The next morning, 'making only a transcript of the grim terrors of [her] waking dream', she began to write *Frankenstein*.

Later novels and films based very loosely on the idea of the non-human whose creation and vengeful acts Mary Shelley's book describes are together responsible for the widespread assumption that Frankenstein is the name of her 'horrid thing' or monster. In fact, it is her scientist who is called Frankenstein, and Mary Shelley's main concern throughout the novel is with his conduct and its consequences. Frankenstein is 'the modern Prometheus' in that he is endlessly curious, an intellectual over-reacher who pays the penalty for his daring. But what lends distinction to this idea is the skill with which it is developed in relation to the needs of society, and especially the way in which Mary Shelley suggests that Frankenstein has so compartmentalized his life as not to be aware of the dreadful initial mistake he makes: being single-mindedly absorbed in his scientific experiment, he creates his monster without realizing that in time the monster will feel the need for a mate. It is because the monster resents the lack of another being of its own kind to love him that he eventually becomes consumed with hatred for the human race in general and Frankenstein in particular.

In comparison with this brilliant fable, Aldous Huxley's *Brave New World*, and most other novels with a similar theme, lack depth. *Frankenstein* raises in apt fictional terms a set of problems which have increasingly occupied scientists in recent years. What are the proper limits for investigation in biological fields, and when is man justified in interfering with nature? Is there an ideal form of scientific education which will safeguard society against irresponsible behaviour by persons without a trained moral sense? Mary Shelley was not preaching in *Frankenstein* or even perhaps consciously uttering a warning. But such was her imaginative involvement with her theme that what began casually as an attempt to 'write a ghost story' became nothing less than a parable describing the radical loss of freedom which can overtake any individual or group placing too blind a trust in modern science.

The same year, 1818, when both *Northanger Abbey* and *Franken-stein* were published, saw the appearance of a third decidedly unusual work of fiction with a title which indicates a connection with the Gothic novel. This was *Nightmare Abbey* by Thomas Love Peacock, whose first novel, *Headlong Hall*, had come out two years earlier. Peacock was a sardonic observer of the Regency intellectual and social scene, a friend of the poet Shelley who nevertheless found the conduct of Shelley, Byron and others who left their mark upon the age somewhat amusing, a clever, reserved man who wrote purely for pleasure — his income came from a lucrative post in the East India Company's London office, where he was never expected to turn up before ten oclock in the morning or to stay beyond four in the afternoon. In *Headlong Hall* and *Nightmare Abbey* he created a form of fiction which has since been much imitated, the 'country-house novel' in which a number of eccentric figures come together for a short time and talk, attempting to persuade each other of the inevitable truth of their diverse quaint philosophies. 'Country house extravaganza' might be a more accurate description of Peacock's tales (the last of which, *Gryll Grange*, did not appear until 1860) because the plots count for little, being merely a pretext for conversation.

Peacock is known to have been a keen admirer of Mozart, and one of his recent biographers has suggested that *Nightmare Abbey* and the other books have less in common with novels, in which traditionally storytelling is central, than with opera, where recitative is secondary to varied and brilliant arias. Where *Nightmare Abbey* excels is in its mimicry of Regency voices as a means of eliciting comedy from contemporary literature, which in Peacock's opinion had become 'dark and misanthropic'. The principal characters are all based on living authors, the 'hero' Scythrop being a thinly disguised version of Shelley, Mr Cypress resembling Byron in his gloomiest mood, and the poet-metaphysician Mr Flosky being closely akin to Coleridge, the most prodigious talker of the age. . .

MR FLOSKY Tea, late dinners, and the French Revolution, have played the devil, Mr Listless, and brought the devil into play.

THE HONOURABLE MR LISTLESS Tea, late dinners, and the French Revolution. I cannot exactly see the connection of ideas.

MR FLOSKY I should be sorry if you could; I pity the man who can see the connection of his own ideas. Still more do I pity him, the connection of whose ideas any other person can see. Sir, the great evil is, that there is too much commonplace light in our moral and political literature; and light is a great enemy to mystery, and mystery is a great friend to enthusiasm. . .

MR FLOSKY It is very certain, and much to be rejoiced at, that our literature is hag-ridden. Tea has shattered our nerves; late dinners make us slaves of indigestion; the French Revolution has made us shrink from the name of philosophy, and has destroyed, in the more refined part of the community (of which number I am one), all enthusiasm for political liberty. That part of the *reading public* which shuns the solid food of reason for the light diet of fiction, requires a perpetual adhibition of *sauce piquante* to the palate of its deprived imagination. . .

Such a high-spirited take-off of Coleridge and his ideas must have appealed strongly to one part of the 'reading public' in 1818; Peacock's aim was to supply his contemporaries with *sauce piquante* in the form of a satirical commentary on fashionable notions of the day. As he did not share either the naive belief in social progress of 'political economists' and other representatives of what he called the 'Steam Intellect Society', nor the reminiscent pessimism of conservatives like Coleridge, but instead cultivated the detached stance and oblique methods of the satirist, he was able to mock all points of view with equal readiness. His own personality and 'positive' values remain oddly elusive as a result, but *Nightmare Abbey*, a Gothic tale which is memorable for its sustained wit rather than for 'ghosts, goblins, and skeletons', makes it clear at least that he considered laughter to be the best antidote to excess. In this he was at one with Jane Austen, with Cruikshank, with Rowlandson and with Byron — the poet of *Don Juan*, not 'Mr Cypress'.

*   *   *

Louis James has shown in *Fiction for the Working Man* that it was not until the later 1820s and 1830s that cheap reprints brought novels within reach of the new urban proletariat, who in any case did not have the leisure to read long books. In this sense, Regency fiction was produced not for all, but for the middle and upper classes, to whom it offered a special kind of imaginative freedom. But already there were numerous paper-bound abridgments of Gothic novels ('shilling shockers'), magazines published fiction in serialized form and Scott's novels enjoyed a second life adapted for the stage and enlivened by music. (In 1820, three separate versions of *Ivanhoe* were acted in London.) Thus by one means or another, the escape into fiction made possible by Scott and his fellow Regency novelists was widely shared.

[8]

The Lure of the Road

Whatever else may have changed in one and a half centuries, the British climate has remained fairly stable; and it is a link across the generations that its darker phase has consistently caused the British people to look forward longingly to the return of light and warmth which make it pleasant to go out of doors and take to the road. One of today's social customs which, while inevitably different in detail, would have been familiar enough as an idea in Regency Britain, at least among the well-to-do, is the planning which takes place in many homes in the depths of winter, often with the aid of brochures, newspaper supplements and television programmes, of the coming spring or summer's holiday travel. Indeed, the practice of making journeys in response to the renewal of spring goes back long before the Regency . . . in April, according to Chaucer, 'then longen folke to go on pilgrimages'. But there is an even more specific point of relationship between Regency attitudes towards travel and those which prevail today. Then, as now, unprecedented numbers were keen to go abroad, and to treat the continent of Europe as if it were an extension of their own land. And then, as now, inflation made it impossible for many of those who wished to do this to carry out their plans; and therefore they travelled within Britain instead.

In the eighteenth century, the recognized manner in which a young man of birth and means completed his education was by undertaking the Grand Tour. Usually accompanied by a tutor, and often by one or more friends of his own age, the young aristocrat would spend a period lasting from a few months to two years or more in France, Switzerland and Italy. He began in Paris, and many sprigs of the nobility were tempted to linger on the banks of the Seine, so different were Parisian ways from those at home. But the emphasis,

172

in theory at any rate, was on the acquisition of culture; and culture meant classical as well as recent achievements, so that Italy was held to be more important than France, and the 'grand object' was to become thoroughly acquainted at firsthand with the glories of ancient Roman, and to a lesser extent of Renaissance Italian, civilization, and at the same time, in Robert Burns's disrespectful phrase, to 'learn *bon ton* and see the warl'.

The Grand Tour proper was an experience restricted to a social élite — a typical traveller was Horace Walpole, the Prime Minister's son, who paid both for his own journey and for that of his companion, the future poet Thomas Gray, like himself an old Etonian and Cambridge undergraduate — and to the male sex. But others soon travelled in the footsteps of the privileged minority, including a number of very observant and lively-minded women, whose fresh and entertaining letters and journals made a welcome change from the rather dull literature which at first surrounded the subject. As time went on, the countries through which the lucky few like Walpole and Gray had passed began to attract sections of the middle class who in the 1740s would never have dreamed of stirring abroad. People realized that while it might be very pleasant to stay abroad for a year or longer and to live expensively, with servants and a private carriage, it was possible to see something of western Europe for a much smaller outlay of time and money. By the time Wordsworth visited France in 1790, it had become quite commonplace for people who could never have afforded the luxury of the old Grand Tour to cross the Channel and even — as Wordsworth did himself, on foot — to cross the Alps.

The fact that a taste for European travel had been created *before* the Napoleonic War took place, helps to explain why many Britons looked on the war with resentment as a restriction on their personal liberty. It is not in the least surprising that during the brief peace of Amiens in 1802-3 British travellers should have gone scurrying in their hundreds to France, Italy, Germany, and Switzerland, all of which had been closed to them for the best part of ten years; nor that some of the more reckless travellers should have found themselves stranded in Europe when the peace came to an end. An even longer period of isolation from Europe now began: the fighting dragged on for another twelve years, with remarkable psychological effects in Britain.

173

It may be that islanders are, by heredity, instinctively interested in making long journeys. At any rate, when the British people found themselves robbed of their old freedom to visit Europe by Napoleon's system of blockades, their craving to travel became intense, and led to bold new patterns of behaviour. Byron, as we have seen, created an alternative Grand Tour in the Eastern Mediterranean, which was eagerly pursued by a number of the wealthy with time on their hands, young men who in the old days would have set out on the orthodox mainland route to Italy as a matter of course. Less rich but equally adventurous men in their twenties and thirties felt so strongly about travelling abroad that they joined the Navy or Army with the wish to see the world as their main motive. Those who chose the Navy were generally luckier; for while some army officers, Wellington among them, fought in India, many sailed directly from England to take part in the Peninsular War, and saw no action elsewhere. An alternative to the Navy or Army was a career with one of the great trading corporations, such as the East India Company, which might result sooner or later in a distant foreign posting.

The rest of the population, denied these outlets, had to make up for what they were missing as best they could. Many people became great armchair travellers. Magazines and reviews of the period were full of articles describing journeys overseas or the customs of other lands. Books on every kind of travel multiplied at an astonishing rate in the Regency. It is doubtful, in fact, if there has ever been quite so pronounced a demand in Britain for the literature of travel. This is all the more significant when one takes into account that photography had not yet been invented. Series of topographical engravings could be purchased, while the most expensive travel books were illustrated by hand-coloured plates of excellent quality; but very few periodicals carried illustrations, and those which did offered no more to stimulate the reader's imagination than crudely reproduced line engravings. When this situation is contrasted with today's abundance of 'photojournalism', both in colour and black and white, of film travelogues and television documentaries dealing with overseas countries and their natural history, the Regency is bound to seem visually undernourished.

Two points, however, can be made on the other side. The first is that prints and engravings, sold separately from books, were probably more popular than their modern pictorial equivalents, precisely because they formed the only visual record of geographical (and other) subjects which was available. It was fashionable to frequent print shops in the Regency, just as now the custom is to spend money on records and cassettes. The number of topographical commissions accepted even by artists as distinguished as Turner is proof of the importance of landscape series in the market for original drawings, watercolours and every kind of reproduction. Secondly, and no less important, readers who had to rely on the written word alone for their idea of what places looked like expected very detailed descriptions from travel writers, and they were probably more skilled in visualizing scenes (albeit often in ignorance of what the originals were actually like) than subsequent generations who have been used to copiously illustrated books and magazines. The 'mind's eye' learned to supply its own pictures, encouraging active reading, in the same way that the habit of making sketches in the countryside bred a more alert habit of perception than (with honourable exceptions) the pocket camera does. Schoolboys may have grown up with very inadequate ideas of the appearance of places they had never seen, but they were continually trying to imagine what these places must be like, which in itself was a spur to go and see them.

Similarly, there were advantages as well as drawbacks in methods of travel in the early nineteenth century, painfully slow though these must appear in comparison with modern air, sea and land communications. Floating in James Sadler's air balloon above Oxford in 1810, or sailing in a packet boat on the Mediterranean at a speed of a few knots (a familiar experience for Byron), or journeying up the Great North Road in a mail coach at ten miles an hour did not bring the traveller to his destination quickly, in modern terms; but at least it allowed him to observe more of the passing scene than can be seen clearly from today's fast-moving forms of transport. Moreover, most of those who wrote about their journeys had covered at least some part of the ground they described on horseback or on foot. As a result, they knew intimately the land which their readers wished to learn about, and the human scale of their experience is reflected in their writing. It was the last age of the horse, and of relatively unhurried travelling. With the coming of steam, those who published *Tours* and diaries of their travels would rely more on hastily made notes and on secondhand information, less on thorough familiarity with the villages and fields lying between places large enough to have railway stations.

To Regency Britons, communications seemed immeasurably faster than they had been in the past — speed of transport is always relative to its period. Whether one set out in a mail coach or in a private carriage such as a phaeton, distances between places in Britain appeared to have shrunk since the eighteenth century. This was partly because coachmakers had worked hard to improve the design of every type of vehicle. Carriages were lighter and therefore swifter; and even when the time of a journey was only fractionally reduced, more comfortable suspension made a world of difference to the traveller's feelings. Much was owing to John Palmer, who in 1782 had established for the Post Office a special service of coaches for the conveyance of mails. His conditions were that they should travel at high speed (eight miles an hour), convey a strictly limited number of passengers, carry an armed guard in case of trouble from highwaymen, and be exempt from the tolls exacted from other carriages at turnpikes, the barriers erected by those responsible for maintaining particular stretches of road.

Palmer was a prickly, tenacious individual, who spent his later years pursuing claims for compensation from the Post Office — to such good effect that he had a pension of £3,000 a year from 1793, and then received a lump sum of £50,000 in the Regency — but those who compared the new situation on the roads with the old agreed that not only the mail service but passenger travel had benefited very considerably from his efforts. For one thing, highwaymen, who had preyed on travellers virtually at will in the first half of the eighteenth century, never dared to attack the armed mail coaches of the Post Office; as the profits from this form of crime dwindled, so did the activity of the criminals. But more significant was the pressure for change which the development of Palmer's system placed on the more backward turnpike trusts. With mail coaches running from London in every direction — to Exeter, Doncaster, Brighton and Edinburgh — it was essential that roads should be of uniformly good quality. Palmer's staff were quick to criticize when they were dissatisfied; and this criticism was soon taken seriously because no regional group liked it when their few miles of road were held up to scorn throughout the land.

On the eve of the Regency there occurred an episode destined to

176

have important results for all road travellers in Britain, which brought together, curiously, prominent Irish politicians, the Post Office, rural Wales and a Scottish road engineer. Since the Irish Union of 1801 and the abolition of the Dublin Parliament there had been an increase in the volume of passenger traffic across the St George's Channel as Irish members travelled between their constituencies and Westminster. Their recognized route was through Holyhead. In response to their insistent demands, a mail coach was put on between Holyhead and Shrewsbury in 1808. But so poor were the Welsh roads that it was found impossible to operate the service with any regularity, and within a few months it had to be withdrawn. Neither the politicians nor Palmer's men of the mails were silent about what they described as primitive roads. In 1810 an official survey of the problems involved in making the road from Holyhead satisfactory for coach traffic was entrusted to Thomas Telford.

Telford was the natural choice for the job, because his first post in England had been as County Surveyor of Shropshire, and in addition to being familiar with the roads and waterways of Wales and western England he was experienced in carrying out work for the Government. Even now he was responsible for constructing the massive Caledonian Canal, linking the northern coast of Scotland near Inverness with the western seaboard, as well as for the largest programme of roadbuilding ever undertaken in the Scottish Highlands. Yet there was no fear that he would neglect the new commission; for thoroughness was his watchword in all that he did. Within a year he had submitted a detailed report recommending that a great road be made between London and Holyhead, worthy to become a principal artery of the new United Kingdom. Irish and Welsh interests were both satisfied by his scheme, but nothing could be done until the struggle against Napoleon was over.

In 1815, therefore, a Board of Parliamentary Commissioners was duly appointed, and Telford began to implement his plans with their authority and approval. In 1819 seven Welsh turnpike trusts were incorporated together and placed under the management of the Board. This was an indication of the future pattern in national planning of communications: while there would be no Ministry of Transport for a long time yet, central authority was gradually beginning to counterbalance and in some cases to replace local control. The plan Telford had put forward took many years to execute in full, as it was easily the most ambitious of its kind ever to have got beyond the drawing-board stage — the equivalent in its own terms of Nash's vision of Regent Street. Not only did Telford have to widen and reconstruct seventy miles of highway close to London; there were many poor stretches of road in provincial England and Wales requiring to be remade from the foundations; and above all, he faced the challenge of building twenty-two miles of completely new road from Holyhead across Anglesey. (Thus everyone who travels today on the A5 owes a debt to Telford.) The symbol of his brilliant success in all of this remains the 579 foot iron suspension bridge spanning the Menai Straits, described by a recent transport historian, Jack Simmons, as 'an astonishing exhibition of . . . lightness and grace'.

Telford has claims to be considered as one of the outstanding benefactors of his age. Southey, who travelled with him in Scotland in 1819, described him aptly as 'the Colossus of roads', and it is not surprising that the previous year he had been elected first President of the newly created Institute of Civil Engineers.[1] The public recognized that by his great energy and care for detail he had done more than anyone in living memory to facilitate travel in Britain. But there was one drawback about Telford's new roads, and that was their cost. People readily accepted that there must be a good system of drainage for any road worthy of the name, and admired the way in which Telford's workmen consistently produced an even curved surface made up of small broken stones or gravel; this 'camber' was found to be infinitely superior to an initially flat road, which quickly became rutted. However, some of those who had to finance Telford's improvements dared to question if he was right to insist, as he always did, on the need for a deep foundation of large stones — the costliest part of the road-making process he had devised. They noted that another Scottish road engineer, John Loudon McAdam, who in 1816 was appointed General Surveyor of the 146 miles of road in the vicinity of Bristol, seemed to have invented a method of roadmaking which possessed the same advantages as Telford's but without requiring an expensive base of heavy stones. As a contemporary jingle proves, McAdam in turn came in for criticism . . .

[1] Southey wrote, 'Telford's is a happy life: everywhere making roads, building bridges, forming canals, and creating harbours — works of sure, solid, permanent utility, everywhere employing a great number of persons.'

The Oxford Street natives fierce arguments raise
About the best method of *mending their ways*:
One party contending, 'midst loud altercation,
That nothing will do but Macadamization;
Another declares if their cash is to save meant,
The road must be made o'er a hard stony pavement.

But McAdam's ideas caught on very quickly when he published his *Practical Essay on the Scientific Repair and Preservation of Roads* (1819) and *The Present State of Road-Making* (1820). He had in fact discovered a thoroughly sound and relatively cheap system of road-making, as a result of which it became possible to improve communications in parts of Britain which could not afford Telford's more elaborate approach to the task. Before long he was asked to advise on roadbuilding schemes all over England, and in 1827 was made General Surveyor of Roads for the whole of the United Kingdom.

Early nineteenth-century travellers frequently commented on the pleasure of bowling along a newly-made highway in one of the splendid mail coaches Palmer had made popular. The feeling of exhilaration which many experienced was eloquently described by Thomas De Quincey, who, in *The English Mail Coach*, wrote of an impression made

> first, through velocity, at that time unprecedented — for they first revealed the glory of motion; secondly, through grand effects for the eye between lamplight and the darkness upon solitary roads; thirdly, through animal beauty and power so often displayed in the class of horses selected for this mail service; fourthly, through conscious presence of a central intellect, that, in the midst of vast distances — of storms, of darkness, or danger — overruled all obstacles into one steady co-operation to a national result.

Part of the excitement of riding in a mail coach, according to De Quincey, had to do with a sensation of power, for everything else on the road had to give way to the royal conveyance:

> The connection of the mail with the state and the executive government gave to the whole mail establishment an official grandeur which did us service on the roads, and invested us with seasonable terrors. Not the less impressive were those terrors, because their legal limits were imperfectly ascertained. Look at those turnpike gates; with what deferential hurry, with what an obedient start, they fly open at our approach! Look at that long line of carts and carters ahead, audaciously usurping the very crest of the road. Ah! traitors, they do not hear us yet; but, as soon as the dreadful blast of our horn reaches them with proclamation of our approach, see with what frenzy of trepidation they fly to their horses' heads . . .

179

De Quincey's imaginative cast of mind made him an observant passenger on the Oxford mail, capable of expressing his sense of the romance of making a journey in the new style. Persons who lived more by the clock than this most casual and dilatory of essayists welcomed especially the punctuality of the mail coaches. For the first time in their lives, they were released from the uncertainty of not knowing when they would arrive at the end of their journey. To De Quincey, one suspects, this was not necessarily a liberating thought, for he was a gipsy at heart.

There were, in fact, two distinct groups of British travellers at this period, the practically-minded and the devotees of natural beauty; or to put it another way, students of improvement, and students of the Picturesque. Although the second group was much the larger, including as it did individuals and families in pursuit of pleasure, the tradition of observing agricultural, industrial and social habits in regions other than one's own with a view to becoming more fully informed was also very strong. It had taken hold as a direct result of innovations in farming methods made by the pioneering improvers of the continuing Agricultural Revolution. Much had been written since the publication of Arthur Young's *Annals of Agriculture* (1784) about the methods of cultivation, and the large-scale enclosures, of men like Coke of Norfolk. But while farmers read of the latest experimental techniques of their prominent fellows with keen interest, they liked to see with their own eyes before being persuaded to change their ways; the actual appearance of the land, and not the evidence of the written word, was their test of success. Cobbett's masterpiece, *Rural Rides* (1830), which brings together the facts and impressions noted on several journeys in different parts of Britain, communicates very clearly the English countryman's determination to see and judge for himself. Cobbett takes as much interest in the fate of the unemployed as in the technical developments in agriculture, and observes people's leisure habits no less attentively than their ways of working, for his subject is nothing less than the changing pattern of life of a whole nation. Despite being an exceptional traveller, however, by virtue of his broad experience and lifelong commitment to ideas of political and social reform, he belongs in his general outlook with other progressive farmers in his time who believed in making journeys in order to learn.

It would be fascinating to reconstruct regional maps of Regency

Britain showing how certain farmers became innovators after venturing beyond their own county boundaries on 'fact-finding tours'. Unfortunately, even when they led to changes in local farming practice, the lessons of such journeys were seldom written down; information has to be pieced together from family letters and legal documents, including estate papers, in Local Record Offices. But a number of the farmer travellers did keep journals, a few of which found their way into print, and from a typical example it is possible to understand how the 'spirit of improvement' came to be applied even in remote places. In 1810 Alexander Dennis, a prosperous Cornishman who farmed near Trembath, by Penzance, and who appears never to have travelled very far beyond his home ground before that year, 'took it in [his] head to spend a little time in travelling'.[1] Setting out towards Truro on 4 May, Dennis covered 1,800 miles during the next eighty-four days, noting wherever he went not only what interested him professionally, but anything else which caught his eye. His Tour was in two parts, with London as the link between the two. First, he travelled in the West of England and the Midlands, visiting Bristol, Birmingham and Leicester before going to London. This part of his Journal reveals that oxen were still in constant use in the south-west, although apparently nowhere else in Britain. After visiting Birmingham market, Dennis wrote sadly,

> Farmers seem to be very much in the dark; nothing can be more against their own interest, than their neglecting to rear and work oxen.

The disappearance of oxen from the land clearly had symbolic importance for this Cornish farmer; it was the loss of an essential part of old England. He noted an occasion when he was close to Worcester as 'the last time I saw oxen at work'. And, being a little set in his ways, he found other things to disapprove of, including the behaviour of a courting couple in the public coach between Bridgewater and Bristol:

---

[1] As he explains in the preface to *Journal of a Tour Through Great Part of England and Scotland* (Penzance, 1816) he originally had no thought of publication, but after listening to him speak of his travels his friends persuaded him to change his mind:

> The following Notes . . . taken for the amusement of the writer . . . would never have been printed, had it not been for a motion made by his much respected friend Henry Boase Esq. of Penzance, the 14th October 1813, and which was apparently supported by the unanimous voice of the company.

> Travelled in a long coach that had different apartments. — I was shut up with two lovers, the most insipid fools I ever met with; I was relieved at last by some person getting out of the other part.

On the other hand, there was a great deal to please him, especially in Warwickshire, whose farmers he described as 'a very bold and sprightly people'. He liked the fact that every part of the county had been enclosed, and wrote, 'Had I been young I would certainly endeavour to settle here.'[1] The only shortcoming of the Warwickshire farmers as far as he could see was their disappointing failure to conserve manure in a manner which might provide abundant supply of fertilizer; he noted in his Journal detailed instructions for making a manure pit. Everything else about the farms in the county of Shakespeare's birth delighted him, including the girls. It seems clear that had he been younger, not only would he have settled in Warwickshire, he would also have been tempted to ask one of these pretty and accomplished Warwickshire maidens to become his wife — Mr Palfrey's daughter, for instance . . .

> Mr Palfrey's daughter is a most ingenious girl, she is fond of gardening, plays well on the pianoforte, and her needlework is incomparable.

This is the authentic voice of the eighteenth century, with its admiration for order and serene domesticity, praising a prosperous Regency farmer's daughter who seemed to possess these virtues.

Dennis, being a practical man, was usually content to record what he saw without adding a great deal by way of descriptive detail or personal opinion. The laconic nature of his Journal entries serves at times to bring out very directly the difference between his Britain and that of today. An example occurs in the short section of his Journal which deals with the stay he made in London after completing the first part of his Tour. Part of his entry for 13 June 1810 reads,

> In the evening went to the Old Bailey, where I saw Jones and Solomon tried for robbing a Mr Dodd of his pocket book, and for which they were sentenced to be transported for life.

[1] Cornwall was notorious for having failed to enclose its 'waste' lands. *In Observations and Remarks, During Four Excursions, Made to Various Parts of Great Britain. In the Years 1810 and 1811* (1812) Daniel C. Webb commented severely, 'The great demand for agricultural produce requires us to use our most strenuous effort at improvement in the cultivation of our lands, together with a division and enclosure of what are called wastes, by the authority of the law. The public good should supersede the advantage of individuals.'

Perhaps if the death penalty had been imposed, as by law it could have been, he might have had more to say. As it is, his words convey the impression that while Dennis had found the spectacle of a criminal trial at the Old Bailey of great interest, he was not in any way shocked by what must now seem an extraordinarily harsh sentence. Here is a reminder that laws for the protection of property were designed to instil terror into criminals (according to twentieth-century usage, 'petty' criminals) such as Jones and Solomon. It may well be that Dennis had known of instances of prosecution for infringement of the Game Laws in his own part of Cornwall; although attitudes towards poaching were generally lenient, a few landowners in every county still set man-traps on their estates, and were happy to see poachers sent to prison or to Botany Bay. In London, Dennis may have reasoned, a man's pocket-book was worth much more than a brace of pheasants in the country.

The second stage of Dennis's Tour took him to East Anglia and then north by York and Newcastle to Scotland, where he visited Edinburgh, Dundee and Stirling, before crossing to Glasgow and returning home by way of Carlisle and Lancaster. This part of his Journal gives further proof of how much on face value persons interested primarily in 'improvement' judged places which they approached as strangers. Dennis thought Cambridge, with the single exception of King's College, a 'very poor looking place', but then he liked to see new buildings in a town, rather than buildings of historic interest. He was much more enthusiastic about Tyneside, and especially about Newcastle, which he described as 'a large good town, well built, streets wide and well paved; the houses in general very good'. (He was also impressed by Newcastle's efficient 'police' — the word predates Sir Robert Peel's police force, with which it is usually associated.) Similarly, while he wrote of the Old Town of Edinburgh

> . . . it would make any one smile to see the dirty creatures emerging through a kind of half door into the streets that are as dirty as the houses and occupiers: the walls are as black as my ink-stand

he had nothing but good to say of the well laid-out and notably clean squares and streets of the Georgian New Town.

Although he was scornful of what passed for sheep north of the Border, commenting 'were you to see the sheep in Scotland, you would scarcely know what to call them, whether sheep or goats',

Dennis was in other respects greatly impressed by the superiority of the northern English and Lowland Scottish agriculture over that of Cornwall. The land, he observed, was much more intensively cultivated, there was less waste, and master and men alike worked harder than 'the slothful Cornishman'. He was sorry to have to leave the good houses and beautiful farms set in the countryside to the west of Stirling, but Glasgow won his heart also, because it looked 'like a place very recently built'. Glasgow in fact was a mediaeval city which had already lost many of its older buildings during the first phase of its massive on-going industrial expansion. Here, as in Birmingham with its 'very wonderful' brass foundries, Dennis felt overawed by the scale and variety of typically modern manufacturing processes. Muslin was woven in one factory by a machine which was almost completely automatic in its working, and this took his breath away:

> What astonished me most was the weaving of muslins; — the looms are worked by a steam engine, all going, no hand near them, it almost inclined me to think that they were moved by enchantment; there is allowed one girl to every two looms in case a thread should break to fasten it, when that happens the girl stops the loom by a little trigger, fastens the thread and sets to work again.[1]

Any idea that industrial cities immediately repelled people bred in the country is shown by such travel journals as Dennis's to be false. The great cities of the new age and their manufacturing methods were undoubtedly of interest to those who came to them merely as visitors. But had Dennis been compelled to stay and work in Glasgow or in Manchester (where he observed 'no indigent poor nor loungers'), his reaction would have been less favourable.

Someone with a much more cosmopolitan background who travelled extensively in Britain in the same year as Alexander Dennis was Louis Simond, a shipowner from the United States. Simond had been born into a wealthy Protestant family in Lyon in 1767, but had emigrated from France to America shortly before the outbreak of the Revolution. He had married an English wife, a niece of the

---

[1] Many visitors to factories at this time likened automatic machine weaving to magic. Thus D. C. Webb wrote of cotton-weaving by steam looms at Manchester: 'It appeared like magic, to see weaving thus performed so regularly without hands' (*Observations and Remarks*, 1812, p. 193). Another common comparison was between iron-works and Hell; Webb wrote of the iron-works at Bilson, ten miles from Birmingham, 'The roaring of the furnaces, the clanking of iron-chains, and machinery, reminded the traveller of the poetical descriptions given us of the infernal regions' (*ibid*, p. 186).

radical politician John Wilkes, and it was this family connection with England, along with their interest in shipping, which brought the couple to Falmouth just before Christmas 1809. Their visit, which lasted for twenty-one months, proved to be a turning-point in their lives, for after going back to America to settle up his affairs in 1811, Simond returned to England and lived there until the end of the war with France (what he thought of Britain's naval war of 1812 with America is a topic which invites speculation); then on the restoration of the Bourbons to the French throne, he and his wife went to live on the Continent, first in France, and later in Switzerland, where Simond died in 1831.

So far from being a casual traveller, Simond planned from the beginning to publish his travel diary, and it was entirely in keeping with his thorough approach to things that after *Journal of Tour and Residence in Great Britain by a Native of France* appeared in 1815 and was well received, he should himself immediately have translated the book into French. There was an air of Huguenot severity about Simond. Mrs Grant of Laggan, a writer whom he met in Scotland, described him as 'a dark, gloomy-looking man', and was even less flattering about his wife, saying she was 'the plainest, worst-dressed woman' she had ever set eyes on. But Mrs Grant did have the grace to add that Simond was evidently a man of 'talent, great refinement and agreeable conversation', and judged his character to be 'fastidious and philosophic in the highest sense'.

While waiting in Liverpool in September 1811 before his ship sailed back to America, Simond summed up his impressions of Britain and the British people. The first idea which came into his mind was distinctly hostile:

> ... its political institutions present a detail of corrupt practices — of profusion — and of personal ambition, under the mask of public-spirit very carelessly put on, more disgusting than I should have expected: the workings of the selfish passions are exhibited in all their nakedness and deformity.

What had disgusted him about the British ruling classes was chiefly their conduct towards those less well off than themselves. He felt very strongly that a great deal which ostensibly was done for 'the public good' was actually a form of self-interest on the part of those whose possessions or education gave them the right to control other men's lives. A case in point was the way in which the Government had resisted reform of criminal laws which, after he had heard in a House of Commons debate that someone could be sentenced to death for 'stealing to the value of five shillings out of a shop', Simond thought unjust and arbitrary. Yet, as he freely admitted, there was another and better side to the nation in which he and his wife had been living . . .

> I have found the great mass of the people richer, happier, and more respectable, than any other with which I am acquainted. I have seen prevailing among all ranks of people that emulation of industry and independence which characterize a state of advancing civilization, properly directed. . . The government of England is eminently practical. The one under which I have lived many years [that of the United States] might be defined, on the contrary, a government of abstract principles. The lower people in England hold other nations in thorough contempt. The same rank in France, in the interior of the country at least, scarcely know there are other nations — their geography is that of the Chinese.

While he had disliked living in 'dingy' London, where he thought the concern of people of fashion to have an address in the West End was absurd ('Every minute of longitude east is equal to as many degrees of gentility *minus*, or towards west, *plus*'), almost every other place he had visited in Britain had appealed to him. This is a significant tribute, as he had not only covered the ground of Dennis's Tour, but added to it most of Wales and part of the Scottish Highlands. Simond was well read, and therefore fully conversant with the cult of 'the Picturesque' which had been made popular at the end of the previous century by such writers as William Gilpin, who published *Tours* of a highly idiosyncratic kind, full of praise for the 'rough' and 'pleasantly irregular' qualities of nature. He was capable of entering into the mood for the Picturesque which even now encouraged hosts of British travellers to visit the Welsh mountains, the Lake District and Perthshire hills described by Scott in *The Lady of the Lake,* but he did not allow the fashion for scenery to dull his judgment. A good example of his cool descriptive writing is this passage about a journey through part of Wales:

> We are at Cowbridge, Glamorganshire. Forty miles today through Newport, Cardiff, and Landaff — the country just uneven enough to afford extensive views over an immense extent of cultivation, lost in the blue distance, nothing wild, or, properly speaking, picturesque, but all highly beautiful, and every appearance of prosperity. Wales seems more inhabited, at least more strewed over with habitations of all sorts, scattered or in villages, than any part of England we have seen, and which are rendered more conspicuous by white-washing of the most resplendent

186

whiteness. Every cottage too has its roses, and honeysuckles, and vines, and neat walk to the door; and this attention bestowed on objects of mere pleasurable comforts, is the surest indication of minds at ease, and not under the immediate pressure of poverty.

Simond found it interesting that whereas in the south of England most adults 'above poverty' had visited London, and many indeed did so at least once every year, undertaking a journey of 100 or 200 miles on impulse without troubling like their French counterparts to make their wills before they left to visit their capital city, there was so little travel in north Wales that, at least in the vicinity of Aberystwyth, 'the post-horses [were] commonly employed in husbandry' — which was of course to change in a few years' time when Telford's new road bridge was completed. Nothing in this, however, led him to alter his judgment that the Welsh people in 1811 were 'one of the happiest, if not the happiest, in the world'; he may have thought they were all the happier, though less well informed, for having stayed at home.

The Highlands of Scotland puzzled him at first, when he ventured into Perthshire in the autumn of 1810:

> Sept. 1 — To Killin, only 21 miles to-day, through much the same sort of country as yesterday; glen after glen — green and bare, and deserted, with towering hills all round; one of them seemed to have the form of an immense crater — a hollow cup — but all the detached masses below were granite and schistus, and nothing volcanic. Beautiful pieces of quartz lay about everywhere. Some of the hills could not be less than 2,000 feet high. The Tay, an inconsiderable mountain torrent, descended with us the whole day. The question occurs naturally in traversing these solitudes, where are the men? Where are the Highlanders? And if you are told that the system of sheep-farming has banished them from their country, then you would be apt to ask, where are the sheep? Very few indeed are seen; the grass is evidently not half eaten down — hardly touched, indeed, in many places.

If Simond discovered an answer to the last of these questions during the few days he spent in Perthshire, he failed to record it (at no point in the nineteenth century was the *entire* unforested area of the Highlands given over to sheepwalks, although it is certainly revealing that as early as this a visitor should have been warned to expect to see sheep in place of people); but he did meet and talk with a number of Highland families, including some surviving in circumstances of 'abject poverty', if healthily enough, on a diet of fish, potatoes and oats. Being an unsentimental American businessman, Simond wrote of these people without much insight into the emotional and socio-economic complexities of Scottish history,

> I do not understand what the Highlanders gain by migrating to America. With some labour they can procure here, what is not to be had there without labour.

He was already eager to set foot in Edinburgh, which delighted his Huguenot soul through being cleaner and closer to the country than London, and which he was to describe before he left as 'in a great degree, the Geneva of Britain'.

Dennis and Simond were each in their own ways 'men of science' in that they travelled in pursuit of new knowledge rather than to gratify a taste for the romantic. One further example of a more strictly scientific traveller's exploration of Britain should be mentioned at this point. In 1815 William Smith, an Oxfordshire-born mines surveyor and geologist, published a *Geological Map of England* on the scale of 5 miles to 1 inch which was more accurate and detailed than anything of the kind which had ever appeared before. (Only about 40 or the 400 copies of the *Map*, which was printed for subscribers, now survive; luckily a number of these are in excellent condition.) Such a survey in the twentieth century is almost always the work of a team, but Smith's *Geological Map of England* resulted from systematic journeys which he had made without help between 1800 and 1813. In each of these years he covered about 10,000 miles, usually on horseback, visiting quarries, claypits and every rocky outcrop which offered clues to the geological nature of the countryside. The full title of his *Map* gives an indication of the range — and depth — of his investigations: 'A Delineation of the Strata of England and Wales, With part of Scotland, exhibiting the Collieries and Mines, the Marshes and Fen Lands originally overflowed by the sea, and the Varieties of Soil, According to the Variations in the Substrata.' Thus in the Regency for the first time it became possible for Britons, or those at any rate living south of the Highland line, to know with some confidence what lay beneath familiar hills and fields. Smith, who was to publish further works of a similar kind in the 1820s deserves to be ranked among the most important early practitioners of the earth sciences and of geological map-making in Britain.

But while the secrets of mines and fossilized remains under the earth fascinated the few, most travellers remained happily ignorant of what lay beneath their feet. Their wish was to be uplifted, to gain aesthetic inspiration and a sense of well-being from the contemplation of rugged mountain scenery and lakes of dazzling beauty. They were in search of that intensity of feeling which thanks, among other influences, to William Gilpin and his writings on the Picturesque, the poems of Wordsworth and the landscape art of Turner, was assumed by many to be the proper emotional response to Nature. Snowdonia, and the Trossachs district close to Ellen's Isle in Loch Katrine which had been glowingly described by Scott, already drew them in large and increasing numbers; but the Lake District was their spiritual home. As yet, they were mostly conveyed from the south in carriages, to stay in posting-inns or private lodgings. At Windermere, Simond wrote in September 1810:

> There are no retired places in England, no place where you see only the country and countrymen; you meet, on the contrary, everywhere town-people elegantly dressed and lodged, having a number of servants, and exchanging invitations. England, in short, seems to be the country-house of London; cultivated for amusement only, and where all is subservient to picturesque luxury and ostentation. Here we are, in a remote corner of the country, among mountains, 278 miles from the capital — a place without commerce or manufacturers, not on any high road; yet everything is much the same as in the neighbourhood of London. Land, half-rock, is bought up at any price, merely on account of the beauty of the spot.

Only the boldest tourists (significantly, this word was a very recent coinage) ventured far from the beaten track, for the precipitous slopes and uncertain weather of the region instilled a healthy respect into early nineteenth-century travellers. On the other hand, nearly everyone brought with him or her a diary or sketchbook, and eagerly set down impressions of the surrounding scenery. These, it was hoped, would act as a permanent record of days of freedom spent close to the dwelling-place of the Muses, and brighten up long winter evenings back in Hampstead or Chelsea.

In view of the continuing public interest in the Picturesque, it was inevitable that sooner or later someone should decide to treat the whole subject of travel satirically. The way in which this actually came about illustrates among other things how important art-dealers were in Regency society. In the opening years of the century Rudolph Ackermann had opened a shop, the Repository of Arts, at 101 The Strand — the site today of the Savoy Hotel. He had good contacts both with artists and with other dealers, and quickly established a name for the excellence of his topographical prints and art books, coming to rival such older established firms as Colnaghi's of Bond Street and Boydells' enterprising Shakespeare Gallery in Pall Mall. Ackermann was lucky enough to employ one of the most gifted caricaturists of the age, Thomas Rowlandson, who collaborated with another artist named Pugin (father of the architect) in producing 104 aquatint plates for his three-volume *Microcosm of London*, soon recognized as a remarkably comprehensive and lively visual record of the appearance of the city at this period; Pugin had drawn the architectural details, Rowlandson the human figures in the foreground.

While this work was being compiled, a friend of Rowlandson's, the actor John Bannister, hit on the idea of a series of cartoons depicting an absurd pedant on his travels. 'You must fancy a skin-and-bone hero', Bannister told the caricaturist,

> a pedantic old prig, in a shovel-hat, with a pony, sketching tools, and rattle traps, and place him in such scrapes as travellers frequently meet with, — hedge ale-houses, second and third-rate inns, thieves, gibbets, mad bulls, and the like.

Rowlandson soon dashed off a number of drawings of a long-chinned figure in clerical attire exactly answering this description, and Ackermann made up his mind to publish them. Knowing, however, that cartoons of this type would create more interest if accompanied by a text which matched their spirit of comedy, he approached a writer who had already helped him by composing the 'letterpress' or descriptive commentary for one of his first topographical publications, the *History of the River Thames*. This was an old Etonian called William Combe (he liked to be referred to as 'William Combe, Esq'), who had in his youth spent a considerable fortune inherited from his father, but who now, in his late sixties, was imprisoned for debt in the King's Bench Prison at Southwark. Combe was the author of many books, successful verse satires among them; but the chronic financial problems which had dogged him for most of his mature life had combined with the innocent snobbery of his nature to make him prefer anonymity to literary fame. He was naturally pleased to be visited at Number 2 in the State House of the Bench by so distinguished a person as Ackermann. The two came to a gentleman's agreement that in return for supplying Ackermann with the letterpress for various publications he had planned, including the Rowlandson cartoons, Combe would be entitled to draw on an account controlled by the Repository of Arts — an arrangement which worked very well, although it led Ackermann to comment many years later that Combe never ceased to draw on the account until he ceased to breathe.

Superb though the Rowlandson drawings were, Combe's immediate task was not an easy one, in that he had to write verses which would create a humorous narrative without failing to 'explain' the situation of each particular cartoon. Moreover, he was in the ironical position of being asked to versify about travel when he knew that he would be in prison for the rest of his life. But this was not the first time he had put to the test Dr Johnson's remark that man may write at any time if he will set himself doggedly to it; and his embarrassing lack of freedom merely lent an additional satirical edge to the tale he proceeded to make up of a pendant suddenly possessed of the idea that he might make a fortune out of a book describing his travels:

> The School was done, the bus'ness o'er
> When, tir'd of Greek and Latin lore,
> Old Syntax sought his easy chair,
> And sat in calm composure there.
> His wife was to a neighbour gone,
> To hear the chit-chat of the town;
> And left him the infrequent pow'r
> Of brooding thro' a quiet hour . . .

Having told his wife that he has decided to 'ride and write and sketch and print', Dr Syntax sets out like his distant literary ancestor Don Quixote on an old nag, Grizzle. His route leads him to Oxford, and then by way of York and Castle Howard in Yorkshire (seat of a contemporary of Combe's at Eton) to Keswick. 'The pleasures of the chace', William Gilpin had solemnly written, 'are universal . . . Shall we suppose it a greater pleasure to the sportsman to pursue the beauties of nature?' Combe's learned Doctor is made to express himself a little differently:

> Your sport, my Lord, I cannot take,
> For I must go and hunt a lake;
> And while you chase the flying deer,
> I must fly off to Windermere,
> Instead of hallowing to a fox,
> I much catch echoes from the rocks.
> With curious eye and active scent,

I on the *picturesque* am bent.
This is my game; I must pursue it,
And make it where I cannot view it,
Though in good truth, but do not flout me,
I bear that self-same thing about me.
If in man's form you wish to see
The *picturesque*, pray look at me.
I am myself, without a flaw,
The very *picturesque* I draw.

Combe and Rowlandson did not meet while working on this project, which was first published serially as 'The Schoolmaster's Tour' in Ackermann's *Poetical Magazine* between 1809 and 1811. When in 1812 their joint work was reissued, with a title-page designed by Rowlandson, as *The Tour of Doctor Syntax in Search of the Picturesque*, Combe, who still remained anonymous, explained in an Advertisement how he had carried out his part of the bargain:

> An Etching or Drawing was . . . sent to me every month, and I composed a certain proportion of pages in verse, in which, of course, the subject of the design was included: the rest depended upon what my imagination could furnish. — When the first print was sent to me, I did not know what would be the subject of the second; and in this manner, in a great measure, the Artist continued designing, and I writing, every month for two years, 'till a work containing near ten thousand lines was produced.

Syntax's *Tour* became a firm favourite with the public, who delighted in Rowlandson's portrayal of his hero tumbling into the water while attempting to sketch a ruined castle beside a lake, and in the idea of the regulars in a country pub being sent to sleep by 'Doctor Syntax Reading his Tour'. It would never again be possible after this good-natured send-up to take quite seriously the talk of men and women to whom 'Picturesque' was a holy word, for a free spirit incarcerated in the debtors' prison had mocked the excesses to which this cult could lead.

Within days of Napoleon's abdication in April 1814, people who had never previously had the chance to do so found themselves eagerly packing for the Continent and joining long and excited queues in Passport Offices. Most of those who crossed the Channel in the few weeks which followed were well-to-do members of the middle and upper classes, but nearly every age and walk of life was represented, for the journey to Paris was looked on as a symbol of victory — and therefore as something on which a lifetime's savings were not wasted. Cartoonists turned the new craze to account by mocking John Bull as a traveller of large prejudices and scant respect for the customs of foreigners. Their satire was only just, because a number of British travellers behaved when on French soil in an outrageous manner. Not only did they refer loudly and publicly to every military and naval incident in living memory capable of being described as a French defeat, they stared at the people into whose midst they had come as if they were visiting one of the zoological collections which were becoming popular in Regency Britain.

Such tourists were in the minority, but the travel literature produced in this period and in the post-war years proper shows that even well-educated Britons viewed France with deep cultural suspicion and some contempt. One of the first British journalists to secure a passport and a commission from a leading publisher was John Scott, editor of the Sunday *Champion*. His books *A Visit to Paris in 1814; being a Review of the Moral, Political, Intellectual, and Social Condition of the French Capital* (1815) and *Paris Revisited, in 1815, by way of Brussels: including a walk over the Field of Battle at Waterloo* (1816) went through several editions in two years, and did much to confirm English readers who had stayed at home in their distrust of all things French.

Scott was an alert observer, interested alike in buildings, in works of art in the Louvre (many of them the spoils of Napoleon's campaigns), and in the subtleties of the changing political scene in Paris — but everything was brought to the test of an alien standard, and nearly everything French was found wanting. The French Press, he noticed, failed 'to give a regular announcement of births, marriages, and deaths'; this was proof that France, with all its show of social activity, lacked genuine feeling for individuals. Disappointed at the absence of pleasure boats on the Seine, he made another comparison with England and commented,

> . . . the taste of the Parisians is by no means aquatic. They are not conscious, apparently, that water can be made to conduce pleasure, unless it is in a bath, or squirting jets through pipes.

But his strongest condemnation was reserved for the Palais Royal, 'the focus of the Revolution', and now a place of shops, talk, and vice. Here, John Scott believed, the French character was fully revealed in both its weakness and its strength:

> [The Palais Royal] is dissolute, gay, wretched elegant, paltry, busy, and idle: it suggests recollections of atrocity, and supplies sights of fascina-

193

tion: — it displays virtue and vice living on easy terms, and in immediate neighbourhood with each other. Excitements, indulgencies, and privations, — art and vulgarity, — science and ignorance, — artful conspiracies, and careless debaucheries, — all mingle here, forming an atmosphere of various exhalations, a whirl of the most lively images, a stimulating melange of what is most heating, intoxicating, and subduing.

The chapter of *A Visit to Paris* from which this passage comes was to prove influential in moulding British attitudes towards Parisian life, helping to create a myth of French 'decadence'.[1] More than thirty years later, Thackeray, a keen student of everything to do with the Regency, would make Clive Newcome in *The Newcomes* recall Scott's description of the dangerous allure of the Palais Royal:

... we bought Scott's 'Visit to Paris' and 'Paris Revisited', and read them in the diligence. They are famous good reading; but the Palais Royal is very much altered ... there is none of the fun going on which Scott describes.

Thackeray's use of the word 'fun' suggests that the sternly moralistic commentary of travel-writers like John Scott — or Thomas Raffles, who in *Letters During a Tour* (1817) noted in connection with the Palais Royal, 'The quantity of vice in Paris is, indeed, immense, and its varieties are almost unbounded' — sometimes had a very different effect from that which was intended. Like the Folies Bergères at a later date, the Palais Royal attracted young British travellers who had been specifically warned to avoid a place of sin. If they were not in search of 'fun', they wanted to be shocked; and in either case, to judge by Clive Newcome's response, they were liable to be disappointed, at any rate once the nineteenth century reached middle age.[2]

---

[1] Sir Walter Scott contributed to the myth of France also, in his anonymous *Paul's Letters to his Kinsfolk* (1816). 'The French', he wrote, 'act from feeling, and the British from principle.'

The artist B. R. Haydon, a friend of John Scott's was to write in his *Autobiography* of the degree of mutual strangeness and incomprehension existing at this date between the French and their British visitors: 'The French looked on us as if we had dropped out of the moon, and we upon them as if we were dropping into it. Everything was new and fresh. We had thought of France from youth as forbidden ground, as the abode of the enemies of our country. It was extraordinary. They absolutely had houses, churches, streets, fields and children! Both with English and French twenty-five years of peace and rapid inter-communication have so entirely removed this feeling, that it will be hardly possible for posterity to estimate the intensity of national feelings during the revolutionary war. Boys were born, nursed and grew up hating the name of Frenchmen. On half-holidays in Plymouth we used to be drilled, and often have I led out ten or a dozen boys to the cornfields to cut off Frenchmen's heads, which meant slicing every poppy we met, shouting as each head fell, "There goes a Frenchman! huzza!" ... These feelings in S[cott] and myself were inveterate.'

Post-war visitors to France from 'John Bull's other island' were on the whole much less hostile towards French ways than mainland Britons. The novelist Lady Morgan, widely known in the Regency as 'The Wild Irish Girl' after one of her best-known books, proved an enthusiastic apologist for the French people in *France* (1817). She and her doctor husband had been treated with consideration wherever they went, and her book contained such ringing statements as,

> The society of Paris, taken as a whole, and including all parties and factions, is infinitely superior in point of taste, acquirement, and courtesy, to that of the capital of any other nation.

Such unqualified praise was bound to raise objections in Britain, especially as it was accompanied by an analysis of the effects of the Revolution on the life of the poor which was not at all in line with orthodox anti-French opinion. According to Lady Morgan, the French peasantry, and domestic servants, were far better treated than their British counterparts. In France, she saw no evidence of a social split between master and man, whereas

> There is no contrast more shocking and violent, in English society, than that presented by the situation of master and servants, during the hours of social intercourse of fashionable London. For the one, the air is perfumed with roses, and the chill atmosphere of winter expelled by every artificial contrivance; and comfort, enjoyment, and accommodation, are studiously accumulated. For the other, all hardship, suffering, and endurance. Exposed for hours to all the inclemency of the season, in listless idleness, or in vicious excess (the necessary and inevitable alleviation of their degraded situation), this large and useless class of persons gratify the ostentation of their masters, at the expense of health, and of every better feeling and higher consideration.

Even Byron, who singled out Lady Morgan's next travel book, *Italy* (1821), as one of the best ever published on the subject, would have found it hard to think up an argument more calculated to provoke disagreement among his fellow countrymen. In her own way, the wild Irish girl was asking his question, 'Is Earth more free?', and offering as part of her answer, 'Certainly not for the many poor people in Britain.' *France* aroused a storm of protest. *The Quarterly Review* criticized the book as fundamentally immoral and false, and one indignant reader, William Playfair, went so far as to reply to her in a work considerably longer than her own, *France As It Is, Not Lady Morgan's France* (2 volumes, 1819). The French peasantry, according to Playfair, so far from being surrounded by the fruits of a just social system, had 'a stiff haggard worn out appearance'. Lady Morgan's intention, he asserted, had been 'to create discontent in Britain'; she was that dangerous creature, an admirer of democracy — 'This design is the more evident since democratical principles run through the whole work.' He scoffed at her as a childish admirer of the Picturesque, incapable of appreciating the sterling virtues of the British character:

> Lady Morgan appears to have seen France as a child does Bartholomew fair, everything was new to her, and all was admired . . . There is nothing of the picturesque in an English post chaise and four with two postilions, and two out-riders, sweeping along a fine road; but there is a great deal of it in a French diligence, with all its lumber and luggage, (some degrees heavier and clumsier than a common stage waggon), with half-starved horses, and passengers with their heads all wrapped up, as if they were returning from the Battle of Waterloo.

When Lady Morgan returned to Paris in 1818, she was abused by part of the Royalist Press as someone whose distortion of fact in the name of 'sympathy for the Revolution' had brought the fair name of France into disrepute, but warmly welcomed elsewhere as a kind of latterday Joan of Arc. She repeated many times that she had merely told the truth as she had seen it, and never disguised the liberal political principles which coloured her thinking. While shrewdly aware of the effect of publicity, good or bad, on sales of her books, she noted in her diary in March 1819 shortly before leaving for Italy that the life of a celebrity in Paris was exhausting:

> My popularity here increases daily; and, without either vanity or affectation, my notoriety is now more *à charge* and tiresome to me than the profoundest obscurity could possibly have been. I never know the enjoyment of one day, one hour to myself. Strangers of all countries not only write to me to receive them, but actually force the door, dispute the point with my servant, enter my room, and then they excuse this intrusion by talking to me of my 'reputation European'. You have no idea how I pant for silence, solitude, and a long journey, which thank heaven, we are now about to begin. We have been for the last few weeks in a constant round of gaiety and dissipation.

It has recently been said of Lady Morgan that, like the Wife of Bath in Chaucer's *Canterbury Tales*, she had her world in her time. She had certainly loved the social whirl in Paris before the sheer unrelenting pace of it became oppressive. In this she can be compared to the heroine of her friend and fellow countryman Tom

Moore's extremely popular verse satire on the fashion for travelling to France, *The Fudge Family in Paris* (which reached a ninth edition within a year of being published in 1818). Miss Biddy Fudge is not a professional travel-writer, but she too finds the French capital to her taste . . .

> Where shall I begin with the endless delights
> Of this Eden of milliners, monkies, and sights —
> This dear busy place, where there's nothing transacting
> But dressing and dinnering, dancing and acting,
> Imprimis, the Opera — mercy, my ears!
> Brother Bobby's remark t'other night was a true one; —
> 'This must be the music', said he, 'of the spears,
> For I'm curst if each note of it doesn't run through one!'
> But the dancing — ah! *parlez-moi*, Dolly, *de ça* —
> There, indeed, is a treat which charms all but Papa . . .
> Then, the music — so softly its cadences die,
> So divinely — oh, Dolly! between you and I,
> It's as well for my peace that there's nobody nigh
> To make love to me then — you've a soul, and can judge
> What a crisis 'twould be for your friend Biddy Fudge!
> The next place (which Bobby has near lost his heart in)
> They call it the Play-house — I think — of St Martin;
> Quite charming — and very religious — what folly
> To say that the French are not pious, dear Dolly,
> Where here one beholds, so correctly and rightly,
> The Testament turn'd into melo-dramas nightly;
> And doubtless, so fond they're of scriptural facts,
> They will soon get the Pentateuch up in five acts.
> Here Daniel, in pantomime, buds bold defiance
> To Nebuchadnezzar and all his stuff'd lions,
> While pretty young Israelites dance round the Prophet,
> In very thin clothing, and but little of it; —
> Here Begrand, who shines in this scriptural path,
>
> As lovely Suzanna, without ev'n a relic
> Of drapery round her, comes out of the bath
>
> In a manner that, Bob says, is quite Eve-angelic!
> But in short, dear 'twould take me a month to recite
> All the exquisite places we're at, day and night.

The debate might rage about Napoleon and the restoration of the Bourbon monarchy, about whether Lady Morgan's *France* was a fruitful description of the social and political condition of Britain's nearest Continental neighbour, or an unspeakably inaccurate travesty; but visitors to Paris from the British Isles were determined to have their world in their time, for that was the Regency approach to living.

Epilogue

By the time Queen Victoria came to the throne in 1837, the frivolity and cheerful casualness which are present in Tom Moore's *Fudge Family in Paris* had become things of the past. In early Victorian Britain the rage was all for earnestness, godliness, and the work ethic. Before long, the Royal Pavilion at Brighton was ruthlessly gutted — in the 1840s Queen Victoria ordered that it should be dismantled, most of its contents being distributed between Buckingham Palace and Windsor Castle — and the Regency was no more than a shameful memory of a different age. Characterized as it was by *joie de vivre*, hedonism, and dreams of freedom, the Regency had indeed been different, a breathing-space for the nation before it became enveloped in respectability. It is not that the decade lacked seriousness — it produced tracts by the score, and it is hard to think of public figures more serious in their way than social reformers such as Robert Owen. But, thanks in part to the pace of its events, in part to the escapist buffoonery of the Regent himself, and in part to the satirical genius of men like Byron, Cruikshank and Peacock, Regency Britain did not often fall into the Victorian trap of confusing seriousness with solemnity.

When George III died and the Poet Laureate Southey wrote a very solemn and pompous poem describing his reception into Heaven, Byron responded by producing 'The Vision of Judgement' (1821), a satire which expressed something of the essential irreverence of the decade that had just ended. The poem opens on a note of high-spirited comedy:

> Saint Peter sat by the celestial gate:
> His keys were rusty, and the lock was dull,

198

So little trouble had been given of late;
    Not that the place by any means was full,
But since the Gallic era 'eighty-eight'[1]
    The Devils had ta'en a longer, stronger pull,
And 'a pull together', as they say
At sea — which drew most souls another way.

The Angels all were singing out of tune,
    And hoarse with having little else to do,
Excepting to wind up the sun and moon,
    Or curb a runaway star or two,
Or wild colt of a comet, which too soon
    Broke out of bounds o'er the ethereal blue,
Splitting some planet with its playful tail,
As boats are sometimes by a wanton whale.

'The Vision of Judgement' contains pointed satire — so pointed that the publisher was prosecuted for 'endangering the public peace by a publication calumniating his late majesty'. But Byron's wish to communicate his political views does not prevent him from relaxing and enjoying (and this is a typically insouciant Regency attitude) the joke he has created about Saint Peter and George III:

All that I saw farther, in the last confusion,
    Was, that King George slipped into Heaven for one;
And when the tumult dwindled to a calm,
I left him practising the hundredth psalm.

The emphasis here is on tolerance. One of Byron's favourite passages in Shakespeare was the condemnation of false puritanism in *Twelfth Night*:

SIR TOBY: Dost thou think, because thou art virtuous, there shall be no more cakes and ale?
CLOWN : Yes, by Saint Anne; and ginger shall be hot i' the mouth too.

Byron had detected in British society a growing earnestness and killjoy mood, an ominous liking for straight lines rather than for curves. Hence his many attacks on 'cant', and poems like 'The Vision of Judgement' in which he did his best to warn his contemporaries against the sort of narrow and humourless thinking which is now associated with the worst side of 'Victorianism'.

    Tolerance and freedom belong together. This does not necessarily imply either that Byron's period was exceptional for its realization of these qualities, or that the age which followed the reigns of

---

[1] i.e. the outbreak of the French Revolution.

George IV and William IV was wholly lacking in them. But it is clear at least that during the Regency freedom was *sought* with an intensity which has been rare in history; and the pursuit, if not the degree of attainment, had a certain magnificence.

Freedom stood for many different things to different people in Regency Britain. As Asa Briggs has pointed out, a view of life at this time depended 'on where you were born and when you were born as well as on the background facts of parentage, class, property, income and education'. To William Hazlitt, freedom meant the chance to go and see Edmund Kean play Shylock at Drury Lane — 'Wherever there is a playhouse, the world will not go on amiss.' To Thomas Lord, who opened a cricket ground in St John's Wood in 1814, freedom meant the right to do what he could for his favourite sport; someone might complain that his ground was 'all ridge and furrow' resembling a billiard-table only in respect of its pockets', but Lord was undeterred, and brought in a flock of sheep to crop the grass at weekends. To William Wilberforce, tireless campaigner for the negro, freedom meant bringing about an end to slavery throughout the world. To the soldier who had fought at Waterloo it signified victory over Napoleon and the return home, often to unemployment. To the crofter in Sutherland, it stood for all that he had lost, and, in many cases, for emigration from his native land. To the poet Shelley, learning in Italy of the 'Peterloo Massacre', it meant an angry call to action:

> Rise like Lions after slumber,
> In unvanquishable number,
> Shake your chains to earth like dew
> Which in sleep had fallen on you —
> Ye are many — they are few.

What all these people had experienced in common was the pressure of a revolutionary age. If any period in modern British history can be said to correspond to the French Revolution in terms of social and political ferment, it is the Regency. The parallel is not exact; there was no storming of the Bastille, no major break with the past calling for a new national constitution or decision to begin everything afresh in the 'Year One'. But in Britain between 1811 and 1820, as in France in the years after 1789, nobody did anything by halves, because the pursuit of liberty had become life's chief value. This brought about extremes of happiness and of misery. The

Regency can best be summed up in words used by one of its sons to describe the French Revolutionary period:

> It was the best of times, it was the worst of times, it was the age of wisdom, it was the age of foolishness, it was the epoch of belief, it was the epoch of incredulity, it was the season of Light, it was the season of Darkness, it was the spring of hope, it was the winter of despair. (Charles Dickens, *A Tale of Two Cities*)

Book List

GENERAL

Elie Halévy, *England in 1815* (1913, translated from French 1924) remains the most detailed historical study of the 'political institutions, economic life, religion and culture' of Regency Britain. *The Age of Elegance 1812-1822* (1950), by Sir Arthur Bryant, combines an easy style with a wealth of information. R. J. White, *Waterloo to Peterloo* (1957), is a compelling account of 'social transition [or] suspended revolution'. The same author's *Life in Regency England* (1963), and J. B. Priestley, *The Prince of Pleasure and his Regency 1811-1820* (1969), are stimulating general surveys, the latter profusely illustrated. Volumes xii and xiii of the *Oxford History of England – The Reign of George III* by J. Steven Watson (1960) and *The Age of Reform* by Sir Llewellyn Woodward (2nd edition, 1960) – overlap in the Regency. The period is brought into sharp focus by Asa Briggs in *The Age of Improvement 1783-1867* (1959), by E. P. Thompson in *The Making of the English Working Class* (1963), and by T. C. Smout in *A History of the Scottish People 1560-1830* (1969). Details of who was doing what when may be found in *Chronology of the Modern World: 1763 to the Present Time* (1966) by Neville Williams. The publications of writers of the period, together with books and articles about them, are listed in volume iii [1800-1900] of *The New Cambridge Bibliography of English Literature*, edited by George Watson (1969), which includes long sections on Travel, Sport, Education, and Newspapers and Magazines; see also Ian Jack, *English Literature 1815-1832* (Oxford, 1963). Two useful anthologies are *Romantic Poetry*, edited by G. M. Ridenour (Englewood Cliffs, New Jersey, 1973), and *Romantic Poetry and Prose*, edited by H. Bloom and L. Trilling (New York, 1973). R. D. Altick, *The English Common Reader: A Social History of the Mass Reading Public 1800-1900* (Chicago, 1957) illuminates 'the place of reading in an industrial and increasingly democratic society'.

PARTICULAR TOPICS

THE REGENT   Christopher Hibbert's two volume biography *George IV* (*Prince of Wales 1762-1811*, 1972, and *Regent and King 1811-1830*, 1973) is racy and well documented. A fascinating view of the man and his age emerges from *The Correspondence of George, Prince of Wales 1770-1812*, edited by A. Aspinal (vol. vii [1810-11], 1970, and vol. viii [1811-12], 1971), and from the

202

same editor's *The Letters of King George IV 1812-1830* (vol. i [1812-15] and vol. ii [1815-23], Cambridge 1938). Chapter 5 of J. H. Plumb's *The First Four Georges* (1956) can be enjoyed along with W. M. Thackeray's character sketch in *The Four Georges* (1861).

BYRON   John Jump has edited *Childe Harold's Pilgrimage and Other Romantic Poems* (Dent, 1975), while *Don Juan* is available in the Penguin English Poets series, edited by T. G. Steffan, E. Steffan and W. W. Pratt (1973). The best modern biography of Byron is that by Leslie Marchand (3 vols, 1957); see also Peter Quennell, *Byron: The Years of Fame* (1935) and *Byron in Italy* (1941), and Elizabeth Longford, *Byron* (1976). Marchand has since published *Byron: A Portrait* (1971), and his edition of Byron's *Letters and Journals*, which includes previously unpublished correspondence, is in progress (1973-   ).

MISCELLANEOUS   T. S. R. Boase, *English Art 1800-1870* (Oxford, 1959) deals authoritatively and elegantly with Regency painting, sculpture, and architecture. The achievement of John Nash is examined in two books by Sir John Summerson, *John Nash, Architect to George IV* (1935) and *Georgian London* (1948); see also Stella Margetson, *Regency London* (1971). Two valuable books by Clifford Musgrave, who directed the restoration of Brighton Pavilion in the 1950s, are *Royal Pavilion* (1951) and *Life in Brighton; from the earliest times to the present* (1970). Ellen Moers, *The Dandy: Brummell to Beerbohm* (1960), and *Regency England: The Great Age of the Colour Print* (1960) by Reay Tannahill, treat their respective subjects aptly, and a knowledgeable account of the art of the Regency cartoonists will be found in M. Dorothy George's *Hogarth to Cruikshank: Social Change in Graphic Satire* (1967). Boxing, slang, and popular journalism all fall within the scope of J. C. Reid's admirable *Bucks and Bruisers: Pierce Egan and Regency England* (1971). De Quincey's *Recollections of the Lakes & the Lake Poets*, edited by David Wright (1970), raises gossip to the level of art.

Index